ONE REALM
BEYOND

ONE REALM
BEYOND

BOOK ONE
OF THE

REALM WALKERS

TRILOGY

DONITA K. PAUL

ZONDERVAN®

ZONDERVAN

One Realm Beyond
Copyright © 2014 by Donita K. Paul

This title is also available as a Zondervan ebook. Visit www.zondervan.com/ebooks.

Requests for information should be addressed to:

Zondervan, *Grand Rapids, Michigan* 49530

ISBN 978-0-310-73580-9

Published in association with the literary agency of Alive Communications, Inc., 7680 Goddard Street, Suite 200, Colorado Springs, CO 80920. www.alivecommunications.com

Cover design: Kris Nelson
Cover illustration: Steve Rawlings
Interior design: David Conn

Printed in the United States of America

14 15 16 17 18 /DCI/ 20 19 18 17 16 15 14 13 12 11 10 9 8 7 6 5 4 3 2 1

RAISING A RUCKUS

Cantor straddled the thick tree limb suspended less than three feet over his favorite fishing hole. He'd fished from this spot for more than eighteen years, from the time he could barely straddle the fat limb 'til now, when the tips of his sandals almost brushed the surface of the clear, cold water. He watched the small fish circling below him, waiting for the big one just as he had been taught. His fishing mentor, Odem, probably took him fishing here before he was out of diapers. Cantor wouldn't want to share the limb now. Though the tree had grown with him over the years, he didn't think the branch would hold the weight of two grown men. He wasn't eager for a bath in the frigid water from the mountain's runoff.

Still and patient, Cantor waited for the large carp he called Bully to rise and push the other fish out of the way. A sprinkle of thumb-sized chunks of bread floated on the water. One of the smaller guppies darted off to the side, and a huge, open mouth appeared under the surface. The fish snapped up a sodden crust.

Cantor hurled the stone in his hand. The rock thunked against the skull of his target. All the smaller fish deserted Bully, who floated on his side. With a grin, Cantor threw his leg over the limb and slipped into the knee-high water. He shivered in the icy snowmelt, grabbed his catch, and slogged to the shore.

Exposed roots riddled the steep bank, making irregular hand and foot holds. Cantor threw the fish onto the grass above his head and climbed out. Sitting cross-legged in the tall grass, he removed his sandals and put them on a rock to dry in the sun. He opened the pouch Ahma had sewn into his tunic and removed an undersized scabbard.

He'd owned this small, sharp knife since childhood. Odem had visited on his sixth birthday and, against Ahma's protests, given the tool to him. Cantor'd thought himself very clever when he named the knife Slice, especially when Odem laughed in his loud bray that filled the tiny cabin. Ahma shook her head and fetched another piece of greenberry pie for him and Odem.

She'd caught Cantor that night picking his teeth with the blade. Boxing his ears, she told him if she caught him doing another stupid thing with "that weapon," she'd take it away.

Cantor grinned as he applied Slice to the job of gutting the big carp. A couple of carrion birds landed in a tree nearby. Cantor nodded in their direction. "I'll leave you the tasty insides. I don't suppose you would agree to peaceably share between yourselves."

The bigger of the two mountain crows spread his wings and threatened the smaller, cawing and crowding the other bird off the limb.

Cantor shook his head. "Yeah, I didn't think so."

He pulled a thin string of gut from the innards. With it in his hand, he aimed at the bird and snapped his fingers. The filament wrapped around the large scavenger's beak. The string would work loose after the smaller bird had a chance at Cantor's fishy offering.

He finished his chore and strung the fish on a switch cut from the longleaf tree. Cleaning his blade in the sandy soil, he heard the gentle whoosh of a portal opening. With a casual air he did not feel, he put the knife in its scabbard and the scabbard in his pouch.

Where was Tom? At the cabin with Ahma? He'd last seen his mentor's furry companion sunning himself on the front stoop. But Tom could be a stealthy canine, quiet like a cat sneaking up on a mouse. More often than not, Cantor played the part of the mouse.

With a searching look at the surrounding trees, he propped the switch on his shoulder, the large carp dangling behind him. He angled away from the portal as if it didn't make the hairs on the back of his neck tingle, as if it didn't give off the scent of new horizons, adventure, and intrigue, as if he hadn't a thought in his head about diving through.

Anyone watching would think he had only the intention of taking his catch home to dear Ahma for their dinner. Except Tom, of course. Tom had an uncanny sense of knowing what he planned. And Cantor had just used his talent to enhance his aim, not bothering to disguise the burst of energy. That ripple would be detected by any other being familiar with Primen's gifts. Tom would have felt it.

Cantor made himself wait until the distance to the portal had shortened considerably. With a final, nonchalant inspection of the surrounding meadow, Cantor hauled in a deep breath, dropped the fish, and bolted toward the gaping hole in space. His heart quickened when he saw it was a horizontal portal. Vertical openings presented a shaft, which required scrambling up or plunging down to enter another plane.

If he'd outsmarted Tom, he was in for some fun. He pumped his legs harder.

The distinct sound of leathery wings unfolding caught his ear. He fought back a grin and redoubled the speed of his dash to freedom. The dragon on course to intercept him roared a warning. Accepting the challenge, Cantor pushed his muscles with all his might. If he could reach the portal first, he could dive and roll. The dragon in flight would have to land and squeeze through.

Cantor kept his eye on the opening. On the other side, he could see a street with people hurrying to and fro. A rush of air above him warned him just in time. He ducked and avoided the clutching claws of a brilliantly colored mor dragon as it swooped to catch him. The small, powerful beast was slightly larger than a full-grown cow. Cantor glanced up to see him dip one wing and neatly turn, barely losing momentum as he came back for another pass. Cantor refocused on the portal. Fifteen more feet.

The dragon dropped from the sky, approaching his target face on. He skimmed the high grass and rose to thud against Cantor's chest with his own. The impact knocked Cantor down and pushed the air out of his lungs. He remained on the ground, staring up at the blue sky. Dragging air in with rasping, choking sounds, he rolled to his side and curled up to facilitate at least one life-sustaining breath.

The dragon landed and approached. Cantor would have liked to fake death, be still enough to confuse the beast stalking him, and get the better of the interfering animal. But he concentrated instead on breathing, pulling air in and pushing air out.

The dragon's clawed foot rested on his shoulder, then with a pinch, he forced Cantor to roll onto his back.

In spite of the spasms racking his chest, Cantor recognized the wicked gleam in his tormentor's eyes. The beast all but crowed with glee at having downed his prey. With a hop, the dragon sat on Cantor's chest.

"Oomph," Cantor managed to choke out, "Get off!"

The dragon's lips curled up at the ends in the terrifying smile only a dragon can produce. "Patience, Cantor. Why is it that when you are days from being allowed through the portals on your own, you still persist in trying for a rogue adventure? Ahma is very close to granting your walker status."

"Get off, Tom!" Cantor tried shifting his weight enough to tilt his body and dump the dragon.

A whoosh of air signaled the closing of the portal. The dragon winked, and his snout narrowed and grew a thick, short coat of fur. Pointed horns became floppy ears. Drool dripped from a much smaller mouth than had blown hot air on Cantor a moment before. The pressure on Cantor's chest eased as the mor dragon's body slimmed into the body of a dog. The reptilian tail changed last. Cantor couldn't see it wagging, but since Tom was pleased with himself, it most definitely was.

"I hate it when you do that!"

Tom swiped his face with a pink doggy tongue and jumped off. Cantor sat, pulled up his knees, and buried his head between them, still breathing with ragged gasps.

When he finally could talk without discomfort, he looked up at Tom and grinned. "I almost made it."

"You didn't."

"You completely missed me on the first pass."

"I was toying with you. Establishing false confidence."

Cantor stood and brushed off his clothing. "Yeah, sure. I believe that."

He walked back to the dropped fish with Tom dogging his steps. "You really think Ahma is ready to let me out on my own?"

"I know she thinks *you* think you are ready to be out on your own."

"Now, see, Tom, that's what I don't understand. How do you know what she's thinking? I have no idea whether I'm going to be blessed apprentice or cursed knave each day." He snorted. "Each moment."

The dog considered the young man for a minute before answering. "Ahma blames her rheumatism. But I think it has more to do with how the planes are shifting. When too many of them slide in the same direction, she feels off-kilter."

Cantor nodded, observing clouds drifting in from the western horizon. "She knows things before they happen. How is that? She won't teach me the skill."

Tom responded with a bark of laughter. "She's been a realm walker a very long time. I think you must grow old to acquire that skill."

"Too bad not many realm walkers grow old. Odem and Ahma are the oldest, aren't they?"

"Some on the guild council claim to be older than Odem and Ahma, but there is no way to prove that."

They climbed a steep hill and paused at the rise to catch their breath. Cantor looked over at Tom and noticed his tongue hanging out as he panted.

"What are you grinning about, boy?"

"Your long, wet, dangling, very pink tongue. Poor Tom. It must be deeply humiliating to lose your dignity whenever you're hot."

"I don't keep my dignity on my face, but in my heart. Why is it you allow years of instruction given to you by Ahma and myself to drift from your mind like a dandelion seed on a breeze?"

Cantor shrugged, which reminded him of the big fish on the long stick over his shoulder. "Let's go give this to Ahma."

He started down the hill with Tom trotting beside him, head held high and tail swaying behind. A squirrel ran for the nearest tree and scrambled to a safe branch. Its indignant chatter railed them as they passed. Tom lifted his chin, gave the small animal a direct look, and let out a bark. The squirrel stopped its noise long enough to scamper up to a higher limb, then resumed its scold.

"Before you lose your words altogether," said Cantor, "tell me why you think Ahma is on the verge of letting me go."

"Because Odem is there. They have their heads together and are sniggering over some scheme. Woof .... bother! When they last parted, Odem said he woof — blast! — would return for your initiation."

"So you think that's now?" Cantor couldn't help the enthusiasm taking over his voice.

Tom's yes sounded more like a yap, but it was good enough for Cantor.

INITIATION

Odem's donkey, Nahzy, dozed in the shade of the blacka-more tree. Tom deserted Cantor to wake his old mor dragon friend. He tore down the hill, displaying dog-like enthusiasm. As a dragon, Tom exhibited more decorum. Cantor waved a greeting as Nahzy lifted his head and let out a lazy bray with a yawn.

The door to the cabin stood open. Two calico kittens, one black-and-white and one tabby, basked in the sun on the worn stoop. Cantor stopped at the well, drew up the bucket, and splashed his face, rubbed his hands a bit in the water, and then rinsed the dirt off his fish.

He glanced over his shoulder, wondering if Tom were right. Could Ahma and Odem be plotting his initiation? Cantor didn't even know what the initiation involved. As long as he didn't have to write a report, he'd be okay.

Oral questions didn't bother him. Ahma said he'd been gifted with a tinker's tongue and fingers. Sometimes that was a compliment and sometimes ... it was not. He explained things well, could persuade all but Ahma and Odem to let him have his way.

The physical performance tasks didn't challenge him either. For intricate movement, his nimble fingers could twist and poke and maneuver almost any gadget into working properly. As for agility in games and athletic skills, he could outrun, outjump, outflip, twist, or tumble any animal he'd ever met.

He'd do all right as long as he didn't have to pick up a pen. The skinny little implements made him nervous. If he walked into a room, he knew where pens and pencils hid in drawers or behind cupboard doors. A bit of charcoal from the fire didn't bother him unless someone had made a mark with the black lump. And a paintbrush was just a paintbrush unless someone had strayed from merely whitewashing walls and wrote on the faded siding.

Ahma said he was touched in the head. He laughed to himself. Sometimes she regarded his state of mind favorably, and sometimes, not.

Sitting on the stone wall of the well, he studied the house. He'd seen grander houses in the village, but Ahma always said grander houses required more work. He'd seen drawn pictures of cities and their impressive buildings. His life with Ahma had not included visits to very large cities, but he'd done realm walking with both Ahma and Odem to other planes and towns of various sizes.

The guild held council in Gilead, the largest city on Dairine. He would have liked to have some familiarity with that metropolis. He'd see it soon and on his own.

Would he approach the guild leaders before or after the

initiation? If he passed the initiation, would he go straight to Effram to seek out his dragon companion?

Ahma and Odem kept tight lips when it came to the guild. Every year they talked less about the people in charge of all realm walkers. At least, they didn't *openly* discuss them. Cantor felt the tension rise when the topic skittered around the room and disappeared again.

He rubbed his palms over his trousers, picked up the fish, and headed toward the open door. In that humble abode lurked his future. Adventure. Excitement. He was ready, once he got past this initiation. Ignoring a prick of conscience, he paused just outside the doorway to listen, quietly standing and observing.

Ahma and Odem sat at the table. A large empty bowl sat to the side of Odem's elbow. He tipped a tankard of melonwater to his lips, then set the beverage down.

Between the two old realm walkers, objects from the room floated. Cantor recognized the loose configuration of the nine planes represented by spoons, a couple of knotted napkins, a saltshaker, a ball of string, and woodchips from the kindling box. Of course, in reality, the planes looked more like floating pancakes, suspended over one another in a lopsided, shifting column.

Every planetary system in the galaxy was grouped in individual stacks. At times, columns came within pitching distance of one another. Well, not really. When Cantor was younger, he believed everything Odem told him, but he soon learned to discern when the man stretched a fact out of shape for a bit of fun.

The tales of two columns of planes being shuffled together like two halves of a deck of cards were just legends based on imagination, not truth. The ancient myth of one plane sliding out of its column, traveling through space, and integrating with another was also suspect. The only reason anyone lent these tales credence was Primen. Everyone knew Primen could do impossible things. If He were involved, then mountains might pick up their skirts and dance to the seashore.

Some facts stood on their own: Each plane held a realm. Each realm operated independently of its neighbors. Gravity kept them from floating away from each other, but didn't keep them at a predictable, precise distance.

Many years before, Cantor had seen the plane of Alius when his realm and the other had drifted dangerously close. The other realm looked like a pale, mottled yellow disk floating high in the blue sky.

Odem told him that once, in ancient times, Alius and Dairine had collided. They'd bounced, and each floated out of the other's domain.

Odem had cleared his throat and looked Cantor in the eye, the signal that what he was about to say held great importance. "The terror in the minds of the people far outreached the authentic threat of the situation. Some of our people ran to the other side of the plane and jumped off."

"Couldn't the guild do something? Aren't they in charge of organizing the powerful and defending the weak?"

At the time of the discussion, Odem had wagged his head in disgust as he tried to explain.

"The guild had less power back then. Chomountain the Wise *was* wise. He walked among the people on every plane. Then he disappeared with no one to replace him. He took over from Avamountain. The Age of Ava was tranquil.

Dargamountain passed his mantle down to Ava. And before Darga was Sentarmountain. The Age of Sentar was prosperous.

Cantor sought to impress his mentor. "What about Ladomountain? Didn't he come before Darga?"

Odem scowled at Cantor. "Of course, he did. Between Darga and Sentar, I'm glad to see you're paying attention. I wasn't able to trick you."

The old man rubbed his palms over the thick material of his trousers. "But we're talking about power. Without the check of the right hand of Primen, the guild is powerful beyond common sense. If they've grabbed the power, they took it from someone. Who?"

He cocked an eyebrow in Cantor's direction. "Is it coincidence that no action has been attributed to the old wizard for many, many years? Some say Chomountain is dying."

That was the last time Odem talked openly about the guild. For the last several years, both Ahma and Odem had refused to talk of the guild or the missing wizard. As far as Cantor knew, kind and just Chomountain remained elusive. And from the worry etched on his mentors' brows, he discerned that the guild became ever more a concern. When he asked questions now, Ahma warned him it was better not to talk about those who had the power to harm.

So here he stood, reduced to eavesdropping to glean information. Odem gestured at the model floating over the table. "Ahma, you can see, can you not, that Richra and Derson are edging too close?"

Ahma nodded.

Cantor watched, enrapt, as two spoons lost their bearings, slid sideways, and crashed together. They fell, knocking the saltshaker out of the way. Before the three planes stabilized, the woodchip representing Alius began to spin. Slowly, then with more speed, the plane tilted one way and then to the opposite side.

Ahma gasped. "The worst I've ever seen, Odem. Can we alter the course of Richra and Derson?"

"Perhaps." Odem allowed his replica of the planes to collapse. The items clattered as they fell onto the table.

Cantor took a step into the room. "Will I be allowed to help?"

Odem jerked around, then stood to come pound Cantor on the back. "There you are. Today's the day. By the time you put your head on the pillow tonight, you'll be an official initiate."

"And then I'll be eligible to help, right?"

Odem put his large hand on Cantor's head and rubbed. Cantor tried to duck, but Odem snagged him in a headlock and continued to torture his scalp.

"Ahma! Pull this brute off of me."

The old lady cackled and winked, causing Odem to release Cantor. The old man backed up until he was stuck to the wooden doorframe behind him. He gave Ahma an accusatory look. Cantor slid past and rested one hip against the table. Ahma picked up one of the forks and jabbed his side. "Move. No manners! Did Enid the Cow raise you?"

Cantor straightened and tossed his impudent grin at Ahma and then Odem, who still stood pinned to the entryway.

"Thank you, Ahma." With a bow, Cantor presented the fish to the old lady who stood for grandmother, as well as mentor, in his life. "Our dinner."

"And the only reason I helped you escape that old reprobate. Didn't want you to drop our meal." She nodded at Odem, and he stepped away from the door.

Odem shivered as if shaking his body free of the force that had bound him. Not by word or expression did he show any annoyance at Ahma's prank. He sank into his wooden chair and fingered the utensils he'd used as a model for the problems he'd observed.

The kittens poured through the opening and circled Ahma's legs. She shooed them away, then with the same dismissive voice she ordered Cantor to bathe.

"You smell like fish and sweat and river sludge. I'll not have you at my table, reeking. Especially tonight."

Cantor bobbed her another fancy bow and ran out the door.

Ahma followed and stopped in the entryway to holler. "Brainless boy, come back and get clean clothes!"

Cantor stopped in his tracks, then ran backward to the cabin. He kissed Ahma's cheek as he passed her to enter, and then again, when he left with a wad of clean clothes under his arm.

"The soap!"

He backed up and grabbed a bar beside the front door where a bucket sat ready for washing hands. He winked at Ahma and cartwheeled, using the hand that did not hold soap and clothing.

She grinned. "He'll never grow up."

Cantor twirled in place to give his Ahma a jaunty bow.

"Right." Odem's chortle garbled the words, but Cantor understood him. "And that's what will make him good at his job. Energy, pluck, quick on his feet and in his mind. He'll lead the council in a merry jig."

Cantor did a last cartwheel, but refrained from continuing. His feet now trod over slippery shale on the hill beside the cabin. But he was pleased. He'd worked hard for Ahma's smile. Playing the clown often pulled her out of grumpiness when nothing else would.

Odem was more amenable. But his approving words were a balm to Cantor's doubts. Many times he thought that the ordinary existence he lived did little to guarantee success in his fated profession. But Odem thought highly of what few skills he had. Perhaps he would be an acclaimed realm walker. He'd see soon enough if he was fool or knight. One could not fake being a realm walker.

Cantor took off at a faster pace, eager to finish this chore and get back to a fine fish dinner, more talk of the planes, the initiation, and perhaps an invitation to accompany Odem on his journey to set things right between Richra and Derson.

He did his cleansing in the tepid flow of water from an underground spring that fell from the rocks into a pool deep enough to dive into and wide enough to provide a decent swim. The water from the depths of the plane was warm, unlike the snow run-off in the lake.

He soaped up, rinsed off, and soaped up again. Following the second dive to the bottom to remove every bubble clinging to his skin, he hauled himself out and shook his head. Water splattered the bushes around him. He looked for a towel and realized he'd forgotten to bring one.

Grinning, he pulled on his shirt first, then wrangled the rest of his clothes over his damp skin. He plowed his fingers through his wet hair, taming the curls only marginally. A yellow songbird landed on a branch, tilted its head, and let out a trilling whistle ending with what sounded like a hiccup. It repeated its performance several times.

"I hear you." Cantor leaned back with his hands at his hips, puckered his mouth slightly to whistle, and echoed the yellow bird's song.

The bird hopped about the branches, twittering in excitement. It stopped to sing again. Cantor obliged with a reply.

"I've got to go now, bird. Ahma is fixing dinner and tonight is a special" — he held up a finger — "make that a *very* special night."

He went out of his way to pass through the edge of the forest where he gathered a variety of greens and herbs. Ahma loved fresh greens in a huge bowl of salad. He hoped his old mentor would be in a good mood for the initiation. He plucked sweet tamaron from a vine. The tiny purple buds would spice up the vinaigrette. Another favorite for Ahma.

Perhaps the initiation would be easy, and Ahma would not growl and grumble over all the wasted years she spent educating him. The smell of fried fish and maizy bread wafted from the cabin. Odem played his fiddle. Ahma sang with a pure voice for one so old.

The fiddling stopped as soon as Cantor crossed the threshold.

"There he is," said Odem. "Let's eat."

"You ate a bowl of soup in the middle of the afternoon." Ahma shook her stirring spoon at her guest. A blob of thick gravy splatted on Odem's faded green shirt. Ahma reached over and swiped at the spot with a rag. "You shouldn't be hungry for hours yet."

"Not hungry, dear woman. Craving the taste of your delicious meal on this old deprived tongue."

"Deprived tongue?" She scoffed. "You've a depraved mind, I'm thinking."

Cantor crossed the room, threw his dirty clothes into his

bed closet, and then gave Ahma the produce he had gathered. "The words aren't the same, Ahma. Depraved means he commits evil deeds involving blatant turpitude."

Ahma squinted at him. "I never taught you the word turpitude. Where are you coming up with words I didn't introduce you to? Have you been down to the village on your own? You know that's dangerous."

Before he could remind her of the books Odem left with him, she continued. She addressed the kittens climbing the dog Tom and sliding down his sides as he lay on his blanket in a corner. "This Cantor thinks he's smart. Time he went out into the world to learn how ignorant he really is. I'm hoping he lives through the disappointment of only having a mediocre mind, a limited talent, and no possible means of advancing his lowly life on his own."

Cantor sighed. So his role tonight was scoundrel and knave, not beloved sent by Primen to give her life purpose.

Although the meal smelled and tasted wonderful, Cantor found it difficult to eat with his usual gusto. When would the initiation begin? How long would it take? If he flubbed an answer, would he get a second chance?

He tried to think of a calm night sky filled with stars and distant platters floating in space. Soon he would be traveling to the planes alone. No Ahma to chaperone. No Odem to pull him out of an interesting exploration. Perhaps a mission assigned just to him. He'd helped Odem on several occasions when the old realm walker tackled a problem on some other plane. But in those cases, he'd helped by carrying knapsacks, setting up a camp, and fixing meals.

"Now, son!" Odem's voice boomed in the small cabin. "It is time to commence your initiation."

Ahma rose from the table. "Let me clear off all this clutter first."

Cantor clenched his jaw. That would delay them another hour while the old lady put every blessed object, after being scrubbed and polished, in its right place. Suppressing a sigh, he rose to help. Maybe nurturing a better mood in his mentor would hasten the beginning of his initiation.

"Nah," Odem said. "The boy's waited long enough. Don't exasperate the youth."

Ahma muttered but sat down again. She folded her hands on the tabletop and gave her attention to her friend.

Odem winked her way, then turned a serious face to the initiate. "Question, Cantor. Answer me this. Who has first claim to your allegiance?"

Cantor's mind raced. He'd expected questions about herbs, travel safety, levels of guild standing, diplomatic tactics, history of the realms, but nothing like this. Perhaps it was a trick question. They'd never discussed allegiance. Surely if this concept was important enough to be the first question, they should have discussed it.

Ahma patted his hand and gave him an encouraging smile. "Take your time, Cantor. We can wait as long as it takes for you to get comfortable with your answer."

At least he was back to treasured apprentice. Ahma's kindness permeated her voice, her expression, and even her posture as she sat on the stool. All fine and good, but he had no answer.

Think this through. Think. He must. He could come up with the right answer if he put his mind to it.

Was his first allegiance to Ahma and Odem for the love and care and guidance that had brought him into his twentieth year? The answer would have to be just one of them, so Ahma would be correct. That didn't seem right. The statement seemed too small.

Allegiance to Dairine? His realm? Realm walkers defended the weak, guided those of little talent to solve problems, and cleared away obstacles that caused the same to stumble. But realm walkers worked on various planes, not just the one called home. No, this allegiance needed expanding.

To the guild? That could be it. The guild organized, trained, promoted, and provided for the realm walkers so that they could do their jobs. Odem's distrust of the guild dampened his desire to name the guild. A mystery there tainted an allegiance to these powerful men.

The wizard? An inept, absent, dying wizard? Perhaps when the leader had been in the prime of his life, but now? Odem's voice flowed through his memory. "Even the wizard is under authority."

"Primen!" Cantor blurted out the word, and then hoped it was right. It felt right. It felt big enough. "Primen, He who spun the worlds to life and spins them still."

Both Ahma and Odem nodded with smug pleasure on their faces.

"You did well." She started to rise. "Now we put the house to order before turning in."

"But — but — " Cantor stuttered. "That's it?"

Odem chuckled and picked up dishes to take to the counter. "Allegiance to the proper authority is the only thing that matters, son."

"But I don't remember you teaching me anything at all about Primen."

At that, Odem leaned back his head and laughed. Nahzy, outside, brayed in answer. "Then how'd you learn it, boy?"

Pinpricks awakened memories, songs of praise, songs of thanksgiving, stories of the forefathers, a word here and a word there. Everything Ahma and Odem did reflected their allegiance. He'd absorbed the concept rather than reading it in a book or listening to the particulars in a lecture. He knew to whom he owed his allegiance.

3

DRAGON REALM

Cantor carried split wood to the stack between two massive oak tree trunks. The crude wall of logs towered above him, enough fuel to keep them warm all winter. For a long, frustrating week, Odem had helped Cantor begin the woodpile. Cantor begrudgingly admitted that to leave without making provision for Ahma's winter would dishonor the code of the realm walkers. Even though winter was months away, Cantor wisely refrained from pointing that out. Finally, business lured the old man away from the restful cabin. He left, muttering about retirement.

The young realm walker paused when he saw a portal opening. Through the breach that allowed him to see into another realm, he spied a dragon flying over a thick forest of dark evergreen. He dropped his burden and started toward the arched gap. Tom just as quickly took up guard duty, standing between Cantor and the portal.

With a disgusted sigh, Cantor gave up his rush to adventure. "I know, Tom. I'm ready to go alone, but I have to get permission."

The dog sat with his mouth open and tongue lolling out, a doggy grin. Cantor went to him, knelt, and gave his ears and ruff a sound rubbing. The dog was almost like a brother, a big brother, one who had constantly kept an eye on him since Cantor learned to crawl.

From an early age, Cantor had been fascinated by the gaps in walls, trees, landscapes, lakes, and houses. The images of distant lands filled the gaps. He'd tried to pass through the portals when they appeared and before they snapped shut. But Tom's sole job when watching the crawling babe had been to keep him on this side of the arching doorways. When Cantor toddled, Tom herded him back to Ahma's side. When Cantor ran, Tom shape-shifted from dog to dragon and swooped in to snag the determined boy before he slipped into another realm.

All these years later, Tom still guarded Cantor from his own curiosity. They entered the realms many times, but always with Ahma or Odem at their side.

If legends were true, he'd been born somewhere else. A village wiseman would have recognized a babe's potential to be a realm walker. This sentinel would notify the guild, and the guild would send a messenger to take the child and deliver him or her to a suitable mentor. Cantor would never know of his real parents. He didn't even know which plane he'd been born on. Not that it mattered. He loved Ahma and Odem as if they were written in the records as his ancestors. And Dairine was his home.

Both dog and boy heard Ahma's burbling laugh as she climbed the path, returning from the village.

"I'm coming. I'm coming," she called. "This time you'll go through, Cantor, on your own. It's time you acquired your dragon, so be patient a moment longer."

Cantor raced down the path and gathered Ahma in a big hug, lifting her off her feet and spinning in a circle.

She batted at his shoulder with a free hand. "Put me down, you knuckleheaded oaf. Have some respect for your elders."

He lowered her to the ground and planted a noisy smacker of a kiss on her wrinkled cheek. "We must hurry," he said, pointing back toward their cabin. "It could close any second."

She walked calmly beside him as he explained that the gate had been open for quite a few minutes.

"It will be there when we get there," said Ahma in a raspy voice that rattled with her intake of each breath. "And if it's not, another will open shortly. You're drawing them to you whether you know it or not. That's how I know your time has come."

She limped and wheezed until he could stand the slowness no longer. He plucked her up in his arms, carrying her like he would a child. She weighed less than a big sack of potatoes.

"You should've ridden to market in the cart." He squeezed her. "Whatever possessed you to walk all that way when Midge is perfectly willing to pull you up the mountain path as well as down?"

"Midge is getting old. Her bones ache."

Ahma was old enough to be his great-great-grandmother. "The donkey isn't as old as you are."

She cackled.

He loved her odd laugh as much as he loved the old woman. He put her down beside the tree stump she often used as a stool when she sat in her yard. Her body folded without much grace, and she plunked down with a *whoomph* escaping her lips. She dug in the cloth bag that dangled from a long strap over her shoulders.

"I'm not going to tell you all that I've already told you about finding your own dragon."

Cantor nodded.

"Remember only one is your match, and don't settle for something less than that perfect companion."

"You *are* going to tell me, aren't you?"

She wagged her head. "No, no, only the important things."

"You've lectured me all my life that everything you tell me is important."

She pulled out a small wheel of cheese. "Put this in your knapsack."

He ran into the house to gather up his traveling bag and a few essentials. When he returned, Ahma had several things in her lap. "Hold that bag open."

He did, and she dropped in a flint, a couple of appletons and a pouch of gold and silver traps, coins used in all the realms. She handed him a hat shaped like the top of a mushroom with a bill on the front to shade his eyes. She'd managed to sew the object to a perfect fit, and the colorful patches indicated she'd used a bit of cloth from every scrap in her trimmings bag.

"Put it on." She looked up at him. "Have you got your flute and a bar of soap?"

He shook his head.

"Well?" Ahma prodded when he didn't move.

Cantor made another trip into the house and grabbed his comb as well as the soap, his mouth organ as well as the flute, and a rag to wash with, just in case Ahma asked if he had one.

She stood when he came out again. By stretching she could

loop the strap of his knapsack over his head. He helped by ducking into it and putting one arm through so the sack hung at his side.

She grabbed the front of his shirt and pulled him closer, kissing his cheeks and patting his chest. Today it would seem he was honorable apprentice.

"I'll know you're coming when I see you at the door." She squinted at the portal. "Now get, before the way is closed."

Cantor gathered her frail form in his arms once more for a parting hug. "I love you," he murmured against her scraggly gray hair. "I'll make you proud."

She leaned back. "See? You've forgotten." She pointed a finger at him and gave it a shake. "You don't have to do anything to make me proud. I'm already proud of who you are. You don't need to be anything more." She scrunched up her face in a disapproving grimace. "Should you be anything less, I own I would be disappointed."

He kissed her forehead.

"Go, go!"

He walked through the portal and turned to wave to Ahma and Tom.

The air crinkled, grew cold, and drew into itself until nothing could be seen of his home and Ahma. Cantor thought for a moment that he should feel some regret, some emotion that rang of permanent change. This moment should be marked somehow with sorrow for what was lost. But in truth, joy bubbled inside him. Finally he was free to wander wherever he chose. Adventure awaited him.

He snatched off the hat Ahma had given him and threw it straight up in the air. It rolled as it went up, the different patches blurring into a jumble of colors. On its descent, the hat's material spread out and floated in a lazy, swinging motion that reminded Cantor of a kite riding the wind. He caught it and stuffed it into his shirt.

He whirled around, looking into the distance of north, east, south, and west. He had all the time in the world, and many worlds to spend time in. Where to begin? Which way to strike out on this solo exploration?

His ultimate goal on this first journey was to find a dragon suitable for a lifelong friendship, as Ahma had found Tom many, many years before.

"Here!" a voice came out of nowhere.

He brought his gaze from the distant horizon and examined his immediate surroundings. A few old mounds of hay dotted the field. A tree with new buds promised spring in the days to come. A brook babbled, making enough noise to call attention to itself without being pretentious.

"Here, right in front of you."

"What or who is here, right in front of me?"

"My name's Bridger."

"Pleased to meet you, Bridger." He touched his fingers to his forehead and bowed.

"Not over there. Turn just a bit to your right." The voice added a disgruntled sound, then spoke again. "No, I guess I mean my right. There, stop! You went too far. Go back just a bit. Good, good."

Cantor heard a contented sigh.

"You're looking directly at me."

"I'm looking directly at a haystack."

"What realm are you from, realm walker? Are you so inexperienced that you don't recognize a dragon when you see one?"

30

"I see a haystack."

"I have shape-shifted into a haystack."

"Why?"

"I was waiting for you."

"Me?"

"Well, any realm walker, actually." He paused, and the hay rustled. "You *are* looking for a dragon, are you not?"

"Yes."

"What luck! You've found one."

"I've found a haystack."

"No, no. Use your imagination."

"Why don't you shapeshift back?"

No sound. Not a word. No explanation. Cantor turned to leave.

"Stop!"

Cantor faced the haystack from a little distance and called out. "I'm sorry, but I am going to pass on your companionship. My Ahma told me not to settle for the first dragon I meet."

The haystack roared, and a flicker of fire spewed out from a spot close to the rounded top of the mound.

"Fire!" shouted the hay.

"I know. I saw." Cantor frowned. "It wasn't much of a fire breath for a full-grown dragon."

"Ouch, ouch." The haystack shimmied.

Bits and pieces fell away, and what was left formed into a respectable looking, bronze-colored dragon with indigo wings. The dragon had a beard.

Cantor had never seen a dragon with a beard, not even a picture of a dragon with a beard.

Flames licked in and out of the hairy, scroungy tufts cascading from his face. "Ouch! Don't just stand there! Help me!"

Cantor darted for the brook. "Come closer. You need to splash in the water."

Bridger followed Cantor in a lumbering gait. His beard smoked, but no more flames colored the twisted locks. Cantor tossed his knapsack down on the bank and stepped into the stream.

"Hurry! Get in the brook." Cantor cupped his hands, bent over, and swooped up water, which he splashed in the dragon's direction.

Bridger tripped over an exposed root and fell face first at Cantor's feet, soaking the young man.

Cantor straightened from his crouch and frowned at his dripping shirtfront. "Well, that works too."

The dragon pushed his arms out in front of him and pulled his head out of the bubbling brook. Charred stubs hung from his chin.

Cantor crossed his arms over his chest. "I've never seen a dragon with facial hair."

Bridger turned over and sat with the water diverted by his plump body. One side encroached on the embankment as it continued its course.

He fingered his raggle-taggledy beard. "That was me being clever."

"Clever?"

"Resourceful."

Cantor waited.

"As I shifted, I realized my chin would be aflame, so I added the beard as a buffer between the fire and my skin."

Cantor cocked his head and nodded. "That is rather clever, and quick-thinking as well."

Bridger jumped to his feet. "It was, wasn't it? You do see that I would be an asset to your adventuring, don't you?"

The young realm walker shook his head. "But the idea didn't completely work."

"I know." The dragon hung his head, his wings drooped, and he plodded out of the stream. "I didn't account for the fact that flames go up. If I'd made the beard longer, perhaps."

Cantor went to the bank and snatched his knapsack from the ground. He then turned and walked to the opposite side to climb out.

"Where are you going?" called Bridger.

"Don't know yet."

"I know the way." The dragon stepped into the water, following Cantor.

"What way?"

"Any way. I was born on this plane and know every trail. I know the best cooks, the most hospitable hosts, the cheapest stores, and the kindest healers. You'll need me."

Cantor glanced over his shoulder and almost took pity on the bedraggled and mournful dragon. Almost.

"I don't think so."

"Who's going to light your campfire tonight?"

"I have a piece of flint." He continued walking, refusing to look back at the tag-along.

A hill swelled the earth ahead of him, and he made that his destination. He no longer heard Bridger's breathing or the slight rustle of his leathery wings, but he didn't look. The dragon would take his interest as an encouragement. Cantor envisioned himself with a sophisticated, educated, elegant dragon. Bridger did not fit the image.

At the top of the hill, he paused to survey the countryside.

A forest to the south, an outcropping of rocks or stone buildings against the one green mountain, too far away to see clearly, and farmlands spread as far as he could see.

He heard a whuffle from a horse's nostrils right before he received a nudge between the shoulder blades. He whipped around and confronted a warhorse with a gleaming black coat, four white socks and a star on his forehead.

"I thought you might like to ride," said Bridger. A fine set of leather saddlebags lay across the horse's broad back behind a fancy saddle.

"No, thank you."

"It's a long way to the nearest village of any size."

"I'm used to walking." Cantor turned and continued on his way, taking long strides at a quicker pace than before.

Bridger shuffled his giant hooves and followed. "Walking's okay. You could fly if you had a mor dragon for a constant."

"I will have a mor dragon for a constant. It's my destiny."

The horse shambled closer. Warm, moist air huffed down Cantor's neck. "It's my destiny too."

Cantor grunted and kept walking.

4

A HORSE IS A HORSE, OF COURSE

"Can I ride your horse, Mister?" The voice came from a tree next to the dirt road.

Cantor spotted a child straddling a thick limb. The leaves shook, and he realized a trio of children perched overhead. Two girls and a scruffy boy. The oldest, skinniest girl might have made the inquiry. Her eyes twinkled, and her lips were opening to ask another question.

To forestall any conversation about Bridger, Cantor answered quickly, "I don't have a horse."

"Then why's that horse following you?"

Cantor turned slowly, pretended to start at the sight of Bridger, then scratched his head. "I don't have the faintest idea."

"Well, since he's not yours, we can ride him for sure."

The children scrambled down through many limbs, the oldest helping the smallest child, the grunge-covered boy.

The diverse colors of dried, crusty mud smeared into the boy's hair and coating his skin fascinated Cantor. "How did he get so dirty?"

"Pigs!" said the middle child, a girl who wore a little less dirt than the boy.

The older girl set the boy down and pushed him behind the younger girl. "Stay, Ding-dong, until I see if he's safe."

The boy nodded and opened his mouth in a circle. Just before his lips sealed the gap around the thumb, Cantor noticed how much cleaner that part of the boy was compared to all the other visible parts. Even his clothes looked stiff with dirt.

The oldest girl approached Bridger, whose head towered above Cantor. She barely came up to his flank. One wrong move, and she would be knocked over. Cantor breathed easier when he realized the dragon/horse stood exceptionally still.

"Does he bite?" she asked.

"I have no idea. He's not my horse."

Bridger whinnied and shook his head.

The girl laid a calm hand on the horse's cheek. "He's a fine horse."

Bridger's head bobbed up and down.

"Intelligent and gentle." She kissed him on the nose. "Very gentle." She gestured to the other two to come closer. "We can ride him. Maybe we can even keep him."

The two skipped into the road and stood beside the massive warhorse.

The younger girl pointed to the horse's back. "What's that?"

Cantor had to move to the side to see where she pointed. "I don't know. Saddlebags? I think they're called saddlebags."

"What's in 'em?"

Cantor had just been wondering the same thing. Why would a shape-shifting dragon transform into a horse with saddlebags, in addition to the saddle? "I don't know what's in them."

The oldest pulled the middle child closer. "Come on. That'll be something to hold on to."

"How am I going to get all the way up there? He's huge."

"Climb in the tree and jump on the horse from your sitting branch."

Cantor gasped and held up a hand. The children were about to commit suicide. "Wait. Do you know what kind of horse this is?"

The middle child grinned. "Sure! He's a *good* horse."

Thumb-sucker nodded. Bridger snickered air out of his nostrils and bobbed his head.

Cantor scowled his most fearsome, mature, and judgmental frown. "He's a warhorse. Not a pet."

Hands on her hips and toe tapping, the oldest squinted her disapproval. "How do you know?"

"By the size of him." Cantor reached up to put his hand on Bridger's back. "He's probably trained to charge into battle. It's not likely at all that he's friendly to little children."

Two of the children backed up a step or two. But not the instigator of mischief. The oldest stood her ground.

Cantor chose to change the subject and perhaps divert the children's attention. "What are your names?"

The oldest girl answered. "I'm Ella, my sister is Bella, and Ding-dong's real name is Eddie."

Cantor performed his most elegant bow. "I am Cantor D'Ahma."

Ella and Bella giggled, then curtsied. Eddie removed his thumb, uttered a quiet "hi," and reinserted his personal plug.

Ella moved to stand between her siblings and put an arm around each of their shoulders. "Can we ride your horse now?"

"I told you he's not mine. He's a warhorse, and he's probably not suitable for children."

Bridger moved closer to Cantor and laid his chin on the top of the young realm walker's head. He ducked and moved away. Bridger followed and again put his chin on his head. The small audience laughed.

Cantor sidestepped to get out from under Bridger's nose. The horse merely followed him. When he again shifted, this time in the other direction, Bridger moved to set his chin on Cantor's shoulder. His warm, moist breath tickled his ear.

Cantor jerked away and spun to face the shape-shifted dragon. "Enough already, Bridger. Leave me alone."

Following Ella's lead, the children jumped up and down, clapping their hands.

Bella began a chant. "You *do* know the horse. You know his name. You *do* know the horse. You know his name."

"Be still!" Cantor held up a hand to command their silence. To his surprise, they obeyed and stood quietly awaiting his next pronouncement.

He gestured toward Bridger, who had taken to nibbling all the leaves within range. "He does not belong to me, and I don't know anything about him." He glared at his unwanted companion. "Other than he's a nuisance."

Bridger twisted his neck. With a lower lip pulled up in a

sneer, the dragon snorted. Shaking his head, he went back to his snack.

Ella had her hands on her hips again. "You know his name."

Cantor shrugged. "Lucky guess."

"Ha!" She rolled her eyes.

"You don't want him. Can we keep him?" asked Bella.

Cantor had no right to give away a dragon even if it was presently a horse. He didn't have any claim on the horse, and he didn't want to claim the dragon within. He pondered a moment, hoping to come up with any plausible way to leave the horse with the enthusiastic children. Bridger would certainly have a loving family. He needn't divulge that the horse was really a dragon.

Banishing his dishonest thoughts, he gestured to the scene behind them. "Is that your farmhouse among those trees?"

As if a dozen houses dotted the landscape, all three children twisted to look in the direction he pointed. One two-storied home nestled among a grove of appleton trees.

"Yeah, that's our house." Bella faced him again. "You want to come home with us for lunch?"

"Is that the custom in this land?"

The three children gasped and looked upon him with wide eyes and round mouths dropped open to show their surprise.

"You're from somewhere else!" Bella squealed. "A traveler? A real traveler?"

Ella nudged her sister. "Of course he's a traveler. We knew that." She faced Cantor and lifted her chin in a haughty posture. "In our land, it is customary for you to come *to* the house, but not *into* the house. We'll eat on the porch."

Cantor didn't move. Staring with a frown at their house, he pondered his choices. A free meal was always welcome.

The delay would be minimal. He might get rid of Bridger. He might learn significant news of the local happenings. A realm walker needed to be aware of current events wherever he traveled, thus avoiding a stumble into feuds.

Ella blew out a forceful sigh of exasperation. "Come to our home. Come on! You can tell us where you've traveled. Have you been to Bingar?"

Bella hopped, squealed, and clapped her hands. "There's a stage theater in Bingar."

Without waiting for Cantor's response, the older sister spat out another possibility. "Tommatt?"

"They've a bakery that makes fancy sweets," said Bella.

Eddie nodded his approval of baked treats.

"Gristermeyer?" asked Ella.

Bella's eyes grew big. "Three hotels. Three!"

"Joshnaught?"

The brother's thumb came out of his mouth with a pop. "A fire station with a bell. Brrrrring, ding, ding, ding, ding."

Cantor had not been to any of these places. He didn't wish to lower his status as a respected traveler, so he didn't mention his limited experience of these exciting towns.

To distract his audience, he nodded toward the farmhouse. "It's time to introduce me to your parents. It is unseemly for us to chat away when I'm a stranger."

All three children laughed.

Ella snorted and managed to blurt out, "You're only a little bit strange."

The children raced down the dirt lane leading to the grove of trees. Cantor followed with Bridger breathing down his neck.

"Back off, dragon."

Bridger paused a moment, allowing a gap to form so his nose no longer bumped Cantor between the shoulder blades.

"Good. Thanks."

They walked in silence. Far ahead, the children clambered up the steps of their front porch and disappeared into the house.

Cantor kept walking but threw a question over his shoulder. "What *do* you have in the saddle bags?"

The air behind him became suddenly still and heated. He heard and felt a swoosh. Cantor turned to face Bridger. In his arms, the dragon held a rather large cat of an unusual coloring. While the cat was mostly black, with white front paws and a small, neat white bib, tawny gold tipped its perky ears and distinguished tail. Green eyes glittered through shuttered eyes on a black face.

Bridger stroked the half-asleep feline. "This is my cat. Her name's Jesha."

Cantor looked over his shoulder, but the house was obscured from view by a small shed and tall bushes. He whispered, "You own a cat?"

Bridger ducked his head closer to Cantor's. "I don't know that anyone actually *owns* a cat. The relationship is more like that of a realm walker and a dragon. Comrades, partners, colleagues, or maybe collaborators, but one does not own the other."

Still in hushed tones, Cantor scoffed. "So you have vast familiarity with the liaison between dragon and realm walker, do you?"

"No, but a lot of experience with Jesha. We've been together for four years now."

The cat, with eyes closed, lifted her chin, and Bridger

obligingly stroked along her jaw and down her neck. A purr rumbled in her chest.

Cantor grimaced in disgust. "Who ever heard of a realm walker who has a dragon who has a cat? The image is ridiculous."

"In the *Tales of Bermagot*, Bermagot has a dragon who has an owl."

Cantor shook his head. "No! Bermagot had a dragon and an owl. Bermagot had the owl."

With a smile and a wagging finger, the dragon continued his argument. "Supposition. Anyone knows that a constant is enough companionship for a realm walker. Bermagot had a perfectly good constant so he had no need for an additional friend. The owl was attached to the dragon, not the realm walker."

Impatience raised the pitch of Cantor's tone. "Fine! The owl was not a constant. He was just there. Maybe a traveling companion."

Bridger huffed. A small stream of fire escaped his nostrils. Cantor jumped away before the flame singed his jacket.

Bridger twisted his lips in a moue of disgust before speaking. "Have you not read the *Tales of Bermagot*? I thought every schoolboy knew the exploits of the great realm walker."

Cantor looked out over the pasture. The small windbreak of trees would no longer shield their approach. He wished to get rid of Bridger before anyone saw him in his dragon form. "Of course I've read the *Tales*. I know what he did. He rescued damsels in distress, saved countries being overwhelmed by despots, and built bridges and dams and tunnels for the benefit of the people."

"And the Dragon Allmendor and Owl Espin helped. The owl was a constant just as much as the dragon."

Cantor refused to turn and look the dragon in the eye. "I believe that a dragon is not a constant until he has been called by the realm walker. Therefore the owl was not a constant unless called. And why would Bermagot call an owl when he already had a dragon?"

Bridger did not respond. A press of cold air, a stillness, and then a swoosh.

Cantor turned. The dragon and cat were gone, but so was the horse.

He hissed through his teeth. "Bridger? Bridger? Where are you?"

"Why are you whispering?"

Cantor took a moment to recognize Eddie, standing beside the bushes with his face and hands clean, a fresh set of clothes, and no thumb in his mouth.

"Because we didn't want to wrangle at the top of our voices. Shouting matches are not proper."

The boy looked around. "We?"

"The warhorse and I."

"Where is he?"

"He's not mine, so he went away." Cantor hoped he had gone for good.

"You were shouting with a horse?"

"Not literally; it's a manner of speech. I shouted. The horse made various horsey noises."

Eddie scanned the area once more, shrugged, and slowly shook his head back and forth.

Cantor took the same serious study of his surroundings. Where was Bridger? Where was the cat? He spotted the gold-tipped ears. Ah, in the tree, the tree that had not been a part of the windbreak minutes ago. "Mama says to come." Eddie trotted down the lane without checking to see if the guest followed.

Cantor's stomach gurgled as he strolled behind the boy. For one, Ahma and Odem had drilled into him that he and the rest of the walkers were gentlemen who did not fail to show up after accepting an invitation. Two, realm walkers tried to integrate with the local populace to gain insight into the current conditions of the realm. And three, he didn't want to miss a meal.

His only concern was this bright-eyed boy and his family might be too curious. Though he could handle any prying questions. And Bridger might get impatient and go away. That would be a plus. The horse dragon was sure to be a nuisance.

Eddie stopped and turned. "Horses can't talk. Did you know dragons can talk? It was in a book. Ella read it to me."

The realm walker gave his young companion a searching glance. "I haven't seen many dragons. You?"

"Not even one."

Cantor disguised his relief and sounded legitimately sympathetic. "That's sad."

Eddie stuck his hands into his pockets and skipped a couple of steps before walking. "If Bridger was a dragon instead of a warhorse, would you let me ride him?"

"You think riding a dragon would be safer than riding a warhorse?"

Eddie turned to walk backward as he grinned at Cantor. "No. That's why I want to try."

FINE AND DANDY MEAL

A long, broad table crowded one side of a wraparound porch. Assorted benches and old wooden chairs surrounded it. The smells coming through the open windows made Cantor's mouth water.

An older girl with a kerchief over her long blonde hair and an apron over her pink flowered dress pushed through the screen door with large bowls of food. Cantor bounded up the plank steps to take them from her.

She looked startled, then gave up her burden with a smile. "My name's Tifra Means. I'm the eldest daughter."

With his hands full, he could only nod a formal greeting. "Cantor D'Ahma, at your service."

She laughed and slipped back through the door.

Cantor put the bowls down and lifted the cloths covering them to peek at the contents. Mashed potatoes and creamed corn. He licked his lips, anticipating a meal as grand as the community suppers down at the village near his home. He hadn't often visited the village, a result of Ahma's rules for untrained realm walkers. His favorite part of venturing into civilization was the food. Ahma's cooking was tasty but repetitive. He'd probably eaten more corn and mushroom swatch than any raccoon on the plane.

He glanced around, wondering where the pesky Bridger had settled. The warhorse sat in the shade of the appleton trees. Dragons looked comfortable sitting; the warhorse looked awkward. He had his head turned away from the humans as if he deliberately shunned the activity on the porch since it didn't include him. The cat Jesha rested, curled comfortably beside the tree. Bridger, with his head tilted up, watched the flower-laden branches of the trees.

The awkward situation bothered Cantor. Should he claim the horse? Ask for feed? Reveal to the family that Bridger was a dragon? This was Effram. Surely there was some protocol for dealing with new acquaintances when one was a dragon and the other human. But Bridger held the form of the horse. Did he not want to be recognized as a mor dragon? If so, what was his purpose?

The door swung open again. Three young women and the mother streamed out, chattering and giggling. They carried more food and set their dishes in a row down the center of the table. At the same time, a group of men rounded the corner of the house. Their heavy boots thudded on the wooden steps as they joined the people on the porch. The younger family members rushed to their seats and stood at attention behind a chair or bench.

Tifra motioned Cantor to a seat next to hers. She smiled

at him as he came to stand beside her and nodded toward the man at the head of the table.

"My father," she whispered.

Tifra indicated another man. "My grandfather." As the older man began a prayer to Primen, she dutifully lowered her gaze to her folded hands.

The porch erupted with noise two seconds after the patriarch of the family said, "Amen."

Chairs and benches scraped across the floor. Voices that had respectfully remained silent bubbled up in chatter. Cantor sat next to Tifra and became part of the passing of large bowls and platters of food.

"Welcome to our table, young traveler," called Mr. Means from his end of the table.

Evidently bad manners did not include shouting. "Thank you for having me, sir," Cantor yelled back.

"I am Tifra's mother," said the lady across from him. "Our family receives you and the blessing you bring to us through your presence."

Cantor pondered for a moment what words of greeting would be appropriate.

"You are gracious in your hospitality."

Two boys snorted their laughter. Apparently, Cantor had not chosen well. He'd try again.

"I appreciate the hands that have brought this bounty from field and pasture to your kitchen and to the table."

The same two boys bent toward each other and snickered. Cantor wished they'd just give him the line instead of enjoying his embarrassment. Tifra pinched the one sitting next to her, and a sister on the other side of the boys pinched the one beside her.

The mischievous boys sat up straight, but their shoulders shook from suppressed laughter, their faces burnt red, and their mouths twisted in a thin-line, twitching grimace.

The heavy dishes still moved around the table, handed from one person to the next. Cantor's plate overflowed, and he passed the next plate without spooning out a serving. Though he hadn't tasted anything, he swallowed, trying to dislodge his chagrin at not being able to come up with a courteous reply.

"Didn't I say I would be useful?" Bridger's voice whispered through Cantor's mind.

He sat up straighter and leaned slightly so he could see around Goodwife Means to the warhorse under the tree. Bridger remained in the same position. Again his voice interrupted Cantor's thoughts.

"Say to the goodwife, 'Primen blesses us all. I thank you for sharing the blessing. Primen multiplies this good thing.'"

Cantor repeated the three sentences.

Goodwife Means relaxed, a warm smile came over her face, and she and Tifra sighed in unison.

The goodwife dipped her head, acknowledging his words, and said, "All good things come from Primen."

"You're out of the mire now," said Bridger with a chuckle.

"Can you hear me?" asked Cantor without speaking.

"Yes, I can hear you. I can hear everything you hear. I can see everything you can see. This should prove to you that I am, indeed, your constant, your friend, and your comrade for life."

Cantor spooned warm, buttery potatoes into his mouth. While he savored them, he answered the dragon sitting under the appleton trees. *"Oh, no. I haven't consented to any such thing. I appreciate your help in this instance, but don't make too much of it. I have other plans. We must part ways."*

Bridger muttered one word. "*Stubborn*."

Mr. Means, the grandfather, gave an approving nod to his son. Mr. Means, the father, passed the nod to his wife. She smiled, pleased about something Cantor could not decipher. No tension marred the gathering around the table. He figured the silent communication must have been over a family issue.

The men ignored him and ate with little interaction between them. The food refueled them and gave them an excuse to be off their feet for a while. But their attitude showed they had no time for socializing. The children ate, chattered, and played at the table. No one bid them to mind their manners, eat more, talk less, or be still.

Only Goodwife Means kept up a conversation with Cantor. She asked questions, and to thwart her, Cantor began asking his questions first. The tactic kept his hostess occupied and his secrets safe.

The meal was soon over, and the men vacated the porch with the same speed and noise that had heralded their arrival.

Goodwife Means took the plates from Tifra as she helped clear the table. "Go. Show the young traveler around the farm."

Tifra grinned and scooted around the table, heading for the steps. Cantor followed. They headed toward the barn first. Tifra took off her kerchief, finger-combed her hair, then divided the long golden blonde tresses into sections. She braided her hair as they walked.

"My family raises goats and cows."

Cantor glanced around. "I don't see goats or cattle."

"We have to hide them."

"Where can you possibly hide a herd of cattle?"

Tifra pointed toward the western horizon. "Beyond our

land, the territory is riddled with ravines. Ever seen a poke-matt tree?"

"In a book."

"Well, in person, it stinks, and if you touch it, you get poked. The matted appearance is due to long thorns and closely woven branches. Cows and goats don't mind the smell and don't get caught in the branches. Pokematts are a cross between a bush and a tree, and they cover acres of the rocky fields. Both the cattle and goats hide in the shrub-flats and wander in and out of the ravines."

"Who are you hiding them from?"

Tifra gave Cantor an incredulous look. "The King's Guard, of course. You must be from far away if you aren't troubled by the King's Guard."

Cantor waved his hand in the general direction of the east and upward, since Dairine was higher in the stack of planes than Effram. He would be able to tell the truth and at the same time not reveal he was a realm walker from a different plane. "Mountains. Our home is nestled among some fairly rough mountains."

"And the guards don't come through, taking what they can, claiming that the king requires samples of the harvest?"

Cantor shook his head, wondering how he would talk his way around her suspicion. "We haven't had a king's represen-tative in our village for likely two generations, maybe three if you count the babies born last fall. You see, our community was quarantined a hundred years ago, and we lost touch with the valley people." He spread his hands in a gesture of igno-rance. "I suppose the guard assumed we'd died out when no one came down from the mountains to trade."

"Until you?"

Cantor thought she looked half-convinced, so he continued his tale of half-truth. He smiled with confidence. There was a village in quarantine on Effram. Isolating an area of sickness was common among all the realms. One of his directives from Odem was to visit there and bring back a report. "Oh, scouts have ventured forth and brought back news that the people are better off separated from the rest of Effram."

"And you're a scout?"

"Not exactly."

They had reached the barn. Tifra led them through the massive doors into the cool interior. Another door stood open at the back of the huge structure. The smells and sounds of animals indicated the various stalls held occupants.

Cantor didn't wrinkle his nose, but he wondered if he should tell Tifra Ahma's secret for keeping her stalls sweet-smelling even in the winter. The herb she used might not even exist on this plane. And most of the problem was solved by his constant attention to cleaning the stalls.

For a moment he allowed himself concern for Ahma. Her age kept her from strenuous labor. Odem vowed he would stick closer and enjoy her wonderful meals as he practiced being retired. But Odem had the wanderlust, and he had left a glass eye in many places where he worked in spite of the Realm Walkers Council. In his younger years, Cantor had believed the glass eye phrase literally. It took many visits from the traveling man for the young realm walker to understand the glass eyes were people loyal to Odem.

Cantor brought his attention back to Tifra as she went from stall to stall and pointed out baby pigs, a colt with a wrapped leg, a few sheep, and a nest of newborn kittens.

"A snake bit the colt, so we have him in here until Pa is

certain he is well. The pigs go in and out of the wooden flaps that are open to their sty. The sheep will be brought in for the hot hours in the afternoon."

"Will the King's Guard confiscate these animals?"

"Many of them, along with much of the grain we grow and part of our fruit, chickens, and ducks. They even took one of Pa's herding dogs one time. That really made the menfolk grumble. I thought my brothers might sneak into the camp and steal the dog back, but my uncles talked some sense into them. Better to lose a dog to those scoundrels than have a son pressed into service and lost to the family for ten years."

"You know the Realm Walkers Guild is supposed to take care of such injustice. Have you ever sent a message to them, pleading your case?"

Tifra laughed. "The Realm Walkers Guild? You certainly are out of touch with Effram. The king pays tribute to the council, incentive for them to ignore our plight. My relatives and their older friends all say they can remember when realm walkers came to Effram to acquire their constants. Dragons were seen almost every day. I saw a dragon two years ago."

Cantor did not tell her a dragon sat as a horse in the family's appleton grove. He tried to understand what Tifra told him. A plane estranged from the guild was entirely different from what he had expected. On the other hand, it reflected Ahma and Odem's suspicion of the authorities.

Tifra lifted her arms and let them slap against her sides. "See?"

Cantor surveyed the barn for something out of the ordinary. "See what?"

"Few realm walkers come to Effram to find a mor dragon. No young men and women are answering the noble call to serve Primen. At least, that's what my father says. My uncles say when they were lads, they used to see a dozen young men and women come through during each summer. The travelers dressed in the garb of the council when they were looking for a dragon. Made them easy to spot."

She glanced at Cantor, obviously studying his clothing. With a shake of her head, she leaned against the rails of the pen holding the colt.

The tip of Cantor's tongue danced against his clenched teeth. He very much wanted to announce he was a realm walker, but he knew that would be breaking one of the fundamental instructions he'd received from Ahma and Odem. Apparently in the past, realm walkers did not avoid drawing attention to themselves when they entered a community.

Tifra bid the colt good-bye and led Cantor between two stalls. They exited the barn through a side door. She pointed to a fenced pasture. "That's where we keep a couple of cows for milking. There's a pond with ducks and geese, and my brothers fish there. Closer to the house is a chicken coop. We have the best laying hens in the county."

"Your family has worked hard, and your farm is very impressive."

Tifra screwed up her face, and her words took on a bitter tone. "For all the work we do, this farm should be grander. But a lot of our goods are taken before we go to market. Sometimes, the guard visits the market and takes things from there. It's more convenient to have the choice of the best all at one location."

She took his arm and pulled him toward a well. He turned the handle to bring up the bucket. She gave him the first drink from a cup tied by its handle to a post.

"Thank you," he said after downing the whole cup. "That's sweet and cool."

She laughed and sat on the stone rim with her cup. "It isn't really sweet unless you're comparing it to wells that have that musty taste, or worse, sulfur!" Her merry eyes gleamed. "And it's the one thing the guard has not barreled up and taken away. Although my father predicts that someday that will be part of their collection for the king."

They walked to the porch. Cantor noticed Bridger no longer sat in the appleton orchard. He hoped the dragon had gotten bored and gone off to find some other person to pester.

Tifra touched his arm. He moved away, trying not to be rude, but avoiding personal contact. On different planes, the habit of touching varied tremendously. On Dairine, only family members and close friends hugged or communicated through a hand on the other person's arm.

Cantor breathed a sigh of relief when the farm girl did not take offense. "I best be off. I want to reach a settlement tonight. Can you tell me how far it is to the next village?"

She gave him a sweet smile. "You know they want you to stay."

"Who?"

"My family."

"Why?"

"The work is hard, and another set of hands and a strong back are always welcome." Her cheeks colored faintly. "And they are looking for a husband for me."

She laughed as Cantor gulped, stepped back, and tried to keep his face from twisting into a revelation of his feelings.

"Don't worry. They won't capture you to keep you. They left it to me to send you on or entice you to stay. They figure that a maiden has more chance offering romance than a bunch of burly men offering hard work." Her smile faded. "But you had best be careful as you travel. The King's Guard has no scruples."

She nodded the direction he should go. "Tinamiin is a few houses and three stores. You should be able to walk the distance by nightfall. Ask for the Tinamiin Overseer to put you in a home for the night. Your stay should be pleasant."

"Thank you, Tifra. I feel more confident with the knowledge you've shared. I won't be such a mountain bumpkus as I deal with you flatlanders."

She returned his grin. "You're welcome, Cantor D'Ahma. Be safe in your journey."

He bowed to her with as much formality he would have used in the Realm Walker Council meetings, and then picked up his pack from the steps. Children poured out of the door and stood waving and hollering farewells. The goodwife came out, with a frown on her friendly face. Tifra climbed the wooden steps and stood by her mother. She said something, the mother shrugged, and the two joined the smaller ones in friendly waves.

He walked away from the gracious home, occasionally turning to wave again. Until he was beyond the trees and almost to the road, the children stayed to jump in place while they flapped and fluttered their arms and shouted good-byes.

An afternoon stroll in a pleasant countryside and new discoveries just around the corner would occupy the rest of his day. The negative things Tifra had related were probably exaggerations. Odem would have told him if the situation in the Realms were so dire.

Yet her words nagged at him. Though Odem and Ahma

may not have expressed so plainly the dissatisfaction of the people and the villainy of the leaders, they certainly had been cautious for years. Cantor knew the root of their caution lay in a distrust of the council. He'd long had the impression of something being wrong, even if Odem hadn't spelled it out.

He shook as if getting rid of a bad cloak. Politics did not concern Cantor at the moment. The best approach to the problem was to ready himself. He'd find the right dragon soon enough. He'd follow that path set before him and allow life to be simple for a little longer. Enjoying his freedom sounded more enticing than investigating the King's Guard. Diligently searching for a constant should provide enough excitement for now.

6

SURPRISE GREETING

The scattered clouds offered welcome relief from Effram's sun. He'd been walking for several hours with only a stop for a drink from his canteen and another stop to strip off his coat and hook it through the straps of his knapsack. For a time he enjoyed the scenery, congratulating himself as he identified different plants and birds and even some insects as he trudged along the wide dirt path. But as the sun began its descent in earnest and no one had passed him going either way, the hot, dusty road gradually lost much of its charm of being in a foreign land.

Wiping the sweat from his brow with his sleeve, Cantor reviewed the solar systems in his mind. Dairine and Effram shared the same sun, but his home plane was a great deal farther away than the one he walked on now. That accounted for the extra heat.

The sight of a massive forest up ahead encouraged him.

Soon he'd be in the shade. He quickened his step for ten or fifteen minutes and then slowed, as he didn't seem to be getting much closer. To the side of the road, a farmer's peach orchard bloomed. The scent from the small stand of trees wafted on the slight spring breeze.

In a couple of months, juicy peaches would hang from the branches. Cantor stopped, placed his hands on his hips, and acknowledged the turmoil that had swept over him. He'd just had a wonderful meal in a pleasant home, but the thought of gathering greens for Ahma and doing ordinary chores sucked that enthusiasm from his heart. He admitted a little melancholy over leaving the first part of his life behind with only memories to warm his heart.

Looking ahead, Cantor judged the distance again and acknowledged to himself that the woods had turned out to be farther away than he'd thought. He realized the trees were also taller than he expected. Plodding past the flowered orchard, he spotted a huge rock nestled in the grass. His boot had rubbed a blister on his heel, and he sat on the boulder to ease the pain.

At that moment, he would have welcomed Bridger back. Riding a horse or a dragon would have saved his foot and quickened the journey. But he hadn't seen dragon, haystack, or horse since he left the Means' farm. Encouraging the dragon to follow him hadn't been an option. Bridger didn't have the qualifications to be his constant. His usefulness would be hampered by his limited ability.

Shape-shifting dragons typically had three or four shapes they could easily form. Ahma's Tom had lost some of his agility in his old age. He basically held the form of a dog, switched to dragon when the need arose, and rarely became the huge fish that graced some of Ahma's tales of youthful adventure.

Odem's Nahzy shifted into a dragon or a large owl. The owl, fish, and dog shapes lent themselves to accomplishing missions. What could Bridger do as a haystack? Granted, the horse would come in handy, but in Cantor's opinion, Bridger's personality would not help in any situation.

The dragon had not shown himself all afternoon, and Cantor figured he'd taken the hint and gone looking for another partner. Being lonely on his first quest had never crossed Cantor's mind. Ahma said he was cocky and didn't know how much he didn't know. She was right. As usual.

He took a large swallow from his canteen, then dug in his knapsack to find the box containing ointment and a small roll of linen strip for his sore foot. Odem had impressed him with the need to keep his feet in good shape. The blister had burst, so Cantor applied the ointment and secured the wad of linen to protect the sore. Within a few minutes, he shouldered the bag and resumed his trek across Effram.

The road took on a bit of an incline, making his hike a trifle more arduous. But this was nothing compared to the climb from the village to Ahma's cabin. He puzzled over the type of tree that made up the bulk of the forest ahead. As he came closer he recognized the ladder elm, a tree he had seen only in books Odem had brought for his education. Cantor laughed out loud. He excelled in tree-climbing, and that ladder elms would be no challenge didn't negate the fact that he had wanted to climb one from the very first time he'd seen a picture.

Cantor forgot his sore heel, the heat, and the late afternoon dragging on his energy. A smile lifted the corners of his mouth as he trotted the last hundred yards. He dropped his knapsack on the ground and scaled the side of the tree.

The ladder elm's roots growing closest to the surface turned upward and wrapped around the trunk of the tree. These roots looked more like vines. They crisscrossed each other, interweaving to make a latticework design of a thick leafless covering. Over the years, the vines melded with the bark of the tree, and the trunk appeared to have a zigzagging ladder network.

Cantor climbed the root-vines to the lowest branches, which grew a full twenty feet above the ground. He settled himself on the first bough and scrutinized the horizon.

Peering down the dirt road, he spotted the many crops, pastures, and untended fields that he had passed. He squinted to bring into focus the convenient boulder where he'd stopped. It should have been just after the small peach orchard. He could see the stand of twenty or so peach trees, but the rock next to the road had vanished.

Either the rounded boulder had become invisible or it had walked off. Of course, the rock must have been a shape-shifting dragon. Cantor laughed at himself for missing the opportunity to become acquainted with another dragon. But if the beast had shunned him, it wouldn't have made a good constant.

A disturbance off to the east caught his eye. He watched for a moment before deciding the dark mass was a group of horses with riders, traveling without regard to the fields they trampled. Hooves pounded crops into the ground. Fences went down ahead of them as foreriders swung battering rails against the wood, smashing the supports. Cattle scattered.

Cantor scowled. If the men rode single file, their passing would leave less damage. If Tifra's stories were any indication, these must be the King's Guard. Soon they would reach the road. Would they turn in Cantor's direction or continue across country, ignoring the wide dirt path? Cantor decided he did not want to waste time conversing with the captain of these men. An explanation of his journey might not sit well with these arrogant ruffians.

Glancing down, he saw his knapsack in plain sight. That would never do. He scrambled down the tree, grabbed his belongings, and ran farther into the forest. Hopefully, he hadn't been seen. Where the trees grew thicker, he once again scaled a ladder elm. In his new perch, he had to lean away from the trunk to have a better view of the road. The unpleasant men threatening his peaceful walk through Effram still rode across some poor farmer's newly sprouted field of grain.

Settling back for a long stay if needed, he strapped his knapsack to another limb. The squadron of men continued until they came to the road. One man got down and examined the dirt. He pointed toward the ladder elm forest, then remounted, and the men turned to follow the road.

Cantor groaned softly and whispered, "Now why would they be interested in following my tracks?"

He unhitched his belongings from the limb and climbed another fifteen feet into the higher branches of the tree. He resettled himself. Anyone passing beneath would not spot him through the foliage. The problem was he couldn't see without twisting and leaning away from his comfy spot.

The bough he perched on was narrower than those below and not as comfortable to sit upon. He shifted to ease the pain in his backside and dangled his feet. From his pack, he pulled out a packet of dried fruit and sucked on a thin wedge of apple as he waited. Hopefully, the men would ride past him and keep going.

"That smells good. Do you have another?"

Who'd said that? His first thought was Bridger, but the soft voice sounded like a female. Cantor whipped his head around.

In a neighboring tree, just six feet from where he sat, a young woman waved her fingers at him. He had completely missed her. Her skin was paper white. Her wildly frizzled hair hung over her shoulders, the color so fair it held only a gleam of gold. He thought of the rich cream from Ahma's cow. The girl's blue eyes twinkled with mischief as if she barely held back laughter. She'd enjoyed watching him settle without a clue she was there.

But it was no wonder he hadn't seen her. On her head, she wore a green hat that molded to her madcap hair. Cloth tendrils of brown, rust, and shades of green hung down her back and around her face. Her clothing was multi-layered thin materials of the same woodland colors. She blended into her surroundings.

"I really am hungry." She smiled. "Do you have anything to share?"

He reached in the sack and brought out one of Ahma's food packets. "Can you catch?"

"With the best of them."

He tossed the small package, and she caught it handily.

"Thanks."

"You're welcome."

Cantor watched her for a moment. She wasn't shy about being hungry. Her eyes grew round as she opened the pouch.

She held up a roll and a strip of dried meat. "Oh, yum!" With the bread stuffed in her mouth, she poked around in the packet and brought out sliced cheese and an apple. "Oh, Primen loves me!"

She dropped the bread in her lap and bit into the apple.

Cantor's amazement at the woman's odd attire and stranger behavior flustered him for only a moment. If he was to be a realm walker, he'd have to confront oddities in a straightforward manner. "What are you doing up a tree?"

She spoke around the food she hadn't swallowed yet. "Hiding."

He asked even though he suspected he already knew the answer. "From?"

She waved the cheese toward the road. "Them."

7

NICE TO
MEET YOU

Cantor stared at the oddly clothed young woman. "What did you do?"

Her mouth settled in a grim, straight line. A glare beamed at him from squinted eyes. Her brows lowered, and Cantor thanked Primen that she was in another tree and couldn't reach him.

"I didn't *do* anything."

"Then why are you being hunted by the King's Guard?"

"Because I exist."

"That doesn't seem much of an offense."

"You haven't known me long."

She opened her own canteen, practical gear for a journey but covered with soft and shiny material, lace, and small flat ornaments. She lifted it to her mouth and drank whatever it contained. When she again looked at him, her lips curved in a delicate smile, and her eyes sparkled.

Cantor decided she hadn't given him a good enough answer. "Why don't you tell me the real reason you're up a tree?"

"Oh, I told you the truth. I'm not from this plane, and the King's Guard does not take kindly to visitors."

"Where are you from?"

"Richra." She raised an eyebrow at him. "You?"

"Dairine." His curiosity spurred him on. "Are you traveling alone?"

"Yes." She wrinkled her brow. "It's quite all right. I can take care of myself."

"I'm traveling alone as well."

"My name is Bixby D'Mazeline. I'd shake hands" — she nodded at the space between the trees — "but the distance is just a bit beyond my reach."

"Cantor D'Ahma." He bowed as well as he could from his perch.

She tilted her head to the side. Curly blonde locks and cloth tendrils from her cap shifted, framing her face. Dappled sunlight spotted her cheeks and forehead. She looked as close to a woodland sprite as he had ever imagined. Everything about her was dainty, and he had the odd impression that she was not anchored to the physical world. A fanciful thought, indeed.

"There used to be an Ahma serving as a realm walker." She tossed hair and tendrils over her shoulder with a flip of her hand. "That was a long time ago. Is she one of your ancestors?"

"She's my mentor."

Happiness popped out on Bixby's face with round eyes and round mouth and eyebrows arched up. "You're a realm walker! Are you here to find your dragon?"

Cantor fussed at himself for being careless. He didn't like

having his purpose exposed, but he figured this odd creature would not cause him any harm. "Yes."

"Me too."

Cantor couldn't help his loud response. "What?" Birds erupted from the trees around them.

"Oh, great!" Bixby's face pinched into a frown. "You could have just shouted, 'Here we are,' so the King's Guard won't have to work tracking us."

Cantor twisted around the limbs of his tree to get a view of the road approaching the forest. The squadron still advanced at a fair pace.

He heard Bixby shifting her position.

Her voice chastised him. "Anyone knows when you startle the birds, you've sent up a signal pinpointing your where-abouts. We'll have to move."

Cantor stuffed his snack back in the knapsack and latched the straps in place. "That's probably a good thing in the long run. We're too close to where the road enters the forest."

He started his descent without waiting to see if Bixby D'Mazeline would follow. When his feet touched the ground, she was already standing beside the tree. Her height surprised him, or rather her lack of height surprised him. Ahma, who was short, probably stood a full head taller than the petite blonde.

She bounced on her toes, clearly ready to go. Her skirts hung at varying lengths, some with slanted hems, some with fringe, and one with a ruffle. At least six different fabrics made up her outfit. All of them flimsy, light, and totally inappropriate for running away from the King's Guard through a forest thick with underbrush.

A strap ran over her shoulder and across the front to her

waist, where a flat bag hung. Scraps of fabric, bits of lace, buttons, and ribbons in no discernible order made up the satchel.

Cantor wondered where she carried anything. And if her airy skirts would snag on the bushes. He looked down at her shoes. Unsuitable. Thin leather, more buttons and lace. Lace on half-boots with heels. Bixby D'Mazeline was going to be a hitch in his desire to hurry.

"Can you run?"

"With the best of them."

Cantor pointed away from the road. "That way."

He took off, hoping his body would break a way through the underbrush, leaving openings big enough for her to get through, but small enough to avoid the sharp eyes of the scout tracking them. Every time he glanced over his shoulder, she was no more than two feet behind him. How she did it, he did not know. But he thanked Primen that the girl could, indeed, run with the best of them.

The forest thickened with tree trunks almost touching.

Cantor stopped, pointed to the canopy above and said, "Up?"

She nodded, and he led the way up a ladder elm. He paused where the branches became thick. Bixby, who had climbed with equal skill, stopped directly beside him in another tree.

"Are we going across the crown?" she asked.

"Yes, just below the crest and above the blind."

Her face broke into a radiant smile. "Let's go."

This time she scrambled from branch to branch ahead of Cantor. He marveled at her speed and grace. The limbs barely shook beneath her. But the most startling aspect of this daintily dressed female was how her clothing did not catch on anything. She slipped through foliage, pointy twigs, and leafy boughs with no hindrance. Even Cantor's more serviceable attire snagged upon occasion.

Several times Cantor stopped to pull a broken stem from his waistcoat. Bixby dashed ahead. He lost sight of her for a few minutes and came upon her suddenly. She sat with her back to a trunk, legs stretched out in front of her on a broad bough, and her arm rested across a limb that looked as if it had been designed for that purpose.

He almost passed her, but saw her gesture out of the corner of his eye. She put her finger to her lips and patted a branch very close to her perch. Cantor eased himself down, making little noise.

Bixby cupped her hand behind her ear, then pointed toward the forest floor at some spot farther ahead.

Cantor listened. The rumbling of two men talking reached his ears. He strained to make out the words, but a wall of leaves muffled the conversation. Then Bixby put her hand on his and a blast of woodland noises blared in his head. He jerked his hand away to cover his ears. The noise dropped to normal as soon as he broke contact with Bixby.

He stared at her. Joy and excitement lit her face. By some miracle, she did not burst into giggles.

With a finger over her lips, she whispered, "Could you do that by yourself? Do you have that talent?"

He shook his head. "I hear exceptionally well, but I couldn't pinpoint and magnify a sound like you're doing."

"I'll teach you." She held out her hand, and he gingerly touched her fingertips.

Ordinary sounds of the forest stirred his perception first. He heard soft twitters of birds, rustling of passing small animals in the underbrush, and the wind teasing a song from the highest tips of the branches. Each sound intensified as he isolated it from the others, but he had been able to do this since he was a young boy exploring the mountainside of Ahma's home.

With Bixby's help, he reached a finer clarity. Although she spoke no words, he followed her lead, sensing her mental maneuvers to achieve her goal.

He heard an animal lap water, and something splashed in the same vicinity. Flapping wings caught his attention. Then he heard the two men talking, and nothing else infiltrated his concentration.

"You can't do anything about it, Lem. If you do, it'll stir up more trouble."

"Ruese, we're talking about my boy. If it was your Campe, you'd come to me for help, and I'd help you. You know I would."

"Sure I know that, but our pader always said you were the fool storming the castle, and I was the farmer plowing the field. You act. I prepare."

"My boy, my boy." A sob emphasized the father's despair. "I've got to get him back. My Aria is grieving her son. I don't think she can live, knowing he's turned into a mindless, cruel guardsman."

"It might be too late to get him back. They may have already impressed him."

Lem cried out, "No!"

Cantor imagined from the sounds he heard that Ruese had a sobbing Lem in his arms, and the practical brother thumped the brokenhearted one on the back. "Come now, Lem. You have to be strong for Aria and the other children."

The sobbing and thumping continued.

Ruese's words rose above the wail. "Well, maybe the boy's still whole. They take the captured to Gristermeyer."

Lem caught his breath. Hope lifted his voice. "The new catch was still at Bingar this morning. They won't arrive at Gristermeyer until suppertime."

"If we did break them out, where would they go?"

"Just my boy, just Arend. Perhaps the guards won't notice one thin boy gone."

"You can't leave the others, Lem. For one thing, the guard will know just who to blame. And if we did this foolhardy thing, we couldn't do it for one boy. We'd have to rescue them all. How could you look another man eye to eye if you'd left his son to that purgatory?" Ruese sighed. "And we still would have to think of a place to send them. Nothing will ever be the same, Lem. You know that. It's already too late. Our life will remain smashed to bits by the hand of the King's Court."

"But we'd know Arend's alive. Aria would know our first-born lives."

Cantor glanced at Bixby, and his concentration faded. What little color her face had held had paled, her eyes brimmed with tears, and her breath came in shallow puffs through parted lips. He withdrew his hand.

She lost the faraway stare and focused on him.

He whispered, "Does *impress* mean that the guard changes the character of these captives?"

Bixby nodded.

"How?"

"I don't know how, but I know that the young men forget the loving homes they came from. They forget what their families have taught them."

"And the king does this?"

She half shook her head. "Yes and no. There's another man, called the Croguer. That's not his name, but his position. His duty is to quell those under the king, but it is thought that he also influences the king to do more wickedness. The king is very much under that evil man's thumb."

"Has the Realm Walkers Council been told?"

An expression crossed Bixby's face that reminded Cantor of the looks exchanged between Ahma and Odem.

"Are you going to pursue a career as a realm walker?" she asked.

Cantor nodded.

"Then you will have to know that any good done in the name of the council is done by renegades. These realm walkers follow the urgings of their own conscience and not the orders of the old corrupt hypocrites who rule in Gilead. Surely your mentor has told you this."

"Both Ahma and Odem believed in a student being given the facts and then left to puzzle out the situation so that the learning is embedded more deeply than just at the mind's level."

Bixby bobbed her head as if she had heard of that method of teaching before.

Cantor remained quiet as he contemplated the creature perched in the tree across from him. At this point, he wasn't even sure Bixby was human. Perhaps she really was a sprite. Her gaze had left him. Judging by the concentration displayed on her face, he supposed she listened to the two brothers, not the forest stirrings.

"Let's meet these men," he said. "We should warn them of the approach of the King's Guard. Although I think we have put enough distance between them and us that they aren't an immediate worry."

She agreed. "But these men might stumble into their path."

"So we should caution them."

Her smile came back as she studied him. "And perhaps help them free the captives?"

He felt his whole being respond to the optimism that guided this unusual woman. This was what he wanted, but he hadn't dared let the idea gain solid foothold in his brain. He needed no more encouragement than her suggestion.

Even before finding his dragon and reporting to Gilead, he would begin his life as a realm walker.

He gave one strong, decisive nod of his head. "Yes. We shall see what we can do."

8

WHAT CAN WE DO?

Bixby tamped down the excitement bubbling through her veins. Could this young man, who had blundered into the forest and happened to climb a nearby tree, be one of the companions her mentor hinted would enter her life even before she found her dragon?

Stealing through the forest canopy, Bixby led the way. Cantor followed. His balance matched hers. Neither of them faltered as they used limbs high above the ground as if they were a smooth dirt road. She appreciated his skill and marked it as a plus in her assessment of Cantor as a possible cohort in the plan for the future.

Still, Cantor might not be the type of comrade she wanted. He certainly didn't know much about council politics. Clearly he'd not had the exposure to realm walking that her mentor had insisted she have.

She stopped above the clearing where the two citizens of

Effram bemoaned the fate of Arend and all the young men held prisoners by the King's Guard. Easing down the trunk without stirring so much as a leaf, she got within jumping distance to the men. She looked back at Cantor, caught his eye, nodded once, and dropped silently to the ground.

Lem and Ruese stood together, fully occupied with their scheming. Ruese stroked his chin, his eyes unfocused as he plotted. "First we'd have to break into Gristermeyer. You realize it's a walled city."

"We could go in before the gate closes for the night."

"Fine, excellent, that's a plan. *If* you leave out that we have no business in Gristermeyer, nor money to spend pretending we're gathering supplies." His voice scraped across Bixby's nerves with cutting sarcasm. "No one will notice two country fellows loitering in this city, the one notorious for detaining outsiders and sentencing them to hard labor for no reason."

"We can sit in a tavern and nurse one drink until you think it's the right time to get the boys."

"That'll be hours into the night, Lem. We can't approach the barracks until most everyone is asleep."

"We have the time to wait. I'm not doin' a thing until I can tell Aria her boy is safe."

"So we're going to walk right past the guards in the barracks?" Ruese sighed and ran his fingers through his hair. "You think we can just open a locked door and lead a string of men through the city to the closed and locked, as well as guarded, gate?"

Lem raised his arms above his head, then let them fall. "All you do is think of impossibilities. That's what you've done all your life. My boy's in trouble. Just keep your eyes on that."

The brothers glared at each other.

Cantor landed lightly behind Bixby. She tossed him an encouraging smile and scooted back to stand beside him.

Still wearing the grin, she said, "We'd like to help."

Both men jumped and spun to face them. Ruese, standing taller than his brother, jerked his hand to a leather-wrapped grip sticking out of a long sheath. Bixby gauged the tense muscles in the man's neck and the hard glare in his eyes. He carried a serious dagger and a no-nonsense attitude. She'd not rush in and give the man reason to defend himself. Better to disarm him before his weapon left its case. Caution was an instrument of the wise.

Cantor stepped forward and edged in front of Bixby. "We're not here to do you harm."

Lem relaxed, wiped his hand over his tear-streaked face, and slumped into a round and unimpressive figure.

Ruese cast a wary eye on Cantor and Bixby. "Where did you come from?"

Bixby started to reply, but Cantor straightened his shoulders and said, "We're travelers. But we heard your plight and know that the King's Guard is acting in defiance of Primen's precepts. We offer our assistance."

Ruese gestured toward Cantor. "I can see how you'd be helpful in a brawl." He jabbed his chin forward, toward Bixby. "But what's that wee little girl going to do?"

Bixby passed Cantor so quickly his hair fanned in the breeze. With two cartwheels she closed in on the unsuspecting farmer. A flip at his side gave her the opportunity to grab his knife from its sheath and plant a heel against his chin, knocking him over. She landed and took several steps back so Ruese couldn't grab her ankles and upset her.

"I'm quick," she said. "And I make up for my lack of size with tricks that surprise and confuse my opponents."

She glanced at Cantor. His eyes crinkled at the corners even as he held his lips in a straight line. Another point in his favor. He had a sense of humor.

She couldn't help but grant him her most impish smile. She'd have to ask forgiveness of Primen for her unsuitable pride.

Cantor offered the downed man his hand. Ruese took it and stood.

Brushing the dust and forest debris from his britches, he grinned. "I guess I underestimated your talent, miss."

He made a slight bow as suited a farmer expressing courtesy to a refined lady. "I'm Ruese, miss." He gestured. "My brother Lem. It's Lem who's had a son kidnapped. The boy is Arend."

Bixby curtsied, probably a trifle more formally than was needed to greet a laborer. The fact that she had just battered him to the ground made her feel like being a bit generous with her respect. He displayed good humor after being bested, and that showed character.

She reversed the knife she held, offering the handle as she returned it. "I'm Bixby D'Mazeline. And this is Cantor D'Ahma."

"You aren't natives of Effram."

"No. As Cantor said, we're travelers."

Lem shuffled over to join in the conversation. "Are you realm walkers?"

"Yes," said Cantor.

Bixby nodded and cast an approving glance at Cantor. Of course realm walkers tended to pass through a country as quietly as possible. They didn't call attention to themselves or allow citizens to treat them as special guests. But when they stepped into a fray to protect or guide the people, the realm walkers made sure that the glory went to the established order of realm walkers, to the wizard rulers, and ultimately to Primen. The goal was to serve without taking the credit. Her mentor had said that the more a realm walker avoided the limelight, the more the realm walkers accrued powers and abilities. Humility amplified the gifts given by Primen.

Cantor's affirmation that they were realm walkers had aroused interest in the two farmers.

Ruese slowly shook his head. "We haven't seen many tyros of late."

Lem's chin bobbed up and down, making his speech choppy. "Where's your dragon? Have you selected a constant from Effram? Do you not have one? That's why you came, right? You must be new to it. Real tyros. You look to be as young as my Arend."

Bixby pushed aside disappointment. She'd hoped she'd be mistaken for something higher up in the realm walker ranks. But these two farmers had recognized them for what they were: beginners, tyros. She accepted the label since it was accurate.

"Exactly. We're two tyros," said Bixby. "I haven't met many dragons yet."

"I arrived this morning," said Cantor.

"And he was fortunate," said a voice from the woods, "to find his dragon, Bridger, within feet of the portal. Yes, sir. A good day for a realm walker when his dragon is there at the ready."

Cantor groaned, "Bridger." He closed his eyes, and allowed his head to fall back as if he implored the heavens to intervene.

He looked so put out that Bixby laughed. Cantor wore his attitude on his face and in the postures he adopted. She would have to school him on the unreadable expression necessary in their line of work.

While Cantor suffered the anguish of this dragon showing up again, she and the brothers studied the surrounding trees.

"Where are you?" Bixby asked.

A bush squeezed through the narrow space between two trees. As it progressed into the clearing, leaves fell off the changing form. By the time Bridger stood before them, he was thoroughly dragon.

"You," said Cantor between clenched teeth, "are not my dragon."

A cat wound its way around Bridger's feet, then wandered over to Cantor to rub its sides against his black trousers.

Bixby raised her eyebrows and looked pointedly at the feline beastie. "Your cat?"

"No! Jesha is Bridger's cat."

Her head bobbed up and down. "Good. I've never heard of a realm walker who brought his pet along on his journeys."

"Oh?" Cantor's gaze passed from the cat to the dragon and back to Bixby. "Bermagot had an owl." Before Bridger could jump on that comment, he asked, "Have you ever heard of a dragon that had a pet cat?"

Jesha had gone back to Bridger and sat directly in front of his scaly stomach. The cat groomed her mottled fur, concentrating for the moment on her front paws and pointed ears.

Bixby watched. A realm walker who traveled with a dragon who traveled with a cat. She giggled. A moan from Lem cut her off.

She patted the worrying father's arm. Solid muscle bulged

beneath the cloth of his sleeve. This man worked harder than his soft appearance suggested. If he could control his emotions, he'd be an asset in their raid on the barracks. In his present condition, he wasn't much use. "I'm sorry, Lem. We'll make a plan and get your Arend and the others out tonight."

Cantor moved to Bixby's side. "We should scout the town."

Running his fingers over his hair again, Ruese sighed. His untidy topknot looked worse with every swipe. "With four of us, we'll definitely have to look like we're on some legitimate business."

Bixby ran over the last month in her parents' home. A list of all the reasons someone had been sent to town formed in her mind. She considered each as a possible ruse until one popped out as the most suitable.

"Healer!" She gauged the reaction on the three men's faces. "We can take one of you, or me even, in on a litter. If we say it's an infectious disease, they won't inspect us too closely for fear of catching whatever ails the patient."

"Might not let us in," Ruese said. "The gate sentinels aren't likely to invite a plague into the city."

Bixby remained undaunted. "Injured, then," she said after a moment's contemplation. "We need to fake a wound that would need a healer's care."

Cantor nodded. "That might work."

Ruese shook his head. "We'd need a litter. We'd have to go back to the farm and rig something up. That'll take too much time. The gates would be closed before we got there."

Bridger did a little shuffle in place, clearly excited. "I can be the litter. Just tell me what kind you want, and I'll shapeshift into a litter. I figure it's long, isn't it? Because it's also called a streeeettccchhher."

Cantor's face contorted with annoyance. His words were sharply spoken. "You've shape-shifted into a bush, a horse, a tree, and a haystack."

The dragon held up one pointed claw. "And a boulder."

"So that was you. Six things. That's probably your limit. Very few dragons can shape-shift into more than two things."

"I told you I'm useful. I haven't found any form yet that I can't shape. I admit the ball of yarn was difficult, but only because of the size. I got the color right. And it was fun curling around and around to make the ball."

Bixby clapped her hands. "Oh, good. Primen provides even before we know what we need." She turned to Cantor. "Your dragon will be most useful."

"He's not my dragon. He's a nuisance. He latched onto me and is following me without an invitation. Without permission. Without considering for even one minute that I've told him to go away a half dozen times."

Bixby flapped her hands in a dismissive motion. "Never mind. We'll sort all that out after we rescue the young men."

"I need to warn you, Bridger is a bungler."

"Hey!" Bridger objected. "What bungling have I done? We met this morning. Surely I haven't had time to bungle too much."

Cantor pointed a finger at him. "As a haystack, you caught yourself on fire."

"But by quick thinking, I kept it away from my face and barely got a scorch mark."

"You shape-shifted a beard and nearly lost your entire face in a raging blaze."

"No, I doused it in the creek."

"You fell into the creek."

Bixby decided she'd had enough of the bickering. "A litter is not likely to catch on fire."

This crew needed to be organized. She cast her eye around those gathered in the clearing. No one stepped forward to be boss, which was fine as she liked being in charge. "I'll be the injured one. We'll need blood and something that's been dead for a couple of days, and cloth for bandaging."

Lem swallowed hard. His complexion looked a bit pasty. "Something that's been dead?"

"For the smell," said Bixby. "We'll say I have gangrene and that the healer will probably cut my hand off. And the horrid odor will keep the sentinels at a distance."

Bridger scooped up his cat. "Jesha and I will find something dead."

"Good." Bixby turned to the men. "Find something to make a quick dinner, rabbit or quail or something. We'll use the animal's blood to make a realistic show. I'll tear up one of my petticoats for the bandage."

No one moved.

"Go on. Go!" Bixby motioned for them to get going. "I figure we have three hours until the sun sets and the gate closes. Thank goodness Gristermeyer is not too far."

The others scattered into the woods to fulfill their assignments. The realm walker stood his ground and scrutinized Bixby.

Bixby did not like being examined like a bug held down by a grubby, curious boy. She lifted her skirts, one by one, looking for a slip she wouldn't cry over as she tore it into strips.

Each layer was different. Thin, gauzy material made up most of the skirts and dresses. One skirt was finely crocheted. A silverfish silk showed through a cream dress of fine tatted thread. She wore a ruffled gown with an irregular hemline, three skirts out from the bottom layer. It gave shape to the clothes above. She saved it to wear on the outside when she expected to be entertained in the house of a noble.

Here. A light green slip would do for bandages.

Cantor still hadn't gone off to do something worthwhile. He remained still, watching her, and probably thinking of her as a silly chit. She grinned at that. She was not a silly chit.

"You know where this city is?" Cantor asked. Scowl lines ran across his brow. "How?"

"Maps."

"You've been here long enough to find and study maps?"

Bixby rolled her eyes. "No, I looked at them in the library at home."

"It's illegal to take maps from one plane to another."

"That's one of the council's arbitrary laws to make the common realm walkers' missions harder."

"Why would they do that?"

She shrugged. His ignorance chafed. He really needed an education, and she wanted a comrade who was already savvy. "Why do monkeys eat fleas?"

"Monkeys eat fleas?"

She rolled her eyes again. Reaching under her skirt to her waist, she untied the chosen slip. "Go find something dead. Or catch a rabbit. Or follow Lem and Ruese just to be following Lem and Ruese. I'll start a fire to cook the meat."

"Do you need a flint?"

"You're going to dry out my eyes in their sockets, making me roll 'em all the time." She pulled a tinder box from a flat satchel. "Go!"

"What else is in that flat bag?"

"A thousand necessities and a glass of water. Go!"

Bixby shook her head as she watched Cantor's back disappear into the woods. Aside from the fact that she really liked this new realm walker, she doubted he'd be much help.

On the other hand, fascinating eyes, a charming smile, and a trim physique would be useful in distracting some fair damsel while Bixby engaged in more serious business. She grinned. Cantor would not be cast away before she gave him a chance to show what he could do under treacherous circumstances.

9

GOING IN

Cantor held the handles Bridger provided at the back of the litter. Ruese led the way, walking between the two poles at Bixby's head. Somehow Bridger had shape-shifted his cat, Jesha, into a shabby pillow beneath the girl's head, a feat that had impressed Cantor in spite of himself. Lem clasped Bixby's right hand as he kept close to her side. She appeared to be unconscious. Rabbit blood soaked her linen-wrapped left hand. Occasionally, she moaned.

As for playing their parts, Cantor and Ruese only needed to look solemn. Lem's role as worried father came naturally enough. Bixby had been so excited about their endeavor, Cantor hadn't thought she'd be able to lie still and fake being injured. But she obviously enjoyed her role, to the point she acted as if she was actually about to perish.

A crowd jammed the gateway as the sentinels asked questions of the visitors and inspected carts and larger wagons.

Several people in the queue allowed Bixby and her attendants to advance in the line.

"Poor dear," said one old lady with a cart full of vegetables pulled by a lanky young boy. "She's so pale."

Cantor looked at Bixby's face. Her pallor was her natural color, but she'd rubbed charcoal from the fire under her eyes, leaving sickly shadows. She had crushed leaves in her hands and applied a small amount of green on her face, neck, and one arm. The infected arm received a blush of red from berries. Cantor suppressed a grin. She looked awful.

When they reached the massive wooden gates, a scar-faced soldier stopped them. He peered at Bixby. "What have you got here?"

"My daughter," said Lem. He gestured at Bixby's inert body, then clasped her right hand with both of his. He patted it as he continued to explain.

"She cut her hand on a scythe, and it didn't heal. Now the whole arm's infected. Clear up to her elbow. She fell this morning, right on that hand. Passed out, she did, and hit the table on the way down. The skin burst open, and green and gray pus flowed out with blood, lots of blood, just as bloody as when she first sliced it."

Cantor had to work to keep his face straight. Lem's comments were perfect. He watched the sentinel to see his reaction. The man's stony face disappointed Cantor's desire to see some emotion. Perhaps horror, or at least, disgust.

The guard studied Lem. "So you've come to see the healer."

"Yes, yes, we have." Lem's head bobbed. "My neighbor Shankle Simms said the healer here in Gristermeyer is the best in the realm. We're hoping he won't charge too much or else lets us pay in goods or service."

The sentinel leaned over Bixby, then abruptly stood straight. "She smells like she's rotting."

"Aye, she is," said Lem.

Bixby started quaking. She rolled her head back and forth and moaned. Cantor guessed that she'd been overcome with giggles and disguised her mirth in a display of anguish. He clamped his own lips together and bit the inside of his cheek.

The guard looked away from the writhing patient and scrunched his face in a ferocious glower. "Healer Dukmee tends the regiment. He's not too good and not too bad either. Go on through. Turn right at the first street. It runs around the inside of the wall. Dukmee is on the west side. He's got the herb sign above his shop. Can you read and write?"

Lem looked again to Bixby. "My girl Windsome here knows both reading and writing. But she's not fit to help out."

The guard pointed to a line of people. A citizen stood behind a table where a large book lay open. "Go make your X for Rill. He'll help you get registered."

"Thank you," said Lem as Ruese and Cantor started forward.

They all signed the registry with an X, though Cantor had to grit his teeth to make himself hold the pen long enough even to do that. Lem put an extra X down for Bixby. Rill, in charge of the important log, asked their identities and wrote down the false names they gave.

Finally, they cleared the gate and came to a major intersection. The barracks ran along the east wall, so Ruese turned to the left.

The sentinel's bellow stopped them. "Wrong way! The other direction is right and will lead you to the healer."

Lem nodded and raised a hand in acknowledgement. Ruese swung around as Cantor pivoted. The short walk to the

King's Guard quarters would now be a long walk around the city. Bixby hardly weighed enough to raise a sweat, but the litter-shaped dragon was another matter.

And the people in the streets slowed their progress. Some backed away from the small group as if they hauled a plague between them. Others stood firmly in the way, oblivious to passersby. Still others careened into them in a blind rush.

Ruese slowed to a stop, shifted his burden, and looked over his shoulder. "I'm getting blisters under the calluses on my hands." He nodded at the corner ahead. "We can take one of these cross streets as a shortcut."

"Right," Cantor readily agreed.

Before they had taken another five steps, the sentinel's voice rang in their ears. "Two more blocks and on your right."

Bixby groaned. Lem and Ruese glanced back at Cantor. He forced himself to remain calm for their sakes. The two farmers looked like they would bolt with any more provocation. Surely the guard would not have enough interest in them to go all the way to the healer's shop.

The sentinel lumbered through the crowd, knocking aside people who were too slow to get out of his way. "The captain sent me to make sure what the gal has isn't contagious."

Cantor didn't believe the excuse. "People in Gristermeyer catch scythe cuts like they catch piggypox?"

The guard grinned, stretching the scars on his face into strange lines. "Well, you got to give the captain some slack. He's been late in delivering new soldiers, and he's in a peck of trouble with the command post, and the command post is in trouble with the general, and the general is catching it from the king. And the Croguer? Everyone catches it from him. It all passes down, you know."

Much to Cantor's annoyance, the man strolled beside them, ruining their chance to take a quicker route to the barracks. He paused under the sign of three herbs: parsley, rosemary, and bay. "Here we are." He hammered his mallet-like fist against the elaborately carved wood of the door. "Open up, Dukmee. You've got business to tend to."

Sweat beaded on Cantor's forehead. Now they'd been delivered to the healer's door, and they had little choice but to go in and take their chances. Perhaps a man dedicated to healing would hear them out. Then again, maybe he cared only who buttered his bread. In that case, he'd be likely to expose the charade in short order.

The door opened. A skinny fellow with straight black hair sticking up in all directions had his hand on the doorknob as if he would slam it shut should the need arise. He wore a plain black jacket that reached below his knees with a shiny green shirt beneath and black trousers. He put thick glasses on his nose and peered out at the sentinel.

"Do they need me to come mend a soldier?" His deep voice didn't match the wisp of a body under his neatly pressed clothing.

The soldier stepped aside and indicated Bixby with her attendants. "Your fame is spreading far, Dukmee. A farmer brought his girl to you. She's got a rotting hand. Cut it with a scythe."

Dukmee squinted against the sun. His Adam's apple bobbled as he swallowed. "Bring her in."

Cantor thought the healer far too young to be much good. He'd never met a healer that looked younger than eighty. This one looked to be no more than twenty.

The room they passed straight through smelled a bit musty

with the fragrance of dried herbs. Tidy shelves lined the walls on all four sides of the tiny shop. Small wooden boxes, vials and bottles of all sizes, and cloth sacks held the healer's stock. The soldier came in last and shut the door to the street.

They passed through a curtained doorway into a larger room, this one lined with books upon less orderly shelving. A pitiful fire gave off little heat. Pots and a kettle indicated it was used for cooking. Several stacked books made a neat tower on the floor beside a cushioned chair. A lamp glowed on a side table. No windows allowed light into the inner room.

Dukmee gestured toward a high slab on legs, padded with a chunky mattress, covered with numerous old blankets, and tied with ropes to the tabletop. Ruese and Cantor hoisted the litter and placed Bixby where the healer could examine her hand.

The guard had followed them into the inner room, and Cantor entertained ideas for overpowering him once the healer announced Bixby had no wound.

Dukmee stood beside her, but focused on the litter rather than the girl. He placed a hand on the pole closest to Bixby's head and murmured, "I see."

He turned a frown on the guard. "What are you doing here?" He shooed the burly man toward the shop room. Then Dukmee grabbed Ruese and Lem by the arm and propelled them after the soldier. "I don't need a crowd of people watching."

Lem protested. "I'm Windsome's father."

Dukmee continued to drag him toward the curtained door. "Then you won't want to be watching should I need to cut off her hand."

Color drained from Lem's face. Cantor stepped forward to catch him, but Ruese managed to step in front of the healer and grab his brother.

"I've got him." Ruese wrapped his powerful arms around Lem and dragged him toward the front door. "He needs air. Hey, sentinel, lend me a hand."

The healer returned to his patient, giving a cursory glance at the one remaining male.

"I'm staying," said Cantor.

"Yes, I thought you might." He touched Bixby's sleeve. "You can get up now, girl, and tell me what this is all about."

Bixby sat up and pivoted on the litter, swinging her legs to dangle over the side. With a hop, she stood on the floor, looking up at the healer.

"We needed to get into the city, and we needed to look like we were on legitimate business."

Dukmee picked up the pillow from the litter, stroked it as he crossed the room, and placed the pillow on the stuffed chair. The pillow reformed into Jesha. She meowed and stretched, then settled in the chair as if she needed a nap.

"A cat," said Dukmee. "I couldn't quite figure that one out." He sniffed. "Where is the dead thing? I'd like to get that out of my house, if you don't mind."

Bixby slipped her bandaged hand under the sheet that had covered the litter and pulled out a mauled, deceased rat. She held it between two fingers by the tail. The body had been ravaged by some hungry animal. As she displayed the carcass, the tail separated from its rump, and the main part of it landed on the floor with a thud.

Dukmee's pinched face showed his distaste for the smelly corpse. "Out the back door, please. A garbage barrel. Put the lid back on tightly."

Bixby bent over to pick up the rat. She crinkled her nose. The rodent's mouth gaped open and yellow teeth showed through the drying flesh. She picked him up by two long front teeth. As soon as she straightened, the rat fell. The two teeth remained in her hand.

Cantor came to her rescue. "I'll take it out. Let me have that fake bandage as well."

He scooped up the rat remains and departed through a door along the back wall. Bixby followed him. Soon they sailed back into the healer's examining room minus the nasal offender and the blood-soaked bandage from her hand.

Dukmee pointed at the litter. "And since you have a dragon, one or both of you must be realm walkers."

Cantor grimaced. "We are realm walkers, but Bridger is not our dragon. He's not a constant for either of us. We just arrived."

The healer looked puzzled.

Cantor tried again. "Bixby and I met this afternoon. I met Bridger this morning. He tags along. He — " Cantor stopped before saying the dragon was a nuisance. His forming a litter had been a major part of their plan to get into the city.

"I see," said the healer. He strode through another curtained doorway and returned with a satchel. Setting it on the floor, he began gathering books. He nodded at Bixby. "Hold it open, will you?"

The bag should have filled up, but Dukmee managed to put three times as many volumes in as Cantor thought would fit. Dukmee took the satchel from Bixby, closed it, and pulled another case from a cabinet.

"You can clean up in that room." He pointed out another door covered with a curtain. This one was half the height of the others. "Bixby, isn't it?"

She nodded. "Bixby D'Mazeline."

"Water and towels and soap."

Bixby ducked through the opening and came back out. "It's dark in there."

Dukmee stuck his hand in a pocket and pulled out a fist-sized milky white orb. He shook it, and light radiated from the ball. He tossed it to Bixby. She caught it and grinned. Turning it over and over in her hand, she left to wash up.

Cantor wondered if asking questions of the healer would be prudent. The sentinel mentioned that this man treated the soldiers, which meant he'd likely know a lot about the location of things within the garrison. He hadn't given away their ploy to the sentinel, but did that mean he was trustworthy?

"What are you doing?" asked Cantor as he watched the healer walk back and forth, adding things to another satchel.

"Packing."

"Why?"

"I'm going with you."

"What?" Cantor shook his head as if to clear water out of his ears. "Why?"

"I've been a prisoner in this city for five years. I'm ready to leave."

Cantor let that information sink in. Would they be able to free the captives and get them out of the city? Would one more person complicate their plans enough to cause disaster? Having a healer along might be a great asset should there be a battle.

He wasn't sure. The healer might be more recognizable and give them away just by being one of the many. "What makes you think we can smuggle you out? You don't even know what we came to do."

The healer went through another doorway and reappeared with socks and boots in his hand. He sat on the edge of the big chair, being careful not to bother the cat. As he changed his fine, highly polished shoes to the more common footwear, he explained his reasoning.

"You and your band of oddly assorted friends were clever enough to get into the city without raising suspicions. Your subterfuge points to some nefarious deed you wish to accomplish while you are here. I assume that whatever this task may be will not be pleasing to the authorities. Since you've been successful so far in your endeavor, you're the best chance I've seen in five years to avoid the King's Guard and escape."

He stood and picked up his traveling cases. The book satchel alone should have bent the slight man double, but he stood without effort.

Cantor lowered his chin to his chest and studied the floor. Dukmee was not going to be helpful. The healer expected Cantor and crew to provide the wherewithal for their exit from the city. With a large sigh, he lifted his head.

"We're going to the barracks to set free the new forced recruits before their minds are locked away and they become cruel puppets under the king's despotic rule. Lem's son is among them. Then we'll leave Gristermeyer. No one, so far, has planned the rescue. No one has even a clue as to how we'll get out of the garrison, let alone the city."

"I see," said Dukmee.

He set his satchels down, picked up the cat, and sat in his chair. He placed Jesha in his lap and stroked her. She readily purred, kneaded his waistcoat for a moment, then melted into a puddle of fur. With a hand still petting the cat, Dukmee looked up at Cantor. "May I offer you a meal before we go?"

10

MAKING PLANS

Bixby placed the glowing orb in a cupped wall sconce above a sink in the tiny room. She had ducked through the opening and then straightened, knocking her head on the ceiling. Rubbing the bump, she wondered why the tall healer had a room this short in his establishment.

She'd ask. One needed questions. One of her mentors had primed her to ask questions.

"Never give up your whys, whens, and wherefores," he had said repeatedly as she trained under his tutelage. "Intelligent people never pretend they understand when they do not. Questions are the cure for common stupidity."

A small pump beside the sink provided water, not hot or cold, but pleasantly warm. Something else she would ask about.

The soap smelled like beef stew. She inspected it closely but saw nothing that looked even remotely like carrots, potatoes, or onions. Green flecks dotted the creamy brown bar, but even those couldn't be parts of a vegetable. The soap lathered just like the soaps she had used everywhere else she'd been. But the fragrance made her stomach growl and reminded her she'd only had a smidgen of the roasted rabbit they'd eaten before coming to Gristermeyer.

A good scrubbing returned her face and arms to their natural pale color, though she'd thought it would take days for the green and red tints to fade away. Perhaps beef stew soap had superior qualities.

A mirror showed her she could use freshening in other areas. Stripping off several layers of dresses and shirts and skirts, she reordered them so a tan dress, embroidered with a tiny vine of delicate green leaves, was on top. From her flat bag, she removed a silver crown studded with green jewels and placed it on her head. She scrutinized the effect in the mirror, made a face, and exchanged the modest crown for a smaller gold circlet with dainty leaves on slender vines.

Satisfied, she bent to pass through a curtain-covered door and enter the larger room behind the shop.

Popping noises drew Bixby's attention to the examining table. The poles of the litter wiggled, and the expanse between puffed up. The pieces seemed to pull toward the middle, and slowly the shape took the form of a dragon. Bridger's body fit on the tabletop. In this appearance, his size suited the crowded room.

Dukmee stood, carrying Jesha, and approached Bridger with his right hand extended. "You must be Bridger."

Bixby grinned as the dragon solemnly shook the healer's hand.

"Pleased to meet you," said the dragon. "I believe you mentioned food."

Dukmee laughed. "I did, indeed."

He strode through the curtained door to the front of the shop. Bixby and Cantor followed. Standing in the entrance of his herb store, the healer watched people streaming by.

Bixby heard the sentinel's voice and backed into the other room, where she and Bridger peeked through the curtain. They could no longer see out into the street, but they could hear the conversation.

"How's that farm girl, healer?"

"I didn't have to amputate her hand. Tell the father he can come in now. And that other man. You can run along and give your report. I'll be keeping the girl here until I'm satisfied she'll recover."

"How long will that be?"

Dukmee put his hand to his chin and paused as if considering. "Up to seven days. But her initial response to my treatment looks promising, so it may be sooner."

"Fine." His voice sounded gruff, as if he had left off his friendly demeanor and returned to a guard's mindset. "See that this family doesn't leave without checking in at headquarters."

"Not my concern," said the healer. "I'm only responsible for their health, not their whereabouts. You'll have to find someone else for that job."

"Take care to be cooperative, Dukmee. You know how badly things can turn out for those who have a disobliging spirit."

"Indeed, I do."

A gap in the conversation made Bixby want to run into the room to find out what was happening. She waited, holding her breath. What was going on in the street? Dukmee stood silently. Cantor stood behind him. Dukmee's posture denied anything was amiss, but Cantor looked ready to spring into a fray. Beside her, Bridger moaned.

Suddenly, the two men took a step back from the open door. Bixby cringed, waiting for something bad to happen. Lem and Ruese appeared in the door and entered. She sighed with relief. Now they stood in the way, conversing with Cantor, and she couldn't see the healer.

She vaguely heard them as they compared notes about what had happened during the interval they were out of sight from one another. Bixby closed her eyes and reached with her mind. The circlet warmed on her forehead. She couldn't enter the healer's thoughts, but she did hear him speak.

"Pen, take this coin and go to Widow Apar. Ask her to fix me a lunch for six and wait for her to prepare a basket. Bring the basket back, and there will be a coin for you."

"Yes, sir," said a young voice.

The healer closed his door and ushered the three men into the back room. Bixby abandoned the use of her crown to listen in on Dukmee.

He gave Bixby a scrutinizing stare. "I see," he mumbled. Turning away, Dukmee directed the men to help him lower the examining table and set it up as a place for dining.

Bixby's list of questions bubbled inside her, demanding satisfaction.

"Why was that sentinel so different?"

"How was he different?" asked Dukmee.

"He had personality. He seemed like a friendly sort and not a ruthless killer."

"Don't let his demeanor fool you. He's as coldblooded as the rest of them. And he is not a common soldier. He's one who chose to be a servant to the king. That makes him worse than the conscripted men who lose the life they know and are transformed into mindless instruments of terror."

"You mean he's evil because he wants to be evil, not because something was done to his mind that removed his conscience."

"Exactly. He's the king's man because of the power and fortune it gives him."

The front door opened, and Pen called, "I have your lunch, Healer. There's a second basket, so my friend Tando carried it."

Dukmee hurried through the curtain. "Good job, boys. Here's a coin for each of you. Run along now and buy something good for your families to share. Don't buy candy . . . . Sausages! Sausages are cheap and taste good. Here's another coin for bread. Surprise your mums!"

"Yes, sir."

The front door slammed. Dukmee came into the room carrying a basket in each hand.

"That was quick," said Bridger with a greedy eye on the food.

"Widow Apar's shop is only two doors down."

Dukmee planted his burden on the table and gestured for everyone to sit. Cantor visibly startled when their host indicated the dragon should have a specific chair close to his own.

Bixby offered thanks aloud for their little band of comrades, the food, and their safe entry into the city. She also requested that Primen inspire them with a brilliant plan to rescue the men and help the healer escape the city.

Bixby tried not to laugh when she realized Cantor seemed uneasy about Bridger's joining them at the table. The dragon showed some sophistication. In fact, she'd known courtiers who could have learned a lesson or two about table etiquette from the dragon. The only breach he made was slurping his drink, and given the shape of his mouth, Bixby didn't know whether he was capable of drinking without the noise.

When the first edge of hunger was satisfied, and the party slowed down, Bixby settled back to survey the room and her companions.

Her feet swung as they dangled from the high stool. She relaxed, willing to watch Cantor do the interview. She'd learn a lot from his opinions while he asked diplomatic questions.

"What have they done to imprison you? What would we have to do to get past their guards?"

"Wards," answered the healer. "Wards on each of the gates."

The word startled a grunt out of Ruese. "Wards? You mean a spell cast by a wizard? How can that be?"

Bixby focused on the healer.

Dukmee's deep voice carried his information wrapped in solemnity. "Contrary to what we've been told, there are wizards about. The king has several under his influence. I suspect the Croguer is a powerful wizard, but not under the influence of the king. Quite the opposite."

"But the minor wizards are under the king's influence?" asked Bixby. "Do you mean in the same way the recruits are rendered incapable of their own thoughts? And these wizards succumb to the same influence?"

"No. The king can't use the same treatment on the wizards. The process would destroy their ability to do his bidding. They have to believe they're still in control of their decisions in order to work spells."

Bridger leaned over the table. "But they're not. I've seen one at work."

Lem and Ruese exchanged a look. Lem took a swig of his drink. Ruese pushed back his plate and folded his hands on the table. Everyone at the table listened intently to Bridger's tale, even Cantor.

"This wizard blighted a field of corn. A songbird flew by and distracted him. You could see on his face that he was confused. But as he took a step to leave, he regained his focus. He strode into the middle of the field and smote the plants. Then he walked away with a smile on his face."

Bridger's smile radiated a smug impression. "This is one of the reasons I'm glad to be Cantor D'Ahma's constant."

"The fact remains," said Cantor, "that Cantor D'Ahma is not glad to have you as his constant."

Without paying any regard to the realm walker's interruption, the dragon continued. "Perhaps we'll return when our bond is stronger and right the wrongs that are committed here."

Growling his words, Cantor disputed the dragon's claim. "You are not my constant. I have not chosen my constant."

The dragon ignored him and passed a small piece of meat down to Jesha, who sat at Bridger's feet.

Ruese closed his mouth, then with a light hand, popped his brother on the shoulder. "A realm walker and his dragon, Lem. We'll rescue the boys for sure."

Cantor looked down at his plate and muttered, "Not my dragon."

No one answered his comment and after a moment, Dukmee cleared his throat. "Tell me the news outside the city walls. My sources are unreliable at present."

The conversation continued around the table. They spoke of the food shortage in the larger cities, the immodest clothing style of the king's court that outraged those who followed Primen, and the sudden lack of trade between districts.

Dukmee withdrew his attention and seemed to ponder

some deep thought. Bixby tried again to use the crown and enter his mind. He tossed her a look of annoyance, and she quit.

Lem, too, soon dropped out of the exchange of ideas and pushed his bowl away. Gloom descended on him as evening deepened the shadows in the healer's home.

Ruese noticed his brother's despair and put an arm around his shoulder.

Bixby's sympathy welled and spilled out with the aid of her tongue. "What are we going to do? We need to be planning our mission, not discussing food and clothing and trade and such."

Dukmee smiled and nodded. "Indeed, we do. I have an idea, if you would allow me to be your counselor."

"We'll consider anything you have to say," said Cantor. "I believe you're in a good position to know what will work and what will not. Tell us your idea."

"Merely invisibility for two, freedom for many, escape for me. I think I've done a rather good job of covering all the aspects." He spoke to Bridger. "Tell me, my friend, are you the type of dragon who can blow fire? Or are you of the fire-less breed?"

With a smug glance at Cantor, Bridger nodded. "Oh, yes, I can breathe fire, and I don't even have to be in dragon skin to do so."

Cantor mumbled, "That statement is entirely true."

Dukmee clapped his hands together. "Then I believe our difficulties shall be addressed this night. Tomorrow's moon will look down on a happy resolution of our plight."

11

TRICKS AND DISGUISES

Bixby did her best to remain still, but restless energy filled her after Dukmee left the table to make his preparations for their mission. He'd made it clear that the men and Bixby would be in the way, but the more time passed, the more she fidgeted. How could she learn if she sat with those who merely passed the time? Cantor and the others seemed content to sit around the table, eating a bit here and there, talking a lot, and waiting.

Enough of this. Bixby slid from her stool and followed Dukmee into his workroom. Again she noted the endless shelves filled with jars and boxes of who-knew-what. A table in the middle of the room provided a place to mix his potions. Stools of various heights supplied the only seats.

She took one that looked out of the way. Dukmee glanced up but said nothing.

She watched him with his herbs and oils, hoping to learn

more of the healing arts. After a while, she ventured a question. His answer shook loose an avalanche of further inquiries, until he refused to answer any more and started growling at her when she opened her mouth. She tried again to enter his thoughts, but he threw her a warning glance. Soon after, she switched tiaras to aid her perspicacity. So she watched, just watched, no mind probing. But her mind categorized every move he made, every bottle or bag he picked up. She filed away hours' worth of intriguing information.

Many of the herbs he put in a mortar and ground with a pestle. Her offer of help was ignored. He heated the oil above a little contraption that resembled a lantern without the glass globe over the flame. He mixed the crushed herbs in the oil and then stirred that concoction into a bottle of fluid.

"What's in there?" she asked, risking his haughty glare.

The healer surprised her with an answer. "Water."

Pleased that he'd answered her question, she asked another. "What does the concoction do?"

"Causes something to be invisible. A pity I don't have one that renders vocal cords silent."

"Oh, come now." Bixby sighed. She couldn't suppress the desire to tease him. "You know you're as pleased as doodlebugs in the warm sun. I'm a promising pupil. I have gifts that astound you. You've been itching to reveal the secrets of your trade ever since you recognized my potential."

"You think so?"

"I do." She jumped down and moved to a high stool closer to the table where the healer straightened his equipment. "It is as it always is. I'm introduced to a mentor of one kind or another. They test me in whatever way pleases them. They're amazed. Shortly thereafter, the poor master suffers from flabbergastation."

Dukmee paused a moment in reorganizing his materials. "The symptoms of flabbergastation being ...?"

"The victim presents speechless intervals, with a decided glaze of dumbfoundedness marring his normally intelligent expression."

"I see." The healer went back to his work.

"As I was saying, in the beginning, zeal frizzles, snaps, zings, jazzes in the heart and mind of the learned one. He or she can't wait to have me under his or her tutelage."

"And what blights this happy union?"

"In every case, they discover I am somewhat incorrigible, and their fervor dies in a flood of exasperation." She cocked her head to one side and lifted her shoulders in a dismissive shrug. "I got sent home. More than once."

Dukmee snapped the clasps shut on three wooden boxes he'd finished packing with various containers from his shelves. "Couldn't you endeavor to break the trend? You could choose not to be incorrigible. Isn't your goal to stay longer and learn more?"

"The problem is I get bored. The first weeks go very well." She picked a bottle, read the label, then pulled out the stopper to smell it.

Making a face, she recapped it and replaced it on the shelf. "When I've read everything in the master's library and he's lectured until I'm at wit's end ... well, I start asking questions and trying unapproved experiments without supervision and generally make a nuisance of myself."

"So you've now come to the age of eighteen and discovered you're destined to be a realm walker?"

Bixby didn't reply. She had a great many answers she could give, but she guarded this part of her life. Not many people knew of her extraordinary talents, and she liked it like that. People could be so weird when she changed the color of a piece of cloth. And she could do things much more astonishing than dye manipulation.

Yes, she could easily become a realm walker. She saw the portals that most people could not see. Sometimes she could even hear them. And once, it felt as though she had called one into being, although she told no one that tale. Being labeled lunamatory would further hinder her attempts at being respected.

The problem was so many other things besides realm walking appealed to her sense of adventure. Challenging projects drew her interest. Intriguing, mysterious crimes practically roped, tied, and dragged her into the process of solving the puzzle. She also liked art, but that was a hobby. At this moment, the healer's skill looked enticing.

"How does this concoction work?" she asked.

"The old book in which I found the formula did not explain the chemistry of the potion that alters the physics of the cloth. If we had more time, I would make a huge batch, submerge our clothing, and dry them. The effect lasts a great deal longer when done that way. But since the hour is drawing near for our exploit, I'll use the atomizer. We'll be covered from head to toe, veil, gloves, and a long cloak. "

Bixby considered his answer. Instead of a terse reply, he'd explained. Why? Because he didn't want her to know something else. He focused her attention on something that wasn't important to keep her from exploring a line of thought that would lead her to something he preferred to keep under wraps. What?

She squinted and studied the healer. If only he would let her into his mind.

"Not today." He winked at her.

"What are you hiding?"

"I just don't believe in letting strangers roam around in my mind."

She sat up straighter and tried to make her four-foot frame look intimidating. "You're hiding something."

He returned her gaze, dark eyes latched onto hers. "Aren't we all? Especially you, Miss D'Mazeline."

Well, that hadn't gotten her anywhere.

Cantor stepped through the door. "Are we ready to go? The brothers are getting restless."

Dukmee held up a fist-sized bottle. A tube with a bulb at the end extended from the container's metal top. "I'll spritz Bixby's clothing and my own. Then, we'll be on our way."

Bixby flashed her brightest smile. "Why not make us all invisible?"

Dukmee again held the bottle aloft. "I only have enough potion for two."

Crouched behind three garbage containers and a wooden crate, Cantor looked over his shoulder. The alley afforded little shelter. The wooden crate was Bridger being useful as additional cover to hide behind. The brothers had gone ahead with Dukmee.

A warm breath tickled the hairs on Cantor's neck. Bixby peered over his shoulder, though he couldn't see her.

"I can hear you breathing; I know you're there."

"Where else would I be?" She shifted, her boots scooting gravel beneath their soles. "Dukmee told us to stay here and wait for his signal."

"You don't have to crowd me. You don't have to hide. You're invisible."

"Oh ... right. I'm invisible."

He heard her sharp intake of breath, and she clutched the cloth of his sleeve, giving his arm a shake. "That's it. The signal."

Cantor pulled away from her hand. Feeling contact without seeing anything gave him goose bumps. "What signal?"

"Dukmee says to move into position."

"I didn't hear anything."

"He's talking in my head."

Cantor could think of nothing to say. Dukmee, the healer, talked to Bixby, the novice realm walker, in her head? Neither Ahma nor Odem had ever said anything about people talking without talking. First Bridger spoke to him at the farm, but that was understandable. The dragon was trying to prove that he could be Cantor's constant.

After bonding, after years of being together, man and dragon constants read each other's minds. That was his understanding.

Since arriving in Effram, Cantor's thoughts had skittered from one surprising idea to another. With so much information to process, he hadn't latched on to this wordless communication as something common among certain people. Bixby certainly acted like it was nothing peculiar. So perhaps Bridger's communication with him at the farm was not so extraordinary. Perhaps it meant nothing. He hoped it meant nothing.

It didn't mean he would be stuck with this buffoon of a dragon. As soon as they finished the rescue, he'd make some excuse and detach himself from this motley crew, the whimsical girl, the know-it-all healer, and the boorish dragon.

Their adventure invigorated his heartbeat, and this realm walker venture was nothing like the staid problem solving he'd expected. Ahma and Odem had never mentioned daring rescues perpetrated under the noses of a region's lawful, albeit corrupt, authorities.

He felt a small push against his back.

"Let's go," said Bixby.

Cantor shook himself out of his stupor, put a hand on the big crate, and said, "Let's go, Bridger."

The wooden box glided forward, making a lot less noise than the dragon did in his own form. At the end of the alley, when Bridger abruptly stopped, Cantor and Bixby paused.

Cantor leaned sideways and peered around the box. Two men stood talking under a lantern next to the barracks gate.

"Two? I thought Dukmee said a solitary soldier stood guard at each checkpoint." Cantor pulled back behind Bridger. "I suppose with the conscripted men in the barracks, they're taking extra precautions."

Bixby's voice whispered at his shoulder. "Or it's the changing of the guard. But whatever the case, we're fine. I'll take care of them."

Cantor's ear tickled from her breath, so he stuck a finger in the hole and wiggled away the uncomfortable feeling. "How are you going to do that?"

"We were in such a hurry to leave, Dukmee didn't get a chance to tell you the particulars of his plan."

"Or," said Cantor, allowing sarcasm to spice his words, "he didn't think we needed to know. He's got a pretty arrogant manner."

"I won't fight with you on that one. Right now he's urging us to hurry. When the guards fall, go for the gate."

He heard the slight swish of clothing and knew Bixby had gone ahead. He watched the guards. One man looked astonished as the other fell like a rock to the ground. Then his eyes bugged, and he too collapsed. Wondering what Bixby had done, Cantor urged Bridger forward. "We'll find out soon enough."

Bridger made a wood-twisting-against-wood sound. Cantor answered the crate's unspoken question. "I'll explain later."

Exasperated alarm rattled his thoughts. No, I can't be so in tune with this crazy dragon, this wooden box, that I know what he's thinking. It's too soon, and ... No! not *and*. This dragon is not my dragon. I haven't chosen a dragon yet. I'm not even going to travel with these people after tonight.

One guard's shoulders lifted from the ground with his head lolling back. Cantor dashed forward to help Bixby drag the unconscious man into the shadows. Then they pulled the other man out of the way.

Bridger, as a crate, was too big to go through the gate. He transformed into himself, then leaned down and sniffed the man closest to him. "What did you do to the guards?"

Cantor heard Bixby move, then heard her voice. "Dukmee says they'll sleep until morning and then wake up with a headache." A bottle floated in front of Cantor and Bridger. "This is something Dukmee gave me. I wave it under —"

Bridger thrust his face forward, and his nose passed over the uncorked bottle.

"No!" squealed Bixby.

"What?" Bridger looked puzzled.

"Did you smell it?" Bixby's voice trembled.

"Sure," said the dragon, his word slurring. "It smells baaa ... "

Cantor grabbed Bridger's arm as the dragon's big eyes rolled upward. He broke the creature's fall and gave Bixby a glare.

"What is that stuff?"

"It's a potion that makes whoever sniffs it black out."

"The guards dropped like stones. Bridger held out for a moment. Maybe it won't last until morning."

"We'd better find the others and get those men out of the lockup." A cork came out of nowhere and jammed into the bottle's neck. "You and I alone could never carry a full-grown, incapacitated dragon."

Cantor searched the corners and dark shadows. "Where's his cat?"

"The cat won't help haul the dragon."

"But she can stand watch while we're busy elsewhere." Cantor picked up Bridger's feet and started to pull him toward some crates. "Get his tail and help pull."

"Is it all right to pull a dragon's tail?"

"When he's drugged, I think it's safe."

"Right." The tail rose in the air. "I hope he doesn't snore. He doesn't need to attract attention."

Cantor nodded to the hiding place they'd chosen. "There's the cat."

They tugged a little more and hid Bridger in the dark shadows behind the crates.

"Here, Jesha," said Bixby. "Here, kitty, kitty. Come keep your dragon out of trouble while we're away."

The cat, with tail high, sauntered over and sat next to Bridger's snout. Her regal stance looked like a lion statue next to the entrance of a palace.

Cantor shook his head at the sight. "Come on. Let's go."

12

THE MEN IN THE BARRACKS

Dukmee crept forward, his slow, even breaths hot against his face beneath the veil he wore over his hooded cloak. Invisibility was never a comfortable situation — too close and too warm for his taste. Inside the barrack's walls, the buildings scrunched together in the manner of a small town. Narrow streets and even tighter alleys crisscrossed between the shabby and shabbier structures. Behind Dukmee, the two farmers trailed him closely, watching a small rod he held for them to see. When Dukmee paused to get his bearings, Ruese stepped on his heel.

"Ouch."

Ruese jerked back.

Dukmee hopped on one foot, reaching down to replace the shoe that had slipped off when the farmer's big boot scraped against his heel. He scowled at Ruese, hoping the fine kid leather hadn't been scarred. He'd chosen this pair for their silent tread, not sturdiness. He hadn't chosen these men at all, and they had proven to be clumsy, not silent. They looked sturdy, but they hadn't been tested against the King's Guard.

In the dimly lit passages, Lem bumped into his brother. "Hey, Ruese! I can't be running into you like that. The guards will hear us."

"Tell him." Ruese pointed in front of him and gingerly explored the space ahead with an outstretched hand. "I can't see when he stops sudden-like."

Dukmee spoke softly to the two farmers, "Quiet. We'll remain here for a moment while I survey the route ahead."

Lem, the father of the kidnapped boy, touched his cap and bobbed his head as if acknowledging someone from a higher class. "Right. We'll wait for you here."

Dukmee frowned and shook his head. Remembering that Lem couldn't see his gestures, he spoke. "You don't have to be subservient to me, Lem."

"What?"

"Don't tip your hat," explained Ruese.

Lem shook his head. "I didn't."

"You touched the brim. It's the same thing."

"It's not, you know." Lem faced his brother and glared. "It's not nearly as subs-zer, whatever, as doffing my hat."

Dukmee's whisper hissed one word. "Silence."

Both men jumped.

Ruese narrowed his eyes as if that would help him see Dukmee. "Shouldn't whisper, you know. All the hissing travels farther than the sounds of words spoken quiet-like. You learn that hunting in the woods." He firmed his lips in a straight line as if keeping back more words. With a sigh, he relaxed. "Weren't you going to scout the route?"

"I can do that from here." For a moment, Dukmee

considered surrounding them with a sound bubble so that these loud farmers would not be heard. He discarded the idea as too time-consuming. "I'm using my senses to locate the people inside the castle, as well as the barracks. I can tell if they're moving, if they're sleeping, and if they're directly in our path."

Ruese scratched his head. "How?"

"It would take me too long to explain. Simply put, I smell, hear, or taste what is in that tunnel and beyond. The tunnel leads to a more secure part of the barracks. So far, we've not encountered any formidable resistance to our meandering within these confines."

Lem scratched his head. "What'd that mean?"

"I don't know. But I can smell the sewage." Ruese shrugged. "Not as fragrant as manure in a hot barn."

Lem pushed his brother aside and addressed the empty space before him. "Do you know where my son is?"

Dukmee nodded, then scoffed at himself. Stupid mistake. It had been way too long since he'd been invisible.

"Yes," he said.

"By that sensing thing, smelling him?"

"No, I already knew where prisoners are kept."

"He's no prisoner," objected the father. "He committed no crime."

Ruese agreed. "Except being in the wrong place at the wrong time."

Dukmee closed his eyes, gathering patience. Perhaps he should have left these two back in his healer's shop. "Be quiet now. I have to concentrate."

The farmers obeyed to the point that they scarcely moved to breathe. For a moment, the healer noticed the acrid scent of anxiety surrounding the two men, underpinned by the earthy smell of determination. They were scared, but their mission to save Arend would carry them through.

Pushing the farmers and their problems aside, Dukmee focused his attention in the other direction. His perceptive skill slid through the sewage tunnel where fluid sludged in a canal down the center.

Dukmee slowed his breathing. In his mind, he saw a crude map of the barracks based on his visits to render medical assistance to the occupants. His senses gathered information, and colored dots appeared where people occupied small spaces.

"We're blessed tonight, gentlemen." He spoke in hushed tones but allowed the smile on his lips to lighten his words. "The soldiers worked hard today and filled their bellies with heavy food. Most of them are sleeping, and those at their posts are nodding, not fully alert."

Lem breathed a sigh of relief. "Primen is with us. He has drugged those who would stop us from freeing the young men."

Dukmee didn't comment. Too many things could go wrong during this mission. "Remember my signals. We'll not speak once inside the barracks."

He turned to face the men and displayed the short carved rod. He held the baton in front of the farmers. They could see only the two ends as they extended from the invisible glove that covered his hand.

"When the rod is perpendicular from the ground, stop." He turned his wrist. "If it's horizontal, take cover." He rotated the tip of the baton in a wide, slow circle. "Come, cautiously."

Both men nodded with each new position of the stick in his demonstration.

Dukmee placed the rod in an upright status again and twirled it with speed. "Come, hurry, no need to hide."

And last, he jerked the baton in a motion that clearly meant go that way, go fast.

"That's it," said Dukmee. "I'll be a few yards ahead of you so I can spot danger before you come into sight. Remember, we knock them out. We're not here to kill anyone, even soldiers."

Could he trust them? Father and uncle had reason to be brutal if a guard got in their way of rescuing Arend and the others. He read the aura around each man. Serious, determined, but no red-hot anger, no revenge. He hoped no wild emotion would surge to the surface if their plans met resistance.

"We're ready," said Ruese.

"Let's go get my boy," said Lem.

Dukmee believed they were as ready as he could make them. He'd trust Primen to supply the rest.

The sewer tunnel reeked, but Dukmee had practice at blocking unpleasant odors. He couldn't help the farmers, though. He traveled quickly, hoping to avoid his accomplices being overcome with nausea. They trotted behind him. Deciding that farmers who mucked out stalls had sturdy stomachs, he quit monitoring their physical state.

It was time to narrow his focus. At present, his mind followed the placement of each live being in the barracks. Surmising that three were canines, he sent a compulsion to sleep to their minds and dropped them from his running tab.

He knew when Bixby and Cantor entered the front gate, but he couldn't find the dragon. He narrowed his focus to pick up just the dragon. Then he scoped for any dragon-like being. Nothing.

With a sigh, Dukmee went back to his more general reckoning of the opposition within the barracks. Soon he would be close enough to the intriguing girl to hand off some of the mental work. He assumed she could handle the constant input of information. A suspicion that they shared a heritage grew with each observation of Bixby. Whether she understood her standing or not, he couldn't say.

Bixby's voice entered his thoughts. *"Bridger's unconscious."*

"Have you engaged the enemy?" Before he could form another question, images of the dragon sniffing the bottle containing his sleeping potion spun in his mind. The dragon hit the ground.

"So that explains why I haven't been able to locate Bridger; the dragon sleeps in an unnatural stupor, beyond my ken."

"That's right." Bixby sounded slightly apologetic. *"We'll have to carry him after the rescue."*

Dukmee sighed. *"Quite all right. We'll manage."*

Was everyone on this mission inadequate? Thankful that Cantor and Bixby followed orders competently, Dukmee instructed Bixby how to reach the prisoner lockup within the barracks. Staying alert to the undercurrent of many minds, he led the farmers through the shoddy wooden maze behind the stone walls that fronted the building. Each time they approached a guard, Dukmee sent a calming wave of thought and put the man into a deep sleep.

A disturbance within the chamber where the captured young men were kept interrupted Dukmee's carefully monitored assessment of their progress. On his signal, the brothers stopped. He groaned as he realized the full implication of the frantic energy farther down the passage.

Of course, the prisoners had not been fed a heavy meal. They were anxious about the morning, when they would be taken to some unknown destination and turned into emotionless guards. Instead of sleeping, they had plotted an escape.

Dukmee attempted to communicate with them all, a mass message, as he couldn't allow them to run loose in the barracks. His thoughts practically bounced off the turmoil of their minds. He read panic and frenzy. He tried a single word command. "Stay." No use.

"What's wrong?" asked Lem.

"The young men are escaping."

Ruese chuckled. "What's wrong with that? Isn't that just what we were planning to do this night?"

Dukmee sighed, loudly enough that both men realized something was very wrong.

"They're breaking out, planning to fight all the way to the gate. That will get men hurt, both the soldiers and your boys. They have the determination to get out." He blew out an exasperated sigh. "But they've made no plans as to where to go, where to hide, and have no idea of how to get food or how far they must flee to be safe." Dukmee waved his baton. "Hurry. We must get to them before they get out of the prison area."

He ran, leading Lem and Ruese by the shortest route. He liked subtlety, and this race to the rescue had not an ounce of discretion. If he had time, he could muffle the clomping of their heavy boots. If Bixby had worked with him for more than a few hours, she could be relied on to step in and follow his hasty directives.

And Cantor? Well, Cantor seemed a ready young lad.

Cantor breathed as he did when he went hunting, a quiet, slow, shallow rhythm. The passages of the barracks opened to the star-filled sky, and the dirt alleyways felt like forest paths.

But there the likeness ended. To either side, rough wooden structures rose with a stark ugliness unlike anything Cantor had found in the forest back home.

With his breathing hushed, he could hear Bixby, her soft breath and the slight swish of cloth against cloth as she moved. He heard her heartbeat, slow and steady. That surprised him. He'd only heard an animal's heart when the creature was scared or had been running to escape danger.

The light fragrance of some flower tickled his nose. Lavender? No, honeysuckle. The scent had surrounded them earlier in the day when they sat in the ladder elms. He'd noticed the vine wrapped around the tree where he'd first seen her, camouflaged by her unusual apparel. Now she wore an invisible cloak and gloves, but he knew where she was by two senses other than his sight. And another sense, not one of the five. He'd have to explore this awareness. Was it an awakening power or just something special between him and another realm walker?

Waiting did not appeal to him. Words to encourage Bixby to move toward the trapped men formed on his tongue.

She slowed to a halt in front of him. Her hand touched his arm, her fingertips lightly rubbing his shirt sleeve. "We must go now, and hurry. The captives are about to make a horrible mistake and mess up our plan to rescue them."

Cantor leaned toward her to whisper. "How?"

"They plan to break out."

He nodded. "Away from the portal they can't see."

"If they'd just wait two more minutes —" Bixby tugged on his arm. "Let's go. Dukmee says to hurry."

When Dukmee raised the alarm, this time speaking directly to both their minds, he told the two to make haste. Both responded with speed and no silly questions. That one factor might be the saving of this mission turned fiasco. Silly speech reminded him of another of this party of rebels. He made a note to remember to bring along the drugged dragon.

A guard dog staggered to his feet, his sense of duty clawing its way through Dukmee's mental influence. The beast growled low in its throat, but before he could bark the alarm, the healer waved his hand, and the dog sank to the floor, duty forgotten once again.

No sooner had the dog succumbed than another hindrance approached. Dukmee latched on to his last ounce of patience and concentrated on picking up clues from this new problem.

Two men sauntered down a hall, having left a card game. They'd had a bit to drink and still managed to win. How to send them off in another direction so he and his companions were not delayed? Dukmee rolled his eyes at the inanity of the ploy he was about to implement, then he telegraphed a suggestion.

"I left my pouch," said one of the men.

"You weren't carrying one."

"I was! The gray one with the squirrel figured on it with black thread."

"Well, go back and get it."

"Our winnings were in that bag. You come with me. I bet Hankerton hid it and plans to keep our money."

"It was mostly his money to begin with."

"It's our money now. Come on."

The two men turned to retrace their steps.

Dukmee twisted the rod in his hand, beckoning Lem and Ruese to follow.

13

FRESH AIR, BUT WHERE?

The two groups of rescuers converged at the head of the alley leading to the prison. In his state of heightened alertness, Cantor had no trouble pinpointing the position of the healer even with the man still invisible.

Dukmee gave a command, and he and Bixby shed their cloaks.

The healer put his hands on Bixby's shoulders. He drew her nearer so her nose was almost touching his waistcoat. "Have you studied sound barriers?"

She nodded.

"We're going to put up a temporary shield between the barracks and the castle proper. Just follow my lead."

To Cantor, the two looked like they stood still, closed their eyes, and did nothing. Nothing at all. He didn't like Dukmee's assumption that he could order Bixby around. And was it really necessary to stand so close to perform this sound barrier manipulation? Dukmee took his hands off her shoulders. They sighed in unison and stepped apart.

The healer signaled to the others to come closer. He arranged the group as he wanted, taking point for himself. Bixby and Cantor stood behind and away from his shoulders. Farmers Lem and Ruese stood behind them and out. They made a V, and Bixby whispered to Cantor, "It's the V of Force."

He clenched his jaw and controlled the volume of his answer. "I know. The farmers are just for show. It's the three in front who do the work."

"Ever been in one?"

Cantor observed her excited smile and the tremor that vibrated her many layers of lace and thin materials. He hated admitting his inexperience. "No."

Her eyebrows shot up and she grinned. "Neither have I."

He relaxed. She put out her hand, and he took it to shake.

Her face became solemn. "May Primen be with us."

"Indeed."

Ahead of them, Dukmee stiffened. "Oh, conflagragations!"

The double doors at the end of the path banged open, splintered wood flying in all directions. Determined young men poured out, rushing toward the small group of rescuers. With fists raised, they looked as if they would pummel their way through the flimsy barricade of three young scholars and two old men.

The farmers hollered, "Arend!"

As one, Dukmee, Bixby, and Cantor raised their hands, palms up. The rushing men ran into some invisible wall and fell back against those still coming.

One fallen boy struggled against the crowd to gain his footing. "What's going on? These aren't guards."

A burly lad yelled, "Look! Two of them have no hands."

Cantor's attention flickered from the concentration needed to hold the barrier together. He heard both Bixby and Dukmee grunt with the strain, but he couldn't help cringing at the rather sickening sight of arms with no hands in front of his partners.

The scene on the other side of the division erupted into chaos. Some men caught the ones who'd been stunned by their encounter with the invisible wall. A few pushed forward, resolute in their desire to gain freedom. And some turned back as if to seek another way out.

Regaining his focus, Cantor felt his limited ability for combining his strength with others swell. Being part of the V of Force proved he could blend with the others' more extensive power. He felt a quiver of pride over the accomplishment.

Dukmee's strength surged into Cantor and Bixby, and Cantor realized that as their power wove together, the energy increased. Individually as well as corporally. Like the old saying, "A three-strand rope will not break." At this point, he felt confident the might of their dominance would hold against the onslaught of many more than these two dozen men.

Dukmee's next command came in the form of a picture. Step by step, the three walked forward, pushing the barrier and the men behind it. The prisoners returned to the large holding cell with a mixture of protests and curses.

The rescuers followed them through the demolished doors. Dukmee lowered his elbows to his sides but kept his palms facing the desperate men. "Lem and Ruese, close what's left of those doors as best you can. Bixby, help me do some damage control. I'll check the castle. You search the nearby barracks."

Cantor looked from Dukmee to Bixby in time to see her nod and squeeze her eyes shut. What damage control? The question died on his lips as a voice rang out. "Pader? Uncle Ruese?"

Lem pushed between Bixby and Dukmee. "Arend?"

Father and son met at the invisible barrier. "This is my pader," Arend shouted above the clamor. "He's come to save us."

The restless young men calmed. With their eyes pinned on Lem, they waited for some pronouncement.

Dukmee cleared his throat. "Our escape route is a portal, and it's in this room. Stay calm, and we will lower the wall we've used to contain you."

The men glanced around the cell. Their expressions ranged from suspicious to terrified . A boy at the back asked, "How do we know we can trust you?"

Arend had his arms around his father, and they slapped each other on the back as they embraced.

"They are with my pader," said Arend. "Of course we can trust them."

The tallest young man in the crowd stepped forward. "Portals are witchery, and everyone knows Primen hates witchery. These people are evil. They don't even have hands like normal citizens."

Ruese scratched his head. "They did at mealtime."

Dukmee and Bixby looked down at their stubby arms, and Bixby grinned sheepishly. She tossed Dukmee a look, but his expression was inscrutable. The two peeled off their gloves.

"Invisibility." The tall man humphed. "More witchery."

Arend rolled his eyes. "That's Pedran. Pay him no mind. He's the only one of us that's ever studied the Primen Guide. He tries to make us believe he's the authority on everything to do with Primen."

Dukmee didn't pay any attention to the men, now that he seemed intent on finding the portal. He walked to the side of the room where one small window next to the ceiling let in a trickle of fresh air.

The healer motioned for Cantor and Bixby to join him. "Here, I think. I'll need your help to open the portal."

Cantor tried to protest. He'd never summoned a portal, only gone through ones that opened on their own. Before he got the words out, Dukmee reassured him, "It's simple."

The image formed in Cantor's mind of his two hands reaching forward and stretching a small hole into a much larger one. Before him, the portal formed just from his thoughts linked with Dukmee's and Bixby's thoughts.

Cantor was thrilled by the flow of power rushing through his body from his toes to his fingertips. He glanced at Bixby to see if she felt the same surge of excitement. She not only looked happy, but there was something else in her expression. She nodded her head and looked as if "I told you so" was on the tip of her tongue. Now what thought gave her that expression?

Dukmee smiled and turned to the anxious men. "We're ready to go."

"Where?" asked Lem.

"There's a portal here. We need only step through."

Ruese rubbed the back of his neck as he slowly shook his head. "I don't see anything."

"We'll demonstrate." Dukmee held out his hand, and Bixby took it.

The healer walked a few steps with the lace-bedecked girl following. They both disappeared. Moments later, Dukmee re-entered the room with Bixby trailing him.

"Easy." Dukmee dropped Bixby's hand and took Arend's.

He addressed the group. "You must touch the person in front of you in order to follow him through. I suggest we get on with it. A few of the guards are awake enough to figure out something is happening." He spared a glance for his partners in this mission. "Bixby, Cantor, hold this open until we're all on the other side. It will get more difficult as I move farther away from the portal."

Cantor looked at Bixby with one eyebrow cocked. She smiled and nodded. "We can do it."

As Dukmee started to walk, Arend took hold of his father's arm. Ruese latched onto his brother, and another of the young men grabbed Ruese's shoulder. Each man in turn disappeared at the exact same spot as the line moved forward.

Toward the end, one nervous boy thought to ask, "Where are we going?"

Cantor answered, "Derson." A sudden image in his mind of two spoons colliding over Ahma's table flashed through his mind. Was Derson the best place to send these fugitives?

"Derson! Another plane?"

The boy's astonished face looked comical to Cantor, but Bixby showed compassion for his dismay. "You'll be safe there from the king's demand that you serve him and him alone."

Cantor added, "The air's a lot fresher there than in this prison."

As the last man passed through the portal, Dukmee appeared in the gap. "Go rescue the dragon. I'll meet you in Gilead."

Cantor's eyebrows shot up. "We're going to report this to the council?"

"That's the plan." Dukmee gave a jaunty wave as he strolled away.

The portal closed with a swoosh and a snap.

14

MOVING A
DRAGON

Cantor led the way through the maze of corridors, alleys, and streets inside the barracks. It reminded him of a rabbit warren. Right. A rabbit warren with evil bunnies. He wanted to be on point in case they ran into trouble.

Bixby carried the two invisible cloaks. She'd refused his offer to be the beast of burden.

"I want you to protect us with that pointy dagger you have in your belt. Keep your hands free, and I'll carry the load. The cloth gets lighter and lighter as the potion fades."

Cantor still felt queasy when he looked at her. Where the cloaks draped over her arm, he could see nothing. They also blocked part of the front of her skirt. The potion was wearing off. So occasionally instead of Cantor seeing right through the cloak and Bixby, the image had dizzying ripples through it. He shook off the unsettling feeling and concentrated on Bridger.

They slipped out the front gate and surveyed the area with relief. No one had discovered it unattended and replaced the knocked-out sentinels.

Cantor looked behind the stack of crates in the street running in front of the barracks. "Right where we left him."

Bixby squeezed in beside Cantor. She shook her head in dismay. "He's bigger."

"He's a mor dragon. They increase in size as they rest. Ahma has one."

Bixby's head swiveled as she searched the area. "Where's Jesha?"

"Meow." The cat's declaration came from above.

Both looked up to spy her sitting at the edge of the highest crate.

Cantor reached for her, and the cat jumped into his arms. He held her close and rubbed the back of her head. Her soft, smooth fur carried the fragrance of night-blooming heliotrope. He put his nose against her cheek. She purred.

"Bixby, have you ever met a dragon as unusual as Bridger? I've never heard of a dragon having a pet."

"There aren't many dragons on Richra."

"I've been to Richra with Odem." Cantor looked up at the sky as if memories of his trip with Odem floated among the stars. "We checked out a dangerous mine and helped shore up the walls."

"There are a lot of mines. My father says that if the citizens don't find something else to do, the plane will be a shell around extensive catacombs."

Cantor focused once again on the dainty figure beside him. "I heard the council was devising another means of livelihood so Richra wouldn't be destroyed."

"Right, and the progress on that is the same as on any project the council undertakes." She shrugged. "If they don't profit somehow, they don't put any effort into the matter." She shifted the cloaks she carried. "We're going to need a cart to move him."

"I'll go get one." Cantor surveyed the street. Three lamp-posts spaced too far apart gave off inadequate light. No traffic passed in the early morning hours. Where would he find a cart or wagon, plus a mule or horse, before the city life sprang up and caught them unprepared?

"I'll go." Bixby dumped the cloaks on the ground. "I don't want to be here if guards show up and spot our dragon. You might want to cover him up with the cloaks, even though they're losing strength."

"Do you know where to look for a cart?"

"I have an idea."

"What if you run into guards?"

"If I can move, I can hide. Standing here beside a lump of comatose dragon would hamper my style." She smiled at him. "It shouldn't take long. I'm going to the market. The vendors should be getting ready for the day."

He nodded, and Bixby spun around, her many layers of skirts swirling around her tiny body. Her departure looked to be part dance and part sprint.

Cantor brought his attention back to the matter at hand. He put Jesha down and used the cloaks to cover what he could of the growing dragon. Bridger's growth exposed his hindquarters as they pushed out from behind the crates. The dragon also made grunty noises. Perhaps he would regain consciousness before Bixby returned.

The cat rubbed against Cantor's legs, and he sat with his

back against the wall both to make himself unobtrusive and to accommodate Jesha, who wanted a lap.

While he waited, Cantor thought about what Bixby had said about the overmining of Richra, and he wondered if the problem had anything to do with Odem's prediction regarding the plane. The old man had said that Richra and Derson were varying from their orbits. Could the problem be attributed to the loss of mass as the ore is mined and escorted through portals to foreign planes?

Third from the top, Richra boasted rich soil and warm temperatures, with almost too much rain. It was home to many interesting animals that lived nowhere else in the system. Yet of all its resources, the rich mineral deposits below the surface were the most valued. Though Richra's citizens grew what they needed and basically had no reason to look elsewhere for their sustenance, the minerals lured other planes to seek trade agreements, sparking greed, envy, and territoriality.

Trading between planets required realm walkers traveling through portals. Some unscrupulous realm walkers denounced their duty to protect and guide in favor of participation in black market trade. Cantor had overheard Odem telling Ahma that these people had grown rich and devious. Feuds between them often resulted in innocents being killed. Yet the council did nothing to curb their avarice.

More and more, people of other planes had begun to regard Richra and her citizens with envy. As was often the case, legends instead of facts fueled discontent. In reality, Primen had not set up the universe to be a place of strife and conflict, granting each of the planes luxuries and difficulties in equal measure.

Realm walkers supposedly recognized the balance of livelihood from one plane to another. But many principles had faded into oblivion as the years marched on without a wizard to guide the populace.

Cantor had enjoyed his visit to Richra with its fetes and glitz and fashion, but in truth, he preferred the less structured society of Dairine.

Rattles and squeaks heralded the arrival of a rickety conveyance for the sleeping dragon. Cantor stood to get a better look. Bixby came around the corner, leading a donkey and a two-wheeled cart. A limping, gray-headed man trailed behind.

Cantor walked down the street to greet her. "Where'd you find it?"

She pointed with her thumb behind her. "Two streets away. That man was sleeping in it. He's going to help us lift Bridger."

Cantor turned and walked beside her. "You aren't wearing the same dress you had on when you left."

"Yes, I am."

"No, the dress you had on was a yellowish white lace with little pink things in it. And hanging out below that was a pale green thing. And hanging out from under that was a pink-striped thing. And on the top—"

"All right, all right. You noticed what I was wearing."

"I've never seen anyone dress like you. Even when I visited Richra."

A smug smile lifted Bixby's cheeks. As they passed under one of the three lamps, Cantor saw her eyes twinkle.

"I have my own style. Part of it is that I wear everything that I take with me. The dress on top was the next to the bottom layer earlier. I decided the cream lace was too bright to wear on these gloomy streets."

"Why?"

"Because I wanted to blend in and not draw attention."

"No, why do you wear all your clothes?"

She shrugged, and Cantor realized the gesture was part of her personality. "Of course, I have other clothes in a hamper, but rather than dipping into that closet, I prefer to have what most likely will be needed on my body. I don't like to keep my clothes in storage. Sometimes they don't smell fresh and need to be aired out before they are fit. And, actually, I like the way the layers look, and ..."

"And?"

"Well, there isn't much to me, and all the layers make me look a bit more substantial."

Cantor laughed. "I see. That makes sense. I guess. You better stow that head-thing though — it attracts attention."

Bixby snatched the finely crafted circlet from her head and poked it into a pouch that she hid in her skirts.

"How many of those pouches do you have?"

"They're hampers, and I have a lot."

He nodded and decided he didn't need to know. "So, we put Bridger into the cart. Then what?"

"We get out of this town, find my dragon, and go to Gilead."

"Sounds simple enough."

"Right." Her voice didn't hold much conviction. "Soon as we get past the first part, it should be easy." She made a face as if thinking. "To tell the truth, the second part might be a bit of a problem as well. But going to Gilead. *That* should be easy."

Cantor needed to make one thing clear. "I'm still looking for my dragon as well."

They stopped beside the sleeping beast and watched the cloaks rise and fall as he breathed. Only a vestige of the potion still worked. The changing image hurt Cantor's eyes. He reached down and pulled the offending garments off.

Bixby took them and tossed them into the cart. Jesha jumped in as if anticipating the loading of her dragon. She skirted the circumference of the small wagon, sniffing as she made her inspection. She then sat down in a corner and proceeded to groom her paws, face, and head.

Bixby stood over the dragon. "You and Bridger would make good partners."

"I want to take some time." Cantor moved to stand at Bridger's head. "I want to consider carefully and choose a dragon I can work with."

"You can work with Bridger. You've already done that. I have the feeling he's very gifted."

Cantor just grunted as a reply. He smelled rather than saw the approach of the cart's owner.

The man came around the wagon. "It really is a dragon. Used to see dragons a lot when I was a lad. Don't hardly see them at all anymore. Especially not in the city."

"Let's get him loaded and away from here," said Cantor.

Bridger turned out to be a more awkward load than heavy. His unwieldy, limp body sagged and slipped and defied a proper grip. Trying to be quiet, trying *not* to break the flimsy old cart, and trying not to hurt the dragon as they shoved him over the brittle wood side made the task challenging.

When they stood panting by the cart, winded by the effort, the man held out his hand in a gesture that clearly meant he wanted to be paid.

Bixby spoke through shallow gasps for air. "Are you sure you want to sell your cart? We could just rent it from you. Come along, and you can take the cart back with a nice fee for obliging us."

"I don't need it anymore. I was going to try to sell it at market this morning."

His lack of heavy breathing told Cantor why lifting Bridger had been more difficult. This helper hadn't helped much.

"Really." The man's tone became urgent. "I'm going to retire."

Bixby pulled out a bulging, frilly purse and gave the man three gold coins. He bit each one, then put them in his pocket. Tipping his hat, the gent turned on his heel and left.

Cantor stood with his mouth open as the man walked quickly away. As he neared the end of the street, his pace quickened until he ran the last few yards to the corner.

Bixby looked up at Cantor and gave another little shrug, then poked the purse back in the folds of her skirts.

"I guess I better tell you. My family is rich."

Cantor closed his mouth. "Bixby, where did you say you found the cart?"

Her face folded in a frown. "On the way to the market."

"And the donkey was already harnessed to it?"

"No, the donkey was in his stable."

"And the man?"

"Was sleeping in the cart."

"He got the donkey from the stable?"

She nodded.

"How did the donkey act?"

"Like it didn't want to leave its home and work in the middle of the night."

Cantor went to the donkey's head, roughed its fur-covered forehead, and clicked his tongue. "Let's go, little lady."

"What's wrong, Cantor? Why are you acting so strangely?"

"If I'm not mistaken, you've just stolen a cart and donkey."

15

GET GOING

Bixby liked Cantor. He didn't get all loud and contrary when calm and order disintegrated into chaos and mayhem. He'd not said one condemning word about her gullibility.

She hadn't thought twice about whether or not the old man owned the cart and donkey. If she had, she could have easily read his nature beneath the surface impression of laziness. But her mind had been on the adventure of escaping the city. She sighed. Several of her mentors had stressed the necessity to not only plan ahead, but to observe the immediate.

Now she and Cantor walked at the head of the donkey, leading it down the least occupied streets, zigzagging back to Dukmee's shop in hopes of avoiding any authorities looking for a stolen cart pulled by a stolen donkey.

They walked in silence until Bridger groaned.

"Great," Cantor whispered. "He's waking up."

Another loud moan stretched out into the sleeping town.

Bixby ran back and climbed into the cart, throwing

her body down on the dragon. "Hush! Bridger, be quiet. Everything's going to be all right."

He mumbled. The only word she caught was *wing*.

She shifted and saw that in her haste, she'd landed behind his left shoulder, directly on his wing.

Bixby rolled off the dragon into the narrow crevasse between him and the side of the cart. "Oh, I'm sorry, so sorry. Did I hurt you? Is it broken? Are you all right?"

Bridger snorted twice, then settled into a soft, rhythmic snore.

The cart stopped, and Cantor looked in from the other side. "Are you okay?"

Bixby tried to rise up to see better over the mountain of dragon, but she was stuck. She collapsed back into the wedge and found she'd slipped farther into the gap. Annoyance stiffened her response. "I'm fine."

Cantor stepped on the wheel. The cart creaked and sagged in his direction. Now Bixby could see him better.

He peered down at the dragon between them. "How about Bridger?"

"He's fine."

He paused a moment, and Bixby watched the frown deepen on his face.

He opened and shut his mouth twice before he spoke what he was thinking. "What's wrong then?"

"I didn't say anything is wrong."

"No, you didn't. But ..."

Bixby let out a loud, exasperated sigh. "Would you help me out of here? I'm jammed into this teeny tiny crack, which is probably getting smaller as this mor dragon grows."

Cantor smiled and reached out to her. "Take my hand."

Bixby grunted as she strained to reach it. Cantor climbed over the side of the cart and found two small spaces on that side of the dragon where he could cram his feet. Now he gave her two hands. Bixby and Cantor both grimaced as he tried to pull her out.

He let go. "How'd you get in there?" His eyes wandered over the sleeping dragon, the cat who'd come awake, and his fellow realm walker.

She rolled her eyes. "Does it really matter?"

"No, I guess it doesn't, but I think time is a critical factor. Seems to me I read that as mor dragons get closer to their natural size, the process speeds up. Bridger really is growing faster. You really are in danger."

"Don't tell my parents."

Cantor gave an experimental tug on Bridger's bony spine. He didn't move. "Tell your parents what?"

"They expected so much of me."

Cantor continued the examination of the problem. "Don't tell your parents what?"

"I don't want the herald announcing, 'Bixby D'Mazeline dies in freak accident, squished between a growing, drugged mor dragon and the bottom of a stolen cart. She is survived by another realm walker, the stolen donkey pulling the stolen cart, the cat belonging to the dragon, and the dragon, who eventually woke up.' My mother would not like any of that."

"I don't think Ahma would either. I'm supposed to watch out for my fellow citizens and do what it takes to keep them or remove them from harm's way."

"So what are you going to do?"

"I'm going to take off that side of the cart."

"Do you think you can?"

"Bixby, this cart is held together by dirt. I wouldn't be surprised if it crumbled all together after we get you out."

Cantor moved around the back of the cart and stood where Bixby could not see him. She heard him tugging at the brittle wood boards. His heavy breathing convinced her the job was harder than he'd anticipated. Nails squealed as he forced them out of their embedded places in other old, creaking boards.

"What are you doing, bantling?" The deep, raspy voice surprised both Bixby and Cantor.

Cantor's boots scraped on the cobblestones as he spun around.

"My friend is stuck."

Bixby wanted to look through Cantor's eyes. She tried reaching her hamper to select a tiara. Her predicament limited her maneuverability. She couldn't twist far enough, and her arms didn't bend in the right direction. The right hamper was inches beyond her grasp.

She heard heavy steps approach the cart. "Let me help you."

Jesha stood, arched her back, then squinted a disapproving look at Bixby.

"It's not my fault, cat. Go growl at the stranger."

Jesha hopped up on the edge of the cart. Her bits of white fur glowed in the moonlight. The gold tips of her ears and tail glittered. And her dark fur blended with the night. She looked like a cat with pieces missing.

The cart squeaked. The stranger's reddened face and long, tangled hair hung over her head. If his body matched the size of his head, the man must be one of the giant breeds. Bixby had seen a few during various travels, but only from a distance.

The odor of sweat and gin flowed down. Bixby gagged and turned her face away. Either the pressure of Bridger expanding against her chest or the man's presence choked her. Her lungs ached. Her arms and legs tingled. The imprisonment between wood and dragon became excruciatingly tight.

A grinding chortle introduced a larger, bellowing guffaw. "She's shy." While the uncouth man still raised a ruckus with his unexplainable cheer, he placed his hands on the wood and with one jerk pulled off the side of the cart. Cantor caught Bixby as she tumbled out from her confinement. He dragged her a few feet away from the ratty old cart and the uncouth savior.

His hands grasped her upper arms, and she felt like she'd crumple if he let go.

He bent over to look her in the face. "Are you all right? Anything broken?"

She gratefully pulled in great gulps of air, shaking her head at the same time. "My knees are shaking."

Cantor glanced around and guided her to a low wall around a small bit of lawn in front of a business. She plopped onto the hard surface without any of her usual grace, and she felt blessed not to have collapsed a few steps away from the seat.

A few moments of concentrated, even breathing calmed her nerves and her lungs. Her muscles, however, still felt like they'd been squeezed in a linen press.

"Oh, I haven't hurt like this since I rode a stubborn old mule all the way across Vendasimer Desert. Perhaps there will be a remedy at Dukmee's shop."

Jesha let out a caterwaul that shook the leaves on a bush next to the wall.

Cantor turned abruptly. "What do you think you're doing?"

Bixby leaned way over to get a view around Cantor. "Put him down."

The ill-favored stranger stood with Bridger draped around

the back of his neck like a shepherd would carry a lamb, or a sheep — a huge, full-grown sheep.

"What?" he asked. "This is a dragon. I'm taking him for payment 'cause I helped you."

Bixby stood and took a shaky step to stand by Cantor. "You can't."

"Why not?"

Bixby stuttered a bit. "B-b-because he's not yours to take."

"He belongs to you, right?" The drunken man seemed to have grasped that much. He let go of the dragon for a moment to scratch his oily scalp. "I saved you. You owe me."

"He's not really mine. But I'll give you money, not the dragon."

Bridger slipped, and the man grabbed the ridge along the dragon's back and hoisted him higher onto his shoulder. A fierce scowl darkened his face, and he shook his head with not a bit of the joviality he'd shown earlier.

"I've had money before. I've never had a dragon." He let go of Bridger again to point his huge finger at Bixby. "If he's not your dragon" — the finger shifted to Cantor — "he's yours."

"No, he is *not* my dragon."

Bixby rolled her eyes. For once, his constant denial of Bridger might serve a purpose. She eyed the giant. Or maybe not.

The man shrugged, repositioned Bridger, turned, and whistled as he walked away.

Bixby clipped Cantor's side with her elbow and whispered, "I think you just made a big mistake." She cleared her throat and shouted, "Come back."

The giant raised a hand to acknowledge he'd heard but kept walking. "Seems like this dragon doesn't belong to either of you, so there's no harm in my taking him."

Jesha split the air again with an impressive howl. She leapt off the cart and charged down the street. The donkey shed its obliging demeanor and bolted in the opposite direction.

Bixby shook Cantor's arm. "The cloaks, we need Dukmee's cloaks."

He didn't stop to question but took off after the clattering cart.

Bixby heard the man holler and saw that Jesha had caught up with him and scaled his leg, using sharp claws. With a hand the size of a shovel, he tried to bat her off. Losing his grip on Bridger, the gargantuan man dropped him to the street. The dragon's descent nearly knocked Jesha from where she now clung to the seat of the giant's pants, but she managed to hold on. With the dragon out of the way, the cat clawed up the man's leather waistcoat and sprang higher, landing on his straggly hair.

Jesha had her legs wrapped around the thief's head. As he thrashed against the attack, pivoting and swinging his head around, he tried to pry her paws off his face. Jesha claimed her battlefield with a warlike yowl and clung tenaciously to the big man's head. Blood streaked from under her claws.

Bixby's legs gave way and she sat. The wall was a step or two behind her, so she ended up on the curb. Cantor and the donkey were out of sight in one direction. The man and cat disappeared around a corner in the other. Bridger lay in a heap, not moving.

Bixby put her elbows on her knees and rested her chin in her hands. "Why is it never easy?"

16

A WAY OUT

Out of the darkened side street, Jesha strutted back without the giant she'd vanquished. The cat sprang up on Bridger's back where she settled in to do a thorough grooming. Bixby laughed. If anything, the cat looked more self-satisfied than before.

From the other direction, Cantor came back carrying the cloaks but with no cart or donkey.

Bixby watched him approach.

"No cart?"

"It came all to pieces, leaving a trail of broken boards, nails, and bolts. The donkey ran off with the harness."

"Maybe he'll go home."

Cantor sat on the curb next to her. "Yeah, maybe. Speaking of being in possession of stolen goods …"

Bixby raised her eyebrows at him, waiting for him to continue.

"I got stopped by the night watchman."

"But you didn't have any stolen goods on you?"

"Not a stitch." He held up the cloaks. "He did ask about these. Said I wasn't dressed like a person who wore fancy cloaks."

She tapped his arm. "See?" She touched her head where she'd put on a tiara while he was gone. "One must look like a person of consequence."

Cantor examined his clothes and then looked back at her with a grin. "Ahma drilled into me that being clean was more important than being fancy. With all this dirt, I've let her down for sure."

His gaze went to her delicate crown. "What does that one do?"

Her eyebrows lifted, and she fought back a guilty grin. Her nanny had always been able to read her expressions. Subsequently, Bixby learned to guard what she let her eyes tell even when she controlled her tongue. A lot of lessons were about her tongue.

"I didn't think you realized what they were."

"I've read books, and both Ahma and Odem lectured me, sharing their life experiences, until their voices went out."

Bixby could well sympathize with verbose mentors. She pointed to the glittering ring woven through her hair. "This one enhances my hearing." She pointed at Bridger. "His heart rate is gradually increasing. I think he'll wake up soon."

"So you have both natural ability, as you demonstrated in the forest, and enhanced ability using tools of wizardry."

She nodded, and her tiara slipped in her curls. She righted it with a push from one hand.

Cantor looked back at Bridger. "Will he wake before dawn?"

She shrugged. "I'm not very good at guessing the hour without a timepiece. What time is it now, do you suppose?"

"I'd figure we have an hour and a bit more before the light creeps in. Dark lingers in the city, because the wall blocks the sun when it first climbs over the horizon."

They both turned their heads to watch the sleeping dragon. Jesha perched on the very highest point his body provided. The cat could easily look in a second-story window.

Bixby moaned. He's grown even since he landed on the street.

Cantor laid one cloak across his lap and held up the other with two hands. He snapped the cloak and laid it out in front of him. "Not one eye-boggling inch left. The potion is gone."

Bixby guessed what he was getting at. "We won't be able to hide us or him or anything."

"Bridger would be hard to hide in any case. He's huge."

"Right." She slapped her thighs and stood. "Let's go wake him."

Circling the dragon, she took in how very, very big he'd gotten in the time since they loaded him in the cart. Cantor walked behind her. They stopped in front of his face.

White, pointed teeth showed between the dragon's parted lips. He grunted and mumbled, snorted and snored.

Bixby patted him on the nose. "Wake up."

"He's too far gone for gentle." Cantor punched him in the jaw.

Nothing.

Cantor sighed and shook his head. "Yelling might help, but we still can't be causing a commotion that'll wake people up and draw too much attention."

Bixby dug out two pairs of gloves. First, she put on the pair made of soft kid leather. The second pair, made of sturdier leather, slid over the first to give her another layer of protection. Pulling her skirts up around her knees, Bixby put one foot on the dragon's front arm. "Give me a boost."

She leaned forward and grabbed a neck scale. Cantor placed both hands on her rump and pushed. She sprang up and out of reach.

"Where are you headed?" he called softly.

"To his ear. It's not far."

She saw Cantor nod and transferred her attention to scaling the side of a slippery dragon. Her muscles ached from being squished in the cart. And now they told her she should be in better shape. Too much time reading books, and not enough time climbing trees, running races, and swimming in the lake.

Cantor spoke up again. "Be careful. Stretched like this, his hide will be slick and the scales become sharper as he sleeps. I believe it's a self-protection contrivance."

"I know that. That's why I put on the gloves. Be quiet."

Digging her toes in between scales helped, but the colorful half-disks cut into her shoes. She liked these shoes. They had bright red straps winding around her leg. The color didn't show much in the poor light, but she knew the blue stockings underneath provided just the right background. And the shoe itself was more of a sandal with sides that glittered and a thick heel to make her taller.

The scales also sliced the leather protecting her hands. "Listen, Bridger. You owe me one pair of snazzy shoes and two pairs of gloves."

He didn't even snort in reply.

Cantor moved around. His footsteps scuffed the dirt and soft shale. "How are you doing?"

"Almost there. Looking for a place to perch."

One foot slipped, and she grabbed the leathery flap that made up the dragon's outer ear. No razor-like edges adorned them, so she held on tight with her hands while her feet searched for toeholds.

"Do you need help?"

She grunted. "No. Be patient."

Bixby hooked her leg over one of the twiggy spikes sticking out from Bridger's neck. Another protrusion provided a stable place for her other foot. The hole at the base of the leathery flap looked dark and deep. Confident that she wouldn't fall, she leaned into the dragon's ear canal.

"Bridger," she whispered.

He shivered as if her breath tickled. She raised her voice. "Bridger, wake up."

He raised his head and shook it. "Something's on me. Get off! Get off!"

His head thrashed back and forth, and he raised a skinny arm to swipe at whatever clung to his neck.

"No, Bridger. Stop! It's me."

With the next flick of his head, she went flying through the air. She managed to squelch the scream that rose to her lips and only allowed a strangled, high-pitched squeal.

Strong hands snatched her out of her flight. Cantor pulled her close to his chest. He muttered, "Dragons!" then let her go.

Bridger's deep voice whispered through a puff of hot air. "Are you all right? I'm sorry. I thought you were a big bug."

Somewhere on the street, a door slammed.

"Shift, Bridger." Bixby put fingers on his arm and jiggled his scales. "Before you're seen."

Cantor grabbed Bixby's hand and jerked it away as the dragon shrunk and became the same horse he had formed the day before, only impossibly big.

"Too big," said Cantor.

Bixby tugged her hand out of Cantor's grip and again patted the dragon, but this time on his chest. "You *are* quite massive, Bridger. Could you compact yourself a little more?"

"In a couple of hours, I could. But not right away when I've started from the biggest I can grow as a dragon."

A man sauntered toward them. His dress indicated he was a working man. Bixby's pulse quickened as she realized he probably worked in the textile factory just down the street. If they weren't in such a predicament, she'd take the time to find out what fabrics were being made, where to find the best prices, and which outlets carried quality light materials. She momentarily considered pulling out a different tiara so she could delve into his mind, acquiring the information without bothering the man with her questions.

"Whoa!" the man exclaimed as he drew near. "That is the biggest draft horse I've ever seen." He stopped and pushed his cap back on his head. "How'd you get him in the city without the King's Guard confiscating him? They'd surely prize a giant horse."

"He came in as a baby," said Bixby.

The man walked around Bridger, admiring the horse. "You better get him off the streets if you want to keep him. There's a big bloke lives in this neighborhood. He likes to take things he runs across without bothering to ask."

Bixby thought through her acquisition of cart and donkey. She had asked. She asked the wrong person, but she had asked.

Cantor gave a low laugh. "I think we met him earlier."

"I best be off to work. If you run into trouble that requires eluding the authorities, there's an innkeeper who dislikes the guard with a real boiling anger. He'll help you. Name's Rock, and the inn is The Sundown."

"Thanks."

"You're welcome. I'm off now. Can't be late for my shift. I'm Tooney, should Rock ask who sent you." He turned and sauntered away.

Cantor picked up the cloaks. "We best get moving too."

"Do you think we can get to the healer's shop by alleys and side streets?"

Cantor scratched the back of his head as he eyed the horse. "I think Bridger is too big for some of the alleys. He couldn't squeeze through." He reached to pat the dragon's horsey cheek but pulled his hand back.

Bridger chuckled. "See, you're beginning to like me. We'll be constants. I feel it in my bones."

Cantor grunted. "As we go along, try to make your bones smaller from time to time."

"Sure thing, boss."

"Don't call me boss."

"Right, partner."

"Not partner, either."

Bridger laughed. It sounded rather horsey, like whinnying.

Cantor stopped and looked into the horse-dragon's eyes.

He noticed the pupils were slightly reptilian, not as round as a mammal's. "How long does it take you to lose your voice after you shift?"

"I don't believe I ever have."

Cantor sighed and started walking again. "I should have known."

"Why?" asked Bixby. "What is the significance of losing his voice?"

"Nothing, really." Cantor lowered his voice. "I just hoped for some quiet, a break from the chattering."

"He doesn't talk any more than I do."

"I know that."

"You're saying you don't like my conversation either." She pressed her lips into a thin line, for a moment reminding Cantor of Ahma.

"Don't put words in my mouth or erroneous meaning in my words. That's a sure way to start a disagreement over something that was not said and something that was not meant."

"Is that in the Primen Guide?"

Cantor stopped at an intersection and peered down each road. He led them down the narrower side street.

Bridger groaned.

Bixby patted his side. "What's wrong?"

"Just trying to lose a few inches around my middle. I can't compact any more for an hour or so."

"By then it'll be dawn."

Cantor looked back at the two. The horse looked twice as big as he should, and Bixby fluttered beside him in her jaunty sashay. "Do either of you have an idea as to how we can cross the city any quicker?"

"I do." Bridger tossed his mane. "I can fly us there."

Bixby shook her head, and her bounty of curls bobbed about just as the horse's mane had. "You'll be seen."

"The longer I walk through the town, the more likely I am to be seen. As a dragon, I can shoot straight up, turn and streak down to land on the healer's building. I'll be visible for less than a minute. Seems I'd be less likely to be seen than if we continue this route."

Cantor nodded. Bixby opened her mouth, but before she could give her opinion, Bridger swooshed, crackled, popped, and stretched into his own form. He still stood as tall as the horse, but he looked the right size for a dragon. His scales had lost their razor-sharp edges, and the air around him had warmed with his changing.

"I was about to say," said Bixby, her face red and scrunched into a frown, "I've never actually ridden on a dragon."

"It won't be that hard," said Cantor.

Her eyebrows lifted. "Straight up and straight down in less than sixty seconds?"

Bridger flexed his wings. "Probably forty-two seconds."

Cantor reached for her hand. "You can ride behind and hold on to me."

She stepped out of his reach and put both hands behind her back. "What if you fall off?"

"I won't."

"Straight up. Straight down. Forty-two seconds."

"Maybe forty-one." Bridger grinned.

"You can ride in front, and I'll hold on to you."

She shook her head. He'd never seen such a solemn look on her face. Not afraid, exactly, but definitely stubborn.

Cantor reached in his backpack and pulled out a wide length of colorful material woven into a hat. He snapped it twice, then stretched it with two hands into a huge belt. "This will keep us on."

He showed it to Bridger, who nodded, then went to the dragon's side. He threw one end over his back, ducked under Bridger's belly, and looped the ends together with a silver buckle contraption. He pulled on it, tightened the slack, and tested it again.

"All set. We won't fall."

Drums rolled a steady beat, paused, and rolled again.

"The soldiers' wake-up call." Cantor grabbed Bixby around the waist, tossed her up to the crest of Bridger's shoulders, then scrambled up behind her. "Ready?"

Bridger craned his neck around to look at his passengers. "You know when we went into the shop during the day, I was a stretcher."

"You're saying?"

"I don't know if I know where the healer's shop is."

"On the south wall," squeaked Bixby.

"Her eyes are shut," said Bridger.

"That's probably for the best." Cantor hugged her closer to his chest and caught hold of the colorful cinch. "Let's go, Bridger. I'll try to help pinpoint the shop. But I can't do it from here."

"Right." Bridger spread his wings, coiled the muscles in his legs for a mighty jump, and took a deep breath. "Up!"

Cantor bent his head to speak into Bixby's ear. "Up is a good choice."

He'd hoped she would relax a little. He thought he succeeded. At least she giggled.

17

CLUTTER

Bixby clung to the arm Cantor had wrapped around her waist. The thud as they landed on yet another roof threatened to bring her last meal up.

She swallowed hard. "Are we here? Did we make it this time?"

"Yep." Cantor let go of her and slid away.

She opened her eyes and gave a sigh of relief. In spite of Bridger's optimism, finding the right roof had taken four tries. Even now she didn't know how they had decided this was the healer's shop, and she didn't care. It was one of the flat-roofed structures that were part of the city's wall and therefore part of the battlement, designed so soldiers could stand on these ramparts and shoot the enemy from above. That was good enough for her. She'd walk around the whole wall if she had to, as long as she didn't have to endure the gut-wrenching leaping and plummeting one more time.

"Look." Bridger pointed to a huge nest. "Mizlark eggs. I

love mizlark eggs." He lumbered over to the round collection of old papers, twigs, stolen garments, and mud. Bixby held tight to the multicolored girth. The putrid smell as they approached almost gagged her. Bridger picked up a greenish egg bigger than a grapefruit and popped it in his mouth, shell and all.

Bixby heard the crunch. "Yuck." She threw her leg over his back and, holding on to the cinch to slow her descent, slid down his scales. "How can you eat the eggs of those nasty birds?"

Bridger tossed an egg into the air, opened his mouth, and caught it as it fell. "This is the only time mizlarks are palatable. A roasted full-grown bird tastes like carrion, no matter what care you take in its preparation. You can't use the feathers for anything. They're sticky and smell like moldy socks. The birds sound out constantly with raucous voices. They leave dung in the most inconvenient places. And they harass farm animals. I'm surprised they haven't been eradicated."

Jesha sniffed the nest from a distance, sneezed, and moved away, sitting on the far side of the roof with her back to Bridger.

He popped another egg in his mouth. "But mizlark eggs are delicious."

Bixby gave a quick look around the skies, fearful of spying an angry flock of massive, gawky birds. "Why aren't they here, guarding their eggs?"

Cantor stood over a trap door he'd just opened. "What? And miss the opportunity to raid other birds' nests and eat other birds' young? Mizlarks seem to think stolen food tastes better than anything they can come by honestly."

"Right," said Bridger as he downed the last egg. "And if someone is wailing over their loss, the lament provides dinner music to the brutes."

"I'm glad we don't have any on Richra." Bixby followed Jesha to the wall facing the outside of the city.

Bridger sat and began picking his teeth with a claw. "You two are perfectly matched to be partners. Bixby has a ton of book-learning and city polish. Cantor has the knowledge of nature that can keep you alive in the wild."

He pulled a bit of something green from between his teeth and flicked it over the side of the wall. "And, of course, I am a superior dragon for Cantor. I knew when I first saw him that we'd fit. He emanates vibrations that meld with my own."

Cantor's jaw twitched as he motioned for Bixby to join him. "Bixby and I are going down to the shop to do the packing Dukmee asked her to do. Why don't you stay up here on guard? Let us know if you see someone coming."

Bixby waved to Bridger. He paused in his dental hygiene to wave back. He didn't seem put out by Cantor's cold attitude. And although she liked the odd dragon, she could see how he annoyed Cantor. Words were not going to change the realm walker's attitude, but perhaps in time, Cantor would see Bridger's worth.

Bixby stepped down onto the top step of the ladder within the building. Darkness hid the remaining rungs. She sat on the edge of the trapdoor in order to dig through her hampers.

"Here's a light." She passed a stick to Cantor. "Shake it and it'll glow." With another in her hand, she resumed her descent.

"Ow, ow, ow!"

Bixby popped out of the opening and ran to Bridger. "What's wrong?"

Cantor had raced to his side as well. "Be quiet! You're going to wake all the people within blocks of here."

The dragon muffled his staccato exclamations with a hand clamped over his mouth. Blood ran from one pointed claw.

"You're bleeding." Bixby pulled on his arm. "Let me see where you're wounded."

The dragon moved his hand a couple of inches. Blood trickled from his mouth.

"What did you do?" asked Cantor.

Bixby turned angry eyes on her companion. "You could be a little more sympathetic."

"It's a tiny trickle of blood. He's not dying."

"He's in pain."

Cantor gave an exasperated grunt and pulled the dragon's hand off his mouth. "Show us."

"I stabbed my gum."

Bixby interpreted Cantor's glance her way as, "See? It's nothing."

"All right." Bixby patted Bridger's shoulder. "Let me look."

He opened his mouth. The toasted almond smell surprised her. Compared to the reek from the mizlark's nest, the dragon's breath was pleasant. Up close, his teeth sparkled white but looked too large for his mouth. His dark purple tongue had black ridges running from side to side.

Bixby looked at Cantor. "I didn't know dragons have black and purple striped tongues."

Cantor rolled his eyes and shrugged. "You haven't been around dragons much, have you?"

"I turned down an internship at Tondard Veterinary University."

Bridger groaned again. "Do you see the wound? It feels like it's ten inches long."

With a gentle nudge, Cantor moved Bixby to the side. "It may be one inch, Bridger. You aren't going to die."

"A puncture wound. They get infected. I need some medicine from the healer's stock." Bixby handed the dragon a rolled piece of cloth. "Hold this against your gum to stop the blood. We'll look for something in Dukmee's things to help."

"Thank you, Bixby. You're kind."

The dragon pointedly did not comment on Cantor's disposition.

A rooster crowed.

"Great!" Cantor pulled Bixby away. "Let's go. We should get everything done before it's time to open the shop."

Bixby climbed down the ladder first with Cantor following.

He called down to her. "Do you have a list of things he wants? When did you have time to write it down?"

"In my head," she answered. Would now be a good time to tell him she remembered details for years? Clutter filled her mind. She knew what the visiting prince from an outlying province had for breakfast when he stayed with her mother and father six years ago. She could name rivers and towns and draw the borders of any map she'd ever seen. If she read a poem, she could recite it later. Sometimes her brain spun facts around and kept her from sleeping. No, she decided she didn't want to reveal another one of her oddities.

They walked to the regular staircase now that they were on a real floor in the building. "He packed a lot of things, but decided to have someone pick them up and bring them to him. And since he was going to do that, he decided to pack up everything. We just have to put them in containers. There are only a few extra things that he wanted specifically."

The next floor overflowed with abandoned furniture. The next level held piles of books.

Cantor's eyes opened wide as they wound their way through stack after stack of books of all shapes, colors, and sizes. "Does he want these packed?"

Bixby wrinkled her nose at the layer of dust covering most everything. "No, his carrier will take care of the top floors."

As they passed a window where moonlight lit a patch of the corridor wall, Cantor took her arm and turned her to face him. "I don't understand this. You speak of him as if you've known him for years, as if you're familiar with his way of doing things. But you just met him, isn't that right? How have you become so at ease with one another in so short a time?"

Bixby closed her eyes and held her breath as if she could blot out the earnest, confused look on Cantor's face. She hated explaining the ins and outs of her peculiar self. Only her mother slightly understood what it was like to be Bixby D'Mazeline. And that was because her mother was the source of many of her more startling attributes, only, in most cases, they appeared in Bixby a hundredfold.

Bixby opened her eyes to see Cantor still studying her as if she would sprout wings and fly. "It takes a long time to explain something like this, and we don't have the time now."

"I think you could talk while we work."

"Perhaps, but I'm very complicated." She grinned a false grin, too big, too flippant. She could tell by his face that he wasn't being cajoled into forgetting his question. "I promise to try to explain when we've settled somewhere." Something flickered through Cantor's expression. Another crown would have helped her discern what he was thinking. A guess would be that he didn't expect there to be a time when they were settled. Probably just nerves.

She started down the last staircase. "Don't you think we should get this chore done before the King's Guard comes for the healer? A lot of men are going to wake up with bad headaches, and they'll want Dukmee to give aid."

She turned quickly and plunged down the wooden steps, her fancy boots clattering loud enough to wake all the other shop owners on the street.

18

ON HIS OWN

"Let him go." Bixby put a hand on Bridger's shoulder. "We'll run into him again, and maybe by that time, he'll realize how much he needs us."

The dragon sighed. His cat wound around his legs. His constant strode the flat prairie road with determined steps. Away from him.

Bixby patted his scales, trying to ease the pain of rejection. "He always said he was going to go on by himself and find his dragon." She frowned at Cantor's retreating back. In truth, she'd like to wring his neck. His Ahma might have taught him manners, but neglected courtesy. His Odem might have drilled him with ideas on chivalry, but neglected allegiance. He thought he was trained to be a realm walker, but he was underdone, half-baked, and short of cinnamon in his appleton pie. He'd learn soon enough not to slough off true friends in order to be able to stand on his own. He'd fall flat. That's what. And nobody there to help him stand again. Foolhardy.

"I'm his dragon."

"He doesn't think so."

"He's wrong."

Bixby had no words for the circumstance. In all her varied life experiences, she'd never been called upon to console a dragon whose constant didn't acknowledge the relationship.

"Let's just give him some time."

A shuddering sigh rippled through the dragon's back.

Bixby leaned forward to get a better look at Bridger's face. "You aren't going to cry, are you?"

That got a reaction. He stood straighter and frowned at her. "Of course not. I'm a self-respecting dragon, and though I am not one to think higher of myself than I should, I am aware of my duty to uphold a certain standard of behavior."

She nodded vigorously, glad to see she'd stumbled upon something to jar Bridger out of his gloom. "I knew that."

The dragon lifted his tail, looking much more lively. Bixby didn't know how long this new spirit of zeal would last, so she decided to press her advantage. "We should be on about our business."

"Right." Bridger smiled at her. Then the expression dropped off his face. "And that business would be?"

Bixby lifted her arms and let them flap to her sides. "To find my dragon."

Bridger's shoulders drooped as he turned to accompany Bixby. "I don't believe he knows."

"Cantor?"

Bridger nodded, every muscle in his face weighted down by dejection.

"What is it Cantor doesn't know?"

The dragon stopped and looked back at the disappearing

figure of a young man traveling the road alone. "That he very likely is the last real realm walker."

For a moment, Bixby thought Bridger had discovered her secret, that her realm walker days would be limited no matter how hard she tried to fit the mold. Her mouth went dry and she groped for words before she realized the dragon was far too absorbed in his own troubles to be referring to her. "What do you mean? There are many realm walkers rising up out of the populace. There are always plenty."

"No," said Bridger, shaking his head. "Not real realm walkers."

Bixby laid a hand on his arm and pulled him toward her so she could see his face. "Are you trying to say there are false realm walkers?" Another question echoed the first, but she didn't speak it aloud. It hit too close to things she wished to keep to herself. *Are you saying* I'm *not a real realm walker?*

"Probably." The dragon resumed his shuffling walk away from Cantor.

"Where do you get your information? I haven't heard any such rumors."

"Hatchlings. Or rather, no hatchlings."

"Baby dragons? Baby dragons tell you there are fewer realm walkers? Almost none?" Bixby slowed her pace to keep beside the somber dragon. Surely the hatchlings didn't come out of the egg with news of the future. The only possible information they could impart would merely be their existence. "Are you saying someone is keeping track of how many babies are born?"

"Baby mor dragons. No, no one is keeping track. We all just know. There hasn't been a clutch of hatchlings in thirty-seven years."

A zing of understanding skittered through her being, the tiny thrill in strange juxtaposition to the solemnity brought by Bridger's words.

She skipped a few steps to catch up to Bridger's long stride. "So the lack of baby mor dragons indicates the lack of realm walkers?"

"*Real* realm walkers."

Somewhere she registered the emphasis, and a small part of her inquisitive mind demanded explanation, but important obstacles related to her own journey to become a realm walker loomed too large to ignore. "If mor dragons have diminished in number, then how is Cantor going to find a dragon constant? How am *I* going to find a constant?"

"I've got a sister."

Bixby stopped. "Where is she?"

"In Tinendoor."

"Is she a shape-shifter like you?"

"All mor dragons are shape-shifters."

"Like you?"

The corner of Bridger's mouth turned up, creating a self-conscious grin. "I'm the only shape-shifter like me."

Cantor looked back only once. Bridger and Bixby had shrunk in the distance, but they still watched him. A pang of remorse threatened to deflate his elation, but regrets couldn't long stand against the thrill of freedom.

Soon. He felt it in his bones. Soon he'd find his dragon, and when he did, they'd be off after the next milepost — he, inexperienced but eager, his dragon, beautiful, strong, dignified, and ready to right the many wrongs in the realms.

While on Dairine, he'd chafed against the days before he could go to Effram. Now he looked forward to the return to Dairine and his first report to the council.

And beyond that!

Another trip to another realm. His future lurked just beyond a few more stops. He'd finish the mundane business of dealing with particulars, tedious necessities to conform to the standards. Then, he'd reach his first goal. He'd be a genuine realm walker.

Then, then, then ... *then* life would take off, filled with purpose, achievements, goals, triumphs, and satisfaction.

He didn't mind wagonloads of service as long as adventure acted as the wheels carrying the duty. He'd been born to be a realm walker. Primen had smiled upon him even as he was in the womb. His destiny was knitted into his fiber just as Primen's gifts and talents had been woven into his character.

Soon.

He walked long hours each day, stopping at each little hamlet along his way, following leads gleaned from locals, searching, always searching. Each step brought him closer. Each day that passed marked one more off the time separating him from his dragon.

After thirty days, Cantor stood on the cusp of a narrow plain blanketed with high grasses and crowded woods and bordered to the west by the Sea of Joden.

Tinendoor.

The word had become a refrain in his conversations with friendly locals as he passed from one region to another. The farther he wandered from the center of the king's power, the more talkative the citizens became, and nearly all of them said the same thing: Most mor dragons now occupied Tinendoor to the exclusion of all other areas on Effram. He heard this so many times in so many taverns that he stopped pointing out the obvious error: that he had encountered Bridger some distance from the Tinendoor region.

Now, unable to keep the grin from his face, Cantor plunged into the valley at a jog. At the base of the foothill, he entered a narrow grove of frichelmarsh trees. No marsh swamped the intricate interweaving of roots from the randomly spaced trees; instead their soft canopy of tiny leaves extended only a few feet from a sizeable stream that washed out of a stone gully coming from the mountains.

He paused to refill his water flask, wash dust off his face and hands, and rest his weary feet in the slow-flowing brook. With his back against a tree and a biscuit and an apple in his hands, he allowed his mind to ramble through bits of information.

Tinendoor had two organized villages, both small and both nestled in the foothills. No farms, industries, or hamlets edged the Sea of Joden, and for good reason. Although the waves sparkled iridescent blue, the harsh minerals suspended in the thick water corroded anything it touched. An hour's swim would be fatal. A sip to ease an undeniable thirst sent an agony of poison through the drinker's body. If a rain cloud formed over the sea and then drifted over dry land, the people went to extremes to protect property and people from the tainted raindrops.

Having been forewarned, Cantor had sought relief for his aching feet in water from the peaks, not from the sea. When he dried his feet and put on his socks and boots, he traveled close to the mountains, a comfortable distance from the dangerous waters.

As the sun disappeared beyond the Sea of Joden, a golden path beckoned the uninformed traveler to draw near. Whenever Cantor's path took him to the top of a hill, he could look out to the west and see the beach curving along the seashore. The sandy composition of multicolored crystals sparkled in the dying sunlight, its innocent-looking beauty luring visitors to come too close.

Resolute, Cantor kept his eyes to the north, hoping to spot lights from one of two hostels he'd heard of in the last town he'd passed through before entering the mountains. One was recommended, and the other was disparaged.

An hour later, Cantor wondered if he'd misunderstood the directions. He'd seen nothing of human habitats, no houses, no roads, and no cultivated fields. And what was more, no dragons. Had he wandered off course? Had the man said south instead of north?

Coming to the edge of a forested area, he decided the hostel would have to wait 'til morning. One more night in the open wouldn't hurt him. He dropped his pack under a tree and looked all around. The scenery thickened with woods.

Stay on the fringe or move to take advantage of the shelter under the boughs?

He surveyed the sky. No clouds, no halo around the moon. A mild night. As he turned toward the woods, a glimmer in the air caught his eye. Over the trees about a half mile from where he stood, the moon lit up a thin column of smoke. He snatched up his pack. He'd have company, after all, this night.

As he approached the long log building at last, he tried to

remember every scrap of information he'd heard about the two hostels. One was hostile, the other hospitable.

The lodging defamed with tales of evil had no flower beds on the premises, a crude barn to one side and slightly behind the primary building, and a foul, smoldering hill of refuse. Cantor squinted, peering into the shadows around the building. The rising moon cast uneven lighting upon the objects scattered before him.

A large structure to the side could be the barn, but he couldn't determine the level of craftsmanship. He didn't see a burning dump, and only a faint hint of rotting vegetables tainted the air.

He saw what he thought might be a patch of land dedicated to zinnias. The flowers showed no color in the neutralizing light of the moon.

He tuned his ear to the noises coming from within. Someone had lifted several of the many windows. Golden lamplight spilled out between the curtains. A strummer instrument and a reed pipe didn't quite play at the same tempo. Nonetheless, he recognized the tune, "Rainy Memories of a Sunny Day." The piper lagged behind the strummer, and while Cantor listened, he skipped ahead in his part to rejoin the faster musician.

Unexpectedly enticing, the aroma of stew laden with garlic and onions invited him to open the door on the chance that he'd found the hospitable hostel.

Men sat around tables close to the floor. The first clue he was in the wrong place.

All conversation ceased, along with the clatter of dishes and the slightly off music of pipe and strummer. The second clue.

No women anywhere. The entire male gathering stood and inched toward him. Third clue.

Each man bared his teeth in a wide and bright, white grimace that held no joy and plenty of menace. Fourth.

In unison, a growl emanated from the stout throats of the very short tribe. No more clues needed.

Words of wisdom drifted back through his thoughts. "Avoid the hostel that caters to Brinswikkers. They are short, irritable, unstable, rude, and aggressive. And they won't take kindly to your being over five feet tall. Their women don't like the men much, and you'll never see a male and female Brinswikker together outside of their own homes."

A chortle from another informer. "And you won't be invited into one of their homes. Leastwise, no one's ever come out of a Brinkswikker get-together and told a tale of congeniality."

Cantor searched the faces for a hint of benevolence in the sea of hard expressions. Perhaps he could get away with a polite inquiry. He didn't doubt he'd win an unpleasant encounter with one of these Brinkswikkers. He could probably conquer three or four. But not fifteen.

First he needed to burst this bubble of tension. With all eyes focused on him, there'd be no escape. Cantor cleared his throat. "I was looking for a place to stay for the night."

The grin on the burly little man right in front of him managed to stretch farther into his ruddy cheeks. "You've come to the wrong place."

"I was thinking that."

19

TROUBLE

Beauty appealed to Bixby. She loved fine threads, intricately woven fabric, elaborate lace, delicate tatting, refined patterns of crochet, and artful combinations of color and textures. Hats, shoes, and tiaras fascinated her. And she took great pleasure in adorning her diminutive self with an abundance of clothing in her own distinctive style.

She also favored delicate jewelry and delighted in wearing as much as possible. No one would say she was averse to glitz and glimmer.

Therefore, when Bridger called his sister out of a gathering of dragons at a country al fresco, Bixby felt the curls in her blonde hair tighten in a severe case of fashion envy. Totobee-Rodolow sashayed from the crowd. Her shining, iridescent scales chimed like a tree full of exquisite, petite bells.

The dragon's coloring undulated in shades of red, pink, purple, silver, and ivory. At the tip of every ridge of her wings, embedded gems gleamed in her skin. The jewels caught the sun and reflected the colors back into the air. Spots of rainbows hovered around Totobee-Rodolow. Bixby set her mind to figuring out how the refracted light hung in the air.

Underlining both the dragon's eyes, emeralds dotted a curved row in graduated sizes, starting with tiny cut stones just below her tear ducts and ending with a coin-sized glittering rock at the height of each cheekbone.

Totobee-Rodolow's figure tapered from narrow shoulders to understated hips. Bixby blinked twice, trying to determine how the large dragon managed to maintain coordination on such a slim foundation. She laughed to herself when she realized the shape-shifter had shifted herself into a shape she deemed attractive.

If Bixby could shape-shift, she'd bulk up. Her body type was more twiggy than willowy and on the lanky side of lithe. She *had* been blown away by the wind. *And* she had fallen through a crack in the pavement. Being slender had drawbacks.

Totobee-Rodolow extended her hand for a greeting just long enough to be polite. "Bridger tells me you're looking for a constant. I don't suppose he told you I've already had my opportunity. I'm content with my present life. My constant died."

"Oh, I'm so sorry." Bixby raised her fingertips to her lips. "Not that you're content, but that your constant died."

"Don't be. He was pompous and not a real realm walker by any means. He'd bought the power. Can you imagine the cheekiness of thinking you could pay for another realm walker to do your bidding?

"Then the man had the audacity to think he could engage me as a constant and I wouldn't be clever enough to figure out his sham."

Bixby slowly shook her head in incredulous sympathy. What a horrible experience. No wonder Bridger had been skeptical of his sister's willingness to help.

Totobee-Rodolow continued, talking softly at a great speed and tossing her hands around in a profusion of gestures. "And even the realm walker he had tied to a leash was an old, worn-out, second-rate has-been." The dragon's eyes rolled expressively toward the sky.

"He could barely locate a portal, and more than once the imbecile only just managed to squeeze us through before it slammed shut. I nearly lost my tail between Dairine and Richra. I saw Rackama had lost his hold and jerked my beautiful tail out before it was smashed." She sighed. "A girl must look out for herself."

Bixby felt she should contribute a bit more to the conversation. "Rackama was the name of the realm walker?"

"An old, worn-out, second-rate, has-been realm walker. Hilarill was supposedly my constant, but an imposter."

"Hilarill died?"

"Yes. I believe I've told you that."

"And Rackama did not die?"

"I left as soon as possible, so I don't know for sure." Her face brightened. "I did hear he's settled in the court of Algore. No one will notice him there." She shifted her shoulders, and her wings fluttered and settled like a glamorous shawl.

"I keep my finger in the pie, just for the gossip and social schemes, you know. I really do not want to participate in the intrigues, but would rather watch from the sidelines. Humph. Not even the sidelines, but more remotely, from the fringe. 'Tis better to be a distance from all the smoldering conspiracies."

Bixby leapt for the opening to her real purpose. "Bridger tells me you are an exceptional dragon."

"In beauty and intellect only, my child." She used one clawed fingertip to tap her chin. The gesture brought attention to fingers encrusted with jewels and a beauty mark next to her lips. The beauty mark looked like a pea-sized purple onyx.

"He says you know about the ins and outs of the various kingdoms, the politics of all the courts and governments, and the temperament of influential citizens in all seven planes."

"Ha! He makes me sound like an old busybody."

"No, that isn't his intention."

A glance at Bridger revealed Cantor's dragon had found something to interest him. He'd acquired a plateful of cheeses, fruits, sandwiches, and nuts. A month with the mor dragon had revealed Bridger's insatiable appetite. He loved food and loved variety.

Jesha sat on his shoulder. Her delicate nose twitched, and she batted the dragon's ear with a white paw. Bridger picked up a piece of cheese and offered it to his cat.

Bixby returned her attention to the beautiful dragon and smiled. "He's quite proud of your head for details and the vast knowledge you've accumulated in such a short time. He believes you have the mind of a prime minister and a more discerning instinct than any premier in history."

Bixby could see she'd chosen the right words. Totobee-Rodolow no longer looked bored.

"Perhaps you'd like to take a tour around your previous sphere of influence. I'd like you to go with me."

Totobee-Rodolow's eyes opened wide and the ridges above them arched. "Darling, I don't want to travel. Traveling is tedious."

"I understand, but this wouldn't be anything more than a sort of vacation. Let me explain before you decide not to visit the castles and palaces of the different realms."

Bixby barely took a breath before plunging on. She didn't want to give Totobee-Rodolow a chance to say no. "Primen has endowed me with many attributes. Being a realm walker is just one possibility. I've other skills, but I'm seeking which is to take precedence. Until I've made a choice, or Primen makes clear His choice, I'm at loose ends."

Bixby looked down at her hands. She had mangled a piece of lace on a front pocket. Forcing her fingers to let loose of the delicate fabric, she clasped her hands at her waist and took a steadying breath. It was necessary to tell Totobee-Rodolow a part of her story, but not all. She was good at telling the truth without including vital information. That was one reason she had been sent.

"Because I'm not sure I'll be a realm walker, it's all difficult. I don't seek the commitment of a constant. But in order to get a taste of what realm walking would be like and whether I'm up to the task, I need the aid of an experienced, sophisticated dragon. Such as yourself."

Totobee-Rodolow gazed at her circle of friends, casually enjoying the food, the weather, and each other. "They aren't mor dragons, you see."

"Your friends are different races of dragons?"

"Yes, there are very few mor dragons left." She waved a hand, indicating the group of socializing dragons. "These do not recognize the responsibility given to one of my kind. And thus, they tend to dismiss the honor of serving."

Bixby repeated words she'd often heard from her father. "There are not many who understand in these times."

Totobee-Rodolow lifted her chin. "Primen is still Primen and will always be. But His followers are no longer *His* followers."

Bixby nodded. Her parents and Totobee-Rodolow would probably back the same causes, join the same forces, and strain to fulfill similar expectations. Surprised to recognize a kindred spirit, Bixby tamped down her desire to bubble. An ally. Her father had emphasized the need for allies. Instead of revealing her eagerness, she kept herself calm and waited to see if Totobee-Rodolow would be curious enough to join Bixby in her mission.

The dragon's eyes narrowed as she thought. Bixby held her breath. After a pause much longer than Bixby could bear, Totobee-Rodolow glanced her way.

"No decision should be made on an empty shopping bag. The Newtowne Faire starts today. Shall we go see what they have in their stalls?"

Bixby let out the air she'd held so tightly. This was her kind of female.

Cantor tasted moldy cheese. His tongue felt the size of a pig's snout. The drought in his mouth might cause permanent attachment of teeth to skin. He tried to swallow and almost gagged.

Water. If he opened his eyes, he might see water. His eyelashes seemed to be glued together. What happened? Where was he?

He moved. Something pinched his arms. Sitting. He sat in

a chair. Tied. Around his arms. Around his legs. Around his waist.

He pulled his head up and felt muscles in his chest and in his neck stretch as if being torn from bones. From stinging lungs, he managed to drag a call for help. He sounded like a wounded cow.

A door scraped open.

"You're awake. I'll be back." A female voice, nasal and unsympathetic.

Light footsteps trotted down the hall. They returned at a slower pace. She stopped a few feet in front of him.

He heard a clatter, then water splashed in his face and down his front. He sputtered and opened his eyes. Images blurred. He wondered if his eyesight was going or coming back.

An out-of-focus Brinswikker woman stood with a bucket in her hand. Short like the male members of her kind, she looked him straight in the eye as he sat in the chair. Her clothes were shades of brown and blue, no patterns in the dye or weave. From what he could tell, all Brinswikkers looked as if a cloth had been wrapped around them, then tied where a tie was needed.

"I saved your life. You owe me one." She turned and walked out, leaving the door open.

He blinked several times, trying to remove the grit from his dry eyes and restore his sight completely. The blinking helped a little bit.

His room contained the chair he sat on, a cot, a table, and a small threadbare rug covering a patch of rough wood floor beside the bed. He ruled out being caught and in prison when he focused on the view beyond the open door.

Through a window on the opposite side of the hall, Cantor

could see a pond too small for the dozens of ducks paddling around or settled on the shore. He'd never seen so many ducks in one place.

Running footsteps approached, and two giggling children arrived with half-full buckets. From the look of their clothes, the pails might have been full when they started toward his room. The littlest, a girl with bangs and a ponytail, grinned and shrieked, "Close eyes!"

She swung her pail and let it fly. It thunked on the floor in front of Cantor, water splashing, then pouring out as her pail rolled on its side. She put her hands on her mouth and laughed. Bright brown eyes sparkled over chubby fingers.

The other child, a boy, scowled. He stepped closer and took aim. The bucket landed in Cantor's lap. The water spilled and ran down his legs. The cool, clean water relieved a slow burn on his skin, one he hadn't acknowledged among all the other discomfort he suffered.

The boy gave a jump of triumph, then dashed in to retrieve his sister's bucket and his own. Their feet on the wooden floor sounded like a half-dozen children instead of only two.

The rascals made two more trips and became a trifle more efficient in dousing their prisoner. Cantor tried to speak, but his swollen tongue still clung to his dry mouth. He'd have said thank you if he could. Every drop of water brought relief to his tortured skin.

When they didn't come back, he strained his ears for clues as to where he was. Outside, a stubby-legged, long-haired cow with curly horns walked between him and the ducks. He could hear chickens and sheep.

A farm.

Children.

And a woman who saved his life.

A head that felt like a broken pot.

A body that burned where it didn't ache.

He knew exactly where he was.

Just past real trouble.

Stymied in the aftermath.

The trouble hadn't killed him.

Perhaps the aftermath wouldn't kill him either.

20

THE FAIRE

Bixby held a length of loosely woven cloth, the color of pink fading as sunset met starry night. Her mind filled with ideas to incorporate the lightweight piece into one of her garments. Contrasting narrow ribbons could be trailed through the weave. The same ribbon, folded and stitched into elaborate flowers, would add the lovely touch of nature to her design. Perhaps a cluster at the waist, and a cascade of smaller flowers to the hem. She raised her head, looking in this stall and along the corridor of vendors for ribbons.

"I'll take this," she said, "and the dusty green silk I chose earlier."

She caught a glimpse of Totobee-Rodolow and waved a brightly colored scarf above her head. Her dragon companion spotted her and leisurely strolled in her direction.

Bixby finished with her purchase, folded the material, and tucked it into a hamper. Then she waltzed in and out of the crowd, making her way to her friend.

The dragon wore new jewelry: rings, bracelets, and a necklace. All glittery and on heavy gold findings. "Oh, Totobee-Rodolow, they're beautiful."

Because of her dainty size, Bixby could not wear massive ornaments, but they certainly looked good on the feminine dragon.

"And I got them for a song, dear." Totobee-Rodolow fingered the large topaz pendant hanging against her chest. Her scales reflected the light of the sun's bright rays.

Bixby squinted. Totobee-Rodolow chuckled, then enclosed the bauble in the palm of her hand. "I thought the stone might be useful under stressful situations."

Bixby frowned and started to ask what she meant, but a young man rushed up to her dragon friend and bowed.

"I can't believe you are in Newtowne." He doffed his hat and bowed again. "I was told you stayed in Tinendoor."

"Bixby D'Mazeline, this is Marcher Limpa, a page in the town hall. Marcher, Bixby D'Mazeline."

"Pleased to meet you, Miss." He bobbed again.

Bixby nodded politely and continued to watch the nervous young man. His hat would never be the same. She had been schooled to keep from fidgeting, and occasionally she lost control of her fingers. She could sympathize with Marcher. He twisted and folded and stretched his poor hat until it started dropping loose pieces of felt.

Totobee-Rodolow's eyes narrowed. She placed a gentle hand on the young man's shoulder. "Tell me, friend. What troubles you?"

He licked his lips. "There's a rumor."

Totobee-Rodolow nodded.

"From Tinendoor."

Totobee-Rodolow's quiet yes spurred the page on.

"A realm walker seeking a mor dragon has been waylaid by Brinswikkers."

"I see." The dragon took a big breath. "Anything else to tell?"

Marcher looked disconcerted for a moment. He swallowed hard. "He's not dead."

"That's a pleasant end to your tale."

Bixby grasped the dragon's arm. Anxiety tightened her throat. She whispered, "Cantor?"

"Undoubtedly so." She stood erect. Purpose stiffening her casual air. "Bridger must be told."

Voices brought Cantor back from oblivion, but he had no idea how long he'd been out. Sunshine still brightened the yard outside. He concluded either it hadn't been long, or it had been a full twenty-four hours. Puddles covered most of the floor of his room. A few scattered towels soaked up some of the water.

The two children, this time without buckets, barreled around the corner and skidded to a stop.

"My brudder's coming," said the brown-eyed moptop.

She giggled and twirled but remained far enough away that Cantor knew she'd been warned to keep clear of the prisoner.

Her brother frowned. "Stop that, Marta."

She gave an extra swift spin with her chubby arms reaching over her head. "No."

"Stop."

She circled him. "Yo don't like my dance, Gimo? Go stick yo nose in a hole."

She stopped to pound her feet in place in a ratta-tat-tat that made Cantor wince.

"Please, Little Miss Marta," he said, "you're hurting my injured ears."

She jumped and landed in one spot. With a sassy grin, she said, "Yo can talk. Good."

She ran to the doorway, held on to the frame and leaned out, then hollered with a voice much too big for such a tiny body. "Come, Ma. Come, Rutzen. He talks."

Heavier footsteps approached. Gimo still scowled, but moved quickly out of the center of the room. The woman who claimed to have saved Cantor's life and an older boy swept into the room. They stopped and studied him.

"More water," the woman ordered.

Marta and Gimo ran from the room.

"I think you've saved him, Ma," the boy, Rutzen, said in a sullen tone. "But I still don't know why."

"Men!" She tossed him a scathing look. "You think too little of life. If you had to bear the child for months and knew the great effort put into bringing new life into the world, you would cherish more and squander less."

Rutzen shrugged his shoulders, apparently not much impressed by his mother's wisdom. "Cherish is a woman's bone."

Outrage stiffened her back. She glared at her son. For one so small, she looked like an explosion of temper would be devastating. "Soon you'll join the men's camp, and this mother will be glad your heathen ways will go with you."

"You'll miss me."

"Ha!"

Rutzen grinned. "You'll miss me. It is another woman's bone."

Cantor caught sight of a pitcher in the woman's hand. Once he'd seen it, nothing the mother and son had to say interested him.

She must have seen his gaze locked on the jug. "I brought you a drink. We've been dousing your outside with water for over two days now. Next is to flush as much water through your insides as we can."

She stepped forward. Without being told, Cantor leaned his head back and opened his mouth. Not all the water went down the inside, but the spillage dribbling off his chin and down his chest felt just as good as the portion sliding down his throat.

Marta and Gimo returned and promptly splashed their burden on Cantor.

"Thank you," he said and even managed a smile.

Marta responded with a giggle and a wave. Gimo scowled and stomped away from him, taking up a post in the corner of the room.

The woman pulled a knife from a scabbard she wore under her apron. "I'm going to cut him loose."

"Too soon," said Rutzen. "He'll savage the lot of us."

"If you think you're old enough to tell your mother what to do, you know where to go."

Marta jumped up and down, clapping her hands. "Men's camp. Men's camp. With Fafada."

Rutzen raised his hand as if to hit her, but she danced away, still chanting.

The older boy sneered. "You'll be sorry when you have to carry wood and water."

Marta picked up her empty bucket and slung it at her older brother. He dodged. She stuck out her tongue.

"Enough," cried the mother. "Rutzen, see to the evening chores."

The boy left, grumbling and casting malicious looks at Marta, who stuck out her tongue again.

The mother leaned closer to Cantor. Her knife turned lazily between her fingers.

"Do you feel any rage?" she asked.

"Rage?" Why would he feel rage? "Do you mean anger? No. There's no one to be angry at."

"They dunked you in the sea, then left you on the shore to suffer and die."

"They?" His voice scratched through his dry mouth.

She tipped up the pitcher again, and he drank.

"The men in the hostel. It wasn't too smart to go in there alone."

"I'd already figured that out. But rage? No, I feel no particular anger toward them."

Marta scooted closer. "The Sea of Joden makes the rage." She put her hands next to her face as if they were claws and twisted her expression. "Aaaargghhh!"

"Go away, Marta," her mother scolded. She narrowed her gaze at Cantor for one more inspection. "Well, if you don't feel the urge to go berserk, I'll cut the ropes."

"I've never felt less like berserking, mistress."

"Yah, and you're probably too weak now." She began to saw on the rope binding his arms. "It'll take a day or two more for the poison to be gone from your insides and your out."

"More? How long have I been here?"

The woman pursed her lips. "How long, Marta?"

"Three days. He stinks, Ma."

"I know. It's the poison from the lake. He can't help it."

"Does he have to take a bath? Do we have to get the water? He's a big man. He should get his own water."

"Yes, he has to take a bath, and he can't get his own water."

As soon as the ropes fell from his wrists, Cantor flexed his fingers, then placed his hands on his arms to rub circulation back to normal.

"No, don't," said the mother.

He'd only made one stroke, but he knew why she'd tried to stop him. His skin reacted as if he'd stripped a layer off.

He grimaced and his eyes teared. She dumped the rest of the jug of cooling water over his arms.

Through gritted teeth, he tried to say something just to prove he wouldn't scream, but nothing came out. He wanted to ask what property in the lake caused so much harm. But he decided breathing in and out was more important than the answer to the question.

"Just rest," said the mother, whose tone sounded more maternal than he'd heard it so far. "We'll help you get to the bed."

After she loosened the rest of his bonds, she stood in front of him. "It's best I don't touch you. Put your hands on my shoulders. Marta and Gimo will help lift your weight by pulling up on the waistband of your trousers. I'm sorry, but it's going to hurt."

By Cantor's reckoning, hurt was a major understatement. Once laid out on the bed, he thought perhaps the chair had been more comfortable. Entirely too much of his body pressed against the mattress. His legs hung off the end since the bed was designed for a much shorter Brinswikker person.

Marta and Gimo fetched a stool for their mother. She put a pillow on it, then propped Cantor's feet on the improvised extension. The children next fetched buckets of water to pour on his aching body. Their mother didn't seem to mind that the water soaked the bed.

"Do you think you can sleep?" she asked.

Surprised by how fatigue had once again smothered him, he nodded.

"I'll be waking you up to make you drink. Other than that, you will rest."

Cantor's last thought before drifting off was about Ahma. Ahma was at times gruff and at others tender. He toyed with the term that was new to him, "It is a woman's bone." Perhaps this Brinswikker woman and Ahma had bones in common.

Snoring woke him. He hadn't been snoring, and now that he was wide awake, the snoring persisted.

His muscles still felt petrified. If he stretched, perhaps he'd crack. He could see the grain in the heavy wood timbers across the ceiling. Light slanted through the open door and one window, but shadows cloaked most of the room. Relieved that his sight had returned to perfect vision, he attempted to find out who was snoring.

With great care, he moved his head, then groaned.

Against the opposite wall, Bridger lay curled up comfortably, snoring deeply. He must have been there awhile, because he had rested long enough to expand to a size too big to walk out the door.

"Bridger, wake up."

The snoring ceased, but the dragon did not open his eyes.

"Bridger, wake up!"

He stirred, opened his eyes, and lifted his scaly chin. "Do you need something?" He rose up on his haunches, his head brushing the timbers above. "A drink? Mistress Dante said you were to drink lots of water."

He shuffled over to the table and poured water from a jug into a cup. At his present size the task looked impossible, but the dragon didn't spill a drop.

"You shouldn't have gone off without me. I could have helped in your confrontation with those Brinswikker men."

"It wasn't much of a confrontation. One minute I realized I had stepped into trouble. The next minute I was tied to ... What did you say that woman's name is?"

"Mistress Dante."

"Tied to Mistress Dante's chair."

Cantor managed to hoist himself into a sitting position. He felt much better than the last time he'd been conscious. He took the cup from Bridger and took a big swig.

Sputtering, he spewed the liquid all over the blanket.

"Ugh. What is that?"

Bridger scratched behind his ear. "I'm not real sure. Bixby and Totobee-Rodolow fixed it up out of some herbs Bixby got from Dukmee's shop."

"Toto — Who?"

"My sister."

"Where did she come from? Why is she here? Why are *you* here?"

"She's going back with us to Dairine. She's going as Bixby's constant."

"I can't go back. I don't have a constant yet."

Bridger's grin exposed teeth that reflected light from the door in the dim room. "I'll be acting as your constant for the time being."

"Who says so?" Cantor spoke in anger, and the abrupt gesture he made with his hands caused him to spill the last of the healing brew on his chest.

"Oh, good," Bridger said. "Bixby said to pour some on your skin."

Cantor clenched his teeth. "Who says you're my constant for the time being?"

"Orders." If possible, his grin grew bigger. "Bixby received a letter from the council. As soon as you can walk, we're on our way."

Cantor collapsed against the pillow behind him. "I may never walk again."

21

ASTOUNDING

Next to her skin, Bixby wore a thermea, a body suit of thin material. Today, she wore the unitard so warmth drained out through the covering and left her cool within. If she turned the garment inside out, her body's warmth would be held and used to keep her comfortable and cozy. She rarely suffered from being too cold or too hot. Only her head, feet, and hands needed protection from the weather.

Now she was warmed by the anticipation of a more festive evening than she'd had since she came to Effram. Cantor was awake and would come to the dinner table at Mistress Dante's home. Although he couldn't travel yet, his prospects for full recovery looked good. The herbs she'd collected at Dukmee's shop had aided in that recovery, and Bixby felt a bit of pleasure at having helped. A friend's improved health was reason enough for her to celebrate. And she would dress accordingly.

In the little room that Mistress Dante had provided for her,

Bixby hummed to herself as she searched through her hampers, getting ready her joy clothes, her most vibrant attire.

Getting dressed was one of her favorite activities. Her list of favorite activities would fill a book, but at the moment, choosing just the right clothes took precedence over the others.

She picked out colorful layers of red, yellow, gold, black, silver, purple, and green. Once she had them arranged to her satisfaction, she couldn't resist a twirl around the room so she could admire the flashes of gorgeous colors and mixtures of fabric, some soft and shiny, some lush and brocaded. And lace! Lots of lace, bunches and streamers and ruffles of lace!

As a final touch, she pulled her tiara hamper from her skirts and tried on several of her larger, flashier crowns. She settled on a circlet in the end, because the dainty gems in vibrant shades hung on fine silver, looking like delicate flowers on a twisted vine. Best of all, some of the vines hung down into her hair and along the sides of her face.

She carefully stored the unchosen headdresses in the proper hamper and pulled out the hamper containing footwear. Finding the boots took only a moment. She'd already decided what to wear with her bright outfit. A pair of high-heeled ankle boots would make her look taller, and these she'd picked up in an Alius market because of their tooled leather accented with beautiful dyes and metal studs.

With everything in place, she felt ready to have a wonderful evening. For only a split second did she mourn the lack of a full-length mirror in which to admire the result of her selections.

A handheld mirror pulled from yet another hamper allowed her to make sure her crown sat on her unruly hair at a proper angle. She jerked a brush through the curls and tangles, leaving her pale blonde hair even wilder than before. Not tangled, but definitely sticking out with a static that snapped as she walked. With a sigh, she plopped the mirror and brush back in the hamper. Bixby never fussed over her hair; she'd long since learned it did what it did, and there was no corralling it.

A knock on the door called her from her preparations.

Totobee-Rodolow smiled her toothy grin. "You look marvelous, darling. Are you wishing to attract the young realm walker's attention?"

Bixby's mouth dropped open, and she snapped it shut so that the very feminine dragon wouldn't guess she knew nothing of attracting young men. It had never crossed her mind that Cantor was anything more than a realm walker initiate.

"Come on, Bixby. Together, you and I, we will dazzle them, whether you want to or not." Totobee-Rodolow wrapped her long fingers around Bixby's arm. She gently guided her toward the door. "It is perfectly all right to be unaware that you are stunning. I am often unaware of my extreme beauty."

The mischievous twinkle in the dragon's eyes made it clear that Totobee-Rodolow enjoyed the outrageous statement she'd made.

Cantor sat at Mistress Dante's kitchen table, exhausted from the walk down the hall. He'd had a real bath before that and no nap. At the moment, he felt like a dillyfish strung too long on his catch string. He was better and itching to continue his hunt for a dragon but not well enough to walk out the door. He'd have to be patient. He hated being patient.

Bridger said he and Bixby had stopped by his home territory and persuaded his sister to join their expedition. Cantor shook his head, wondering what a sibling of his unwanted shadow would be like. Bixby said she was wonderful and made him practice saying her name. It was a mouthful.

His eyes closed, and he couldn't quite get up enough oomph to open them again. He practiced saying the sister dragon's name to keep from falling asleep at the table. He even remembered to stress the Ro syllable. *Totobee. Rodolow. Toto. Bee. Ro. Dolow. Totobeero. Dolow. Totobee. Rodolow. Totobee-Rodolow.* If she was anything like Bridger, he might be able to get by with calling her Toto or Bee.

Someone bumped into his leg, and the jolt sent a shiver of pain down to his toes. Cantor opened his eyes but couldn't identify who had disturbed him. He'd learned Mistress Dante had more children than Marta, Gimo, and Rutzen. Seven children tumbled about the room, some of them actually helping. He tried to ignore the bustle around him as mother and children worked together to fix their feast. He managed very well except for Marta.

Marta claimed she helped by keeping everyone in the room cheerful. She danced and sang and banged on the pots until Cantor thought he'd gladly pay her to entertain the ducks by the pond. But he had no money.

The few traps he'd had were gone. He'd foolishly pinned the coin bag into his shirt. The sea water had disintegrated his clothing, and he only had theories as to what had happened to the traps. Swiped by the Brinswikker men? Dropped out of his pockets somewhere between the hostel and the sea, or between the sea and his present abode? Fallen into the deceptively shimmering waters while the men dunked him? Confiscated by Mistress Dante for the trouble he'd put her through? Fortunately, his knapsack was made by a hampersmith and had protected the things within. His knife, Slice, and the hat Ahma had made were safe.

Mistress Dante had brought him what remained of all his clothes when he asked for them. He could see that the sea had made tatters of the material — in fact, they fell apart when he carefully lifted a corner. He doubted the coins in a pouch ever made it to her home.

With his big toe, he poked at the braided rag rug on the floor. He thought he recognized some of the fabrics as matching the Brinswikker clothes Rutzen had given him. The pants hit just above his knee since he towered over the little men. But the Brinswikker men were round in the middle, so the waist fit Cantor fairly well. They were broad in shoulder and chest, so the shirt Cantor wore buttoned nicely, but the sleeves came to his elbows. If he reached above his head, the shirt lifted to expose his stomach. And of course, there'd been no shoes his size.

He examined the hair on his toes and pondered where a man could acquire suitable clothing. And how to pay for said clothing with no money and nothing to barter with. He wondered if Bixby would take pity on him.

Over the prattle of Marta and her more vocal siblings, Bridger's voice interrupted his thoughts.

In a moment, the dragon came through the door, greeted by squeals from the Dante brood. They tackled him from all sides but couldn't bring him down. He good-naturedly dragged them out the side door to the yard.

Bixby came in next. Cantor's eyes popped at her outfit, layers upon layers of brilliant colors on delicate fabric. He'd always thought her rather untidy and dull, but this array of skirts and tops and the thing on her head made her look spectacular.

Behind her petite form, the new dragon eased into the room with the grace of a sailing ship and the beauty of a well-tended garden. Together, Bixby and Totobee-Rodolow stunned him.

Bixby stepped aside and allowed Totobee-Rodolow to come forward. Even as her dragon smile flashed gleaming teeth, Cantor stood to welcome her as Ahma and Odem had taught him. He suddenly remembered Bixby's summary of Totobee-Rodolow's career, a constant whose partner wanted to climb to the top of society in all seven planes. This dragon had been in many high courts and palaces throughout the known worlds.

He took her outstretched hand and bent over it, hoping his bow passed muster.

She laughed and caressed his chin as he stood straight.

"Darling, you are impeccable, totally suitable for your calling." She withdrew both hands and clasped them at her waist. "And your knees have adorable dimples."

Cantor stood straighter but couldn't help looking down at his legs. "My knees?"

Her arm came around his shoulders. "Never mind, dearest. We'll cover them with proper trousers, so the female populace will be safe from at least that part of your charming person."

Mistress Dante erupted in laughter. The children poured back through the door and joined in without having a clue as to what the joke had been. Totobee-Rodolow left his side to seat herself at the long plank table.

Cantor stood in a stupor until he felt Bixby tugging at his sleeve.

She tiptoed to be closer to his ear as she whispered. "She's the only dragon I could find who will go with us. Besides Bridger."

He looked down at the beautiful girl at his side. He sighed. "To be honest, I did a split second of ruthless scheming. I thought perhaps I could persuade her to be my constant."

Bixby nodded, looking wise. "I thought you might. But I knew once she opened her mouth, you'd change your mind."

Bridger joined his sister at the table. Places had been set with tin plates, wooden bowls, thick ceramic mugs, crudely carved forks and spoons, and burlap cloth napkins. As Bridger settled into the chair next to Totobee-Rodolow, he leaned heavily on the end of the long plank table. The table tipped, and all the dishes slid toward Bridger. They bounced over the rough wood, collided with one another, and rattled an alarm of impending catastrophe.

The dragon stood, jerking his hands away from the disaster coming his way. The other end of the table hit the floor and recoiled once.

Totobee-Rodolow stood and stroked Bridger's shoulder. "You are so clever, dear brother. You stopped the dish-slide before I even knew their world had tilted."

She trailed her hand down his arm and clasped his hand. "Come, Bridger-Bigelow. We shall put the pieces back where they belong."

The children rushed to help.

Cantor barely shook his head as he sighed. "We're going to Dairine, officially summoned by the council, with two — two — "

"Two clever, remarkable, extraordinary dragons." Bixby patted his arm. "Yes, it will be astounding."

22

EQUIPPED

Cantor waffled in his opinion.

Totobee-Rodolow fascinated him. She had a lilting accent that Cantor suspected was an affectation. But he would forget to be put off by this ruse every time she began relating her life as the constant to a diplomat realm walker. Cantor listened intently as she told stories about the aristocrats on Derson. When she veered off topic to gush over the markets and fancy eateries in the city of Peadmahar, the capital of Errinpau, he lost interest.

He couldn't understand why someone given the opportunity to work with the heads of state for the betterment of the people could be passionate about shopping and blasé about trade agreements.

And the tales she told of the two realm walkers who were her companions disturbed him. He'd always thought that realm walkers by definition had committed themselves to a noble way of living. Honor, integrity, courage, compassion, and courtesy marked these men and women as an elite group. The most telling aspect of their character was a devotion to Primen, His teachings and His mandates.

Yet Hilarill stole an identity and forged a lifestyle he couldn't rightfully claim and Rackama, who could have been a realm walker, chose instead to stand behind Hilarill, to feed him the information he needed, do his bidding on the sly, and deceive all those they came in contact with.

Such dishonesty from both men, the arrogance of Hilarill, and the cowardice of Rackama made Cantor's stomach clench. Thinking about all the times Ahma and Odem had whispered exchanges about the Council, Cantor came to the conclusion that they had known about this type of misrepresentation. They'd purposely taught him a lofty view of the chivalry of being a realm walker and hidden the seamy aspect of corruption.

Why? Why had they hidden the truth for so long — gone so far as to release him into the world laboring under such delusions? Bixby's mentor had clearly done no such thing.

He decided to visit Ahma before he reported to Gilead and the Realm Walkers Council.

Cantor got up from the chair where he'd been resting. A feast and the fellowship were fine, but he needed to concentrate on the future. Daily, he pushed himself to walk farther and longer. Soon he would be able to travel. He'd spent a total of ten days with the Dante family, during which time the father had visited from the men's camp and taken Rutzen back with him. He found the family dynamics to be odd and fascinating. And he grew more impressed with his traveling family as well. Their discussions revealed his companions' intelligence. Bixby and both dragons had opinions worth listening to.

Totobee-Rodolow was the only one of them who'd been to the training center for realm walkers. She told him that such friendly discussions were common during the round in which he would study cultural diversity. She warned the discussions at the guild often turned into debates, and the debates sometimes turned into arguments, but still the idea appealed to Cantor and renewed his eagerness to get to the next part of his adventure.

He believed he had recovered enough to take the journey. But he still didn't have any clothes of his own. A minor problem, perhaps, but one that stopped him any time he considered leaving the Dante household.

He stepped out of the long, low building that was Mistress Dante's domain. Being barefoot didn't bother him, as he had spent plenty of his time at Ahma's without shoes. He stepped carefully, mindful of how many ducks used the whole yard to deposit their waste. The ducks came toward him in a frenzy; they expected any two-legged animal to toss them food. Fortunately, he'd grabbed Mistress Dante's refuse bowl and had scraps to throw to the quacking crowd.

He emptied the container, shook it upside down, and tucked it under his arm. The ducks knew the gesture indicating no more food and waddled off, some complaining and others just making noise.

From the Dantes' yard, Cantor had a good view of the treacherous sea, the curve of the mountain range, and the expansive green valley to the west. Three settlements dotted the grassland. In the sky above this tranquil vista, dragons flew, diving and swooping for the pure joy of flight. Cantor counted a dozen. By comparison, even the large hunting birds looked small.

Two of the dragons flew side by side, approaching the Dantes' end of the sea with a more businesslike trajectory than their fellows exhibited. Totobee-Rodolow and Bridger were returning, with Bixby on Totobee-Rodolow's back. They'd been to market. Again. Shopping took up a great deal of Bixby's time, and her female dragon friend aided her in her quest to visit every market and shop in the valley. So far, Cantor had not seen any indication that these three had serious intentions toward the lifetime commitment to the realm walkers' creed.

The dragons swooped in and landed in a lower pasture. Bixby slipped off Totobee-Rodolow's back, and they walked up a hill to the house. Bixby waved to Cantor, and he raised his hand to wave back. She looked excited. Cantor grinned. She always looked excited. Excited, disheveled, and eager. Bixby was fun to be around, even though her presence sometimes wore him out.

Before she reached the crest of the hill, she called out, "We brought you something. You're going to like it." She ran a few steps up the incline. "*Them!* You're going to like them!"

Cantor shook his head, trying to imagine what they could have found at the market that would please him. Let it be clothes.

Bixby stopped and frowned at him. "No fair. You weren't supposed to guess."

He laughed. "I think I read your mind, as you did mine. I never would have thought of clothes on my own."

Bixby lifted one hand to the crown on her head. She pulled the circle of gold and glittering gems off as she reached his side. Her hair clung to the curves crafted in the shining metal, and she had to tug and wiggle it to free the last strands of whitish curls.

"So you did. I forgot I was wearing this crown so Totobee-Rodolow and Bridger could easily find me should we become separated."

"And did you?"

"Get separated? Yes. Mostly, it's Bridger wandering off. He spots something in a booth down the lane and can't forego examining whatever it is up close. We had to rescue him from trouble several times. The merchants know mor dragons rarely buy anything, and they don't like their goods being pawed without good reason. Of course, Bridger and Totobee-Rodolow object to their attitude, and Totobee-Rodolow does buy things." She grabbed his arm and turned him toward the house. "Come on. I can't wait to show you what we got."

They went straight to Cantor's room. Once there, Bixby pulled a hamper from her skirts and laid the innocuous-looking bag on his bed.

She clapped her hands together. "Go ahead. Look."

Cantor picked up the bag and handed it to her. "I'm not sticking my hand in there. You know only you can pull out what you're thinking about. I might pull out a snake."

"You're thinking about snakes?"

"No. That was an example. Don't you know how a hamper works?"

"No, not at all." She took the bag, looked at him, then the bag, and back at him. "I don't have to know how it works to make it work. It just does."

"You puzzle me, Bixby. Sometimes you seem to know everything, and now you don't know a little thing like this?"

She let out a humph of a sigh, pinched her lips, and narrowed her eyes. "What are you talking about?"

"If you put something in a hamper, only you can get it back. You know what it is, you picture it in your mind, and that thing comes to the surface. I can't pull things out because I can't picture what was put in there."

"You're talking about a vault, not a hamper."

"What?"

"A vault. You can't buy a vault just anywhere; it has to be made specifically for you. This is a hamper. Anyone can use it." She handed it back to him. "It's generic. Just think of a shirt in general. Or be even more general than that and think of clothes. Go ahead. Try it."

Cantor scowled but pulled the drawstring opening wide. Putting in his hand, he felt soft cloth and removed a folded shirt — a shirt that would more likely be called a blouse. Lace and pretty buttons, and pale flowers. He cocked an eyebrow at Bixby.

She laughed and plucked it from his fingers. "Sorry! That's mine. I must have tucked it into the wrong hamper."

Cantor waffled again. He felt bubbling amusement trying to escape. But he also felt annoyance that this girl wanted to dress him in fancy clothes. He liked his own clothes just fine — or he had before they rotted. But he understood that part of succeeding at the realm walkers round was to present himself properly dressed and able to engage lofty individuals in conversation.

He gave a great sigh and plunged his hand into the hamper. He should swallow his misgivings and be grateful for the generosity of Bixby and Totobee-Rodolow. At least they'd solved his clothing problem.

And they were willing to advise him, and he should take the opportunity to learn. And he should appear to be gracious about it. He plastered a smile on his face.

He drew out a masculine shirt. Bixby clapped her hands and bounced on her toes. "It's a perfect color for you. Totobee-Rodolow has such good fashion sense. We bought several of those in different colors. Keep going."

He retrieved the other shirts next, probably because Bixby's words brought them to mind and therefore to the surface of the hamper. He rubbed his thumb across the fine weave and admired the different colors, all rich and dark, maroon, blue, green, and gray. They were much nicer than anything he would have chosen, and perfect for a new realm walker looking to properly present himself.

His lungs felt tight, and he breathed in slowly to loosen his muscles. As Ahma had taught him, he named the emotions that affected his body. Anger. Resentment. Chagrin. And he named the source of the emotion. Bixby's grasp of the world of a realm walker far outpaced his own. Yet she was a nonsensical sort of person who didn't seem to value the special gift given to her.

She had showed him up several times in being able to cope with Dukmee's demands and performing manipulations that he had only heard about. He had held firm to the view that she was trifling with the ways of a realm walker. But this knowledge of what he needed to wear showed sophistication he sorely needed. Humility. As Odem often said, "If you don't reach out and take a piece for yourself, someone's going to throw the whole pie in your face."

He expelled the air, and the tension eased. He acknowledged to himself that the ladies' purchases intrigued him. He focused briefly on Bixby's smile and then plunged a hand into the hamper.

His next surprise was shoes and socks. Now he got into the spirit of the unusual gifts. Trousers, tunics, sashes, a slicker, and a coat piled up on the bed. He imagined Ahma's face twisted with disdain, and then an image of Odem bending over and slapping his knees, succumbing to outlandish mirth. Cantor laughed.

"What's funny?" Bridger appeared at the door.

The dragon started to come in, but his sister, Totobee-Rodolow, tapped him on the shoulder.

"Ouch." The dragon rubbed his hand over the place she'd poked. "Why do you have your claws out?"

"To get your attention, dearest. Since we'll be out in the world, you must polish your manners. You're supposed to let the female enter ahead of you."

Bridger made a face and backed out of her way.

"Are you pleased with our selections, dear boy?" Totobee-Rodolow's eyes wandered over the new garments.

"Yes, they're very fine." He didn't think they would be as comfortable as the trousers and shirts made by the village seamstress. Ahma didn't sew.

"And why were you laughing?" she asked.

"I imagined Ahma's and Odem's greetings for me should I come calling dressed up in these fancy duds."

Totobee-Rodolow raised her chin and looked down her elegant snout at Cantor. "Both your mentors have been to courts within the nine realms. You'd be surprised how much experience they have with high society."

Cantor nodded, but his private belief was that Bridger's sister didn't know his Ahma and Odem at all.

"Pack up," ordered Totobee-Rodolow. "It's time we left Effram and headed for Gilead." The two dragons left, but Bixby lingered.

"I have one more thing for you, Cantor." She dug in the folds of her skirt until she came out with a metallic bag the size of a barn cat. She held it out to him.

He took the sagging sack and rubbed his fingers over the surprisingly soft, smooth fabric.

"It's cold like metal, but obviously this material is woven."

"Yes." Bixby's curls bounced in disarray as she nodded. "Totobee-Rodolow and I looked for days before we found a hampersmith with the skills to fashion a vault."

"This is a vault?" He turned it over and over, examining every side. "Where's the opening?"

"You have to make the opening."

"How?"

"Pick a side that you want to be the top. Poke your finger through and pull until you have the size opening you want. You can only do this once, and it has to be you who does it. Otherwise the vault would allow that other person to retrieve things but not you."

The oblong bag didn't seem to have a top or bottom. Cantor decided to make the opening along the longer side, so he could fit larger items he might want to hide away.

Using his index finger, he carefully pushed through the material, then pulled in a straight line. The edges of the gap folded over and sealed the loose strands made by the cut. When Cantor removed his finger from the vault, a heavy string clung to him.

"The drawstring," explained Bixby.

Cantor pulled and the hole drew closed.

"This is amazing." Cantor put an arm around Bixby's shoulders and gave her a quick hug. "Thank you."

With pink cheeks, she shrugged out of his casual embrace and sidled toward the door. "See you outside. I'm going to go say thanks to Mistress Dante."

She slipped out into the hall, and Cantor was left to deal with all the clothes. He dressed quickly and had to admit the new outfit was comfortable. He scratched the back of his head as he surveyed the rest. He had never owned so much in his life. If he'd had to carry this without a hamper, he'd probably have left it all behind. But after Totobee-Rodolow and Bixby had been so kind, he didn't dare forget anything.

He packed quickly, putting the clothes back in the hamper, and tucked the vault inside his shirt, beneath the hip-length tunic he wore.

He looked around the room to see if he'd left anything else. With a grin, he remembered he'd been carried into the room with nothing but the disintegrating clothes he wore. He picked up the hamper that was no bigger than when it had been empty and strode out to the hall, ready for adventures leading him to realms beyond his own.

23

HOME

Bixby and Cantor stood in the pasture beside the Dante home. In a field closer to the lake, the dragons extended their wings, stretching before the flight. Excited children ran between and around the adults and visitors gathered for the momentous occasion.

Bixby leaned closer to Cantor. "Does it seem to you that the number of Dante children has multiplied in the last half hour?"

"Some of them must be neighbors' children."

"It's amazing that they came all this way to see us off. Their abodes are quite a distance from one another."

"Seeing realm walkers teamed with their local dragons must be a big event. Mistress Dante said that there used to be many realm walkers and now, only a few."

A boy cannoned into Cantor's legs, squeezed a short but powerful hug, then took off racing another boy. "It could be they're moving so quickly it just appears there are more of them."

The movement slowed as soon as the realm walkers strolled

down the hill to the dragons. Female adults and children followed Bixby and Cantor to the field.

After a final round of thanks and good-byes, Cantor climbed onto Bridger's back with only a girth to hold on to. Jesha sat between the dragon's ears. Bixby jumped onto the elaborate tooled-leather saddle on Totobee-Rodolow.

"Look at you," he called to Bixby.

She looked down at her dress, the saddle, and the boots that showed with her skirts pulled up to her knees. "What"

"Do you remember how frightened you were the first time you flew?"

"Nervous, not frightened."

He winked and was satisfied by the blush it brought to her cheeks. "You're an old hand at dragon flight now."

She arched her eyebrows. "Shall we race?"

Mistress Dante objected. "You two are to ride safely. You're just like family now."

Cantor waved. "We will, mistress."

"And we'll come back to visit," promised Bixby.

Mistress Dante put a handkerchief to the corner of her eyes, dabbing away some wayward tears. "This is so strange. I never cry when our men go away from home. I'm happy to see them go. But I rather like having Cantor and Bridger around."

Marta stopped skipping and came to her mother's side. "It's 'cause they aren't Brinswikker men, Ma."

Mistress Dante patted the girl's head and called to Cantor. "Come back any time, young man. You have the means to visit again. Totobee-Rodolow and Bridger-Bigelow know every portal in the nine planes."

Totobee-Rodolow stretched her lovely neck and batted her eyelashes at Cantor. "Well, perhaps not all of them, darling, but between Bridger-Bigelow and me, you can choose any destination and we'll know where the portal is on Effram. We could come here first and then on to your intended location."

Amid hoots and hollers, the dragons rose up into the air. Soon the dragons flew together, close enough for their wingtips to brush against each other.

Cantor announced his plans, calling across the expanse to Bixby. "I'm going to stop by my home before we go to Gilead. You can come with me or go on ahead. Dukmee may already be at the Realm Walker Council and wondering what's taking us so long."

"It's been forty days." Bixby's already large eyes grew bigger. "He's probably gone beyond wondering to believing we're captured or dead." Bixby consulted with Totobee-Rodolow. "We're going straight to Gilead."

Bridger and Cantor both nodded their approval of the decision.

Bridger spoke over his shoulder to Cantor. "I'll take you to the portal you came through when you first entered Effram. It's a drifter but probably hasn't moved too far from that point."

The dragons flew over the mountains. Once they reached the other side, Bixby and Totobee-Rodolow turned south, while Cantor and Bridger veered to the northwest.

Bixby shivered as Totobee-Rodolow rose to a higher elevation. With her boots firmly wedged into the stirrups and her knees pressed against the saddle, she felt comfortable enough to pull a hamper out of her skirts and look for something to keep her head warm. Her toes were cozy in the leather boots, but her ears and nose felt icy. And her hair whipped about, making it hard to see.

She found several possibilities for a head covering, but continued digging until she unearthed a crocheted helmet. The cap wasn't lined, so she took a few minutes to rub her fingers along the inside. Her talent allowed her to pull wisps of yarn away from the strands and mold them into a smooth shell.

When she trapped her springy hair under the helmet, a few inches escaped the bottom edge, looking a bit like a frizzy fringe. The front came down over her forehead. She pulled at the center and extended a piece to cover her nose. At that point, she created a split and twisted the yarn outwards until she could tie the strings of the nose covering behind her head. She placed a crown over the helmet, then searched for gloves.

Comfortable with her gloves in place and her hamper safely tucked back in her skirts, she engaged Totobee-Rodolow in a conversation.

"Why are you fidgeting so?" asked Totobee-Rodolow.

"My head and fingers were cold. I didn't have anything appropriate for my head and nose, so I had to alter a knit helmet I had." Bixby stroked the dragon's neck in front of the saddle. *"We're doing splendidly, aren't we? I have no trouble hearing you through my mind. We've bonded more than I expected."*

"Don't get too used to my being around, darling. This is only a temporary soiree into my former life."

Bixby tried her best to not sound like a wheedler. *"I hope you'll continue with me if I decide to follow the realm walker road as my career."*

Totobee-Rodolow merely shrugged her massive shoulders in response. Bixby watched their rise and fall and decided on another tactic.

"Totobee-Rodolow, why are the politics in the council so convoluted? My father is always saying our illustrious leaders muddy their decisions with a lot of sinister subplots."

"Sinister subplots have always been part of the council's management." Totobee-Rodolow gave a trilling laugh, which told Bixby her questions were to be treated lightly. "Hilarill and Rackama had so many schemes in the works. One time, they even had schemes going against each other, and they ended up kerflumoxed and never realized it was the other behind their failure."

Totobee-Rodolow kept up a steady stream of revelations of the unseemly pair. However, the dark deeds of the council apparently were off the approved list of topics for conversations.

Bixby gave up trying to pry information out of the savvy dragon.

According to Bridger, the portal they sought would take three days' flight to reach. The dragon expressed enthusiasm over the time they would spend together and the possibility of deepening their bond. Cantor reminded Bridger that this was a onetime excursion. He hadn't bonded a constant yet.

That first night, Cantor discovered by the campfire that Bridger had a pleasing voice and carried a tune well. His musical aptitude was the first thing that he'd found likeable about the dragon. He chastised himself for that thought. If he was to be honest with himself, he realized the clumsy oaf had done many things to aid in the rescue of the captured young men.

Unfortunately, right after that charitable thought, Bridger turned abruptly and swept his tail through the campfire.

Burning logs, embers, and ash scattered over Cantor's bedroll. His roasting dinner, a rabbit on a spit, rolled through the dirt.

Bridger's help in cleaning up the mess he'd made almost ruined Cantor's blankets, and when he accidentally stepped on the hot rabbit, he hopped on one foot, holding his burnt toes. Cantor dodged the leaping Bridger and took refuge behind a tree until the camp looked like it had been trashed by mean monkeys.

In the middle of the second night, the dragon rudely awoke Cantor by picking him up and running around in circles.

The dragon muttered, "Thunder, lightning, so much water, so much water."

Cantor's kicking and screaming brought Bridger out of his sleepwalking state.

"What were you thinking?" he asked when the dragon put him down.

"You were going to drown. The clouds opened up and rain fell like the whole sky was a waterfall. I had to take you to safety."

Only a hint of sarcasm tripped off of Cantor's tongue. "Thanks for the rescue."

The last night, they found a cave. Cantor suggested strongly that the cave was too small for the both of them. Bridger took the hint and said he would sleep on the wide ledge at the opening. After three days of strenuous flight and lack of sleep the night before, Bridger conked out, his body forming an excellent windbreak against the nippy northern breeze.

Both adventurers slept well. As the night progressed, Bridger relaxed, and in the manner of mor dragons, he grew. Cantor woke late in the morning. No light from the sun reached his corner. He stood slowly, stretching out the kinks from sleeping on rock. He soon discovered why the cave had remained dark. Bridger's body blocked most of the entrance.

"Hey, Bridger, wake up."

The dragon did not stir. But Jesha appeared in the small gap to the outside. She huddled down, and a soft purr resonated through the cave.

Cantor sat on a boulder and tugged on his boots. He called out again, but Bridger responded with a heavy sigh and a snort.

Cantor sauntered up to Bridger and put both hands on the dragon, carefully avoiding the razor-sharp edges of his scales.

"Hey, dragon, we've got to go." He slapped out the simple rhythm of his sister's name. Tap. Tap. Tap. Hard tap. Tap-tap. Still Bridger did not stir. Cantor closed his hands into fists and beat out the same rhythm with more vigor.

Nothing.

He studied the wall of sleeping dragon before him. One whole side blocked the entry. At the top, two small openings appeared — one where Bridger's shoulder curved downward and Jesha sat comfortably. On the other side, sun slipped in where his body sloped off to the tail. Neither opening was big enough to shimmy through, and even if he could, the sharp scales would be a problem.

Frustration welled in his throat. "Bridger!"

He pulled back his leg and swung a full-force kick at the point where Bridger's side became his underbelly. The impact hurt his toes and spread back through the bones to include his entire foot.

Still nothing.

Moving to Bridger's front end, Cantor reached beyond his shoulder to do the drumbeat on the scales of the dragon's neck. He continued yelling, beating, and even kicking until he collapsed against the cave wall. During all that commotion, the dragon uttered two grunts and a long wheeze.

After a huge sigh, he shrugged. "I might as well make coffee and have breakfast. Or perhaps it's already noon, and I'll eat lunch." He glanced up at Jesha. "I can't tell from here, cat. Can't see enough of the outside to know which way the shadows are falling or how short they are. I don't suppose you have a pocket watch."

Jesha stretched and resettled.

Cantor's gaze settled on the bulk of the dragon. Bridger's sides moved up and down as he breathed in and out.

"Dumb beast." Cantor took what little water he had left, brewed his morning drink on a self-heating stone Bixby had given him, and ate the last of the bread and jerky Mistress Dante had provided.

While he packed up his belongings, Bridger stretched.

"Yo, dragon, are you returning to the world of the living?"

Bridger jumped to his feet. He swung his head back and forth. "Huh? What's happening? Trouble?"

Cantor strode to the opening and stepped outside where he could look at Bridger's face. He realized the dragon's muscles quivered, ready for action. His scales quickly lost the cutting edges.

"No, calm down. You overslept. That's all."

"Oh." Bridger shook like a dog, his scales rattling. "Sorry. I'm not used to so much activity. I'll toughen up in a week or so. As my father used to say, 'I need some fine tuning.'"

"That has something to do with stamina?"

"Um." Bridger looked around as if trying to find something to focus on. "Um, I guess not. I think that had to do with my coordination. For stamina, he said, 'Got to go swim upstream with the fishes.'"

"Fish."

"No, my father said, 'fishes.'"

Cantor shrugged, thinking the conversation would go nowhere but downhill from there. "I've already eaten. Can you be ready to fly soon?"

"Sure, I'll go dip in that lake and clean up. I'd like to look fresh when I meet Ahma and Tom."

"You know." Cantor rubbed the whiskers on his chin. "That's a good idea."

A swim and a shave restored Cantor's good humor. They reached the portal in the late afternoon and had to wait a few minutes while Bridger reduced his size to fit through the frame.

The slight swoosh sound announced the opening. The view of Cantor's homeland sent a thrill through his heart. The air crackled a bit as he stepped through, and he thought he heard a rip when the dragon squeezed in.

They'd come home without a hitch. As soon as the dragon stood beside him on the rise beside Ahma's cabin, Cantor pointed toward his home.

"Just beyond that row of blackamore trees."

Bridger sniffed. "I smell old smoke and burnt wood."

Cantor pulled in air through his nose. "So do I. Let's go see what's up." He raced down the hill, foreboding rising in his chest. As he passed the last blackamore, he skidded to a stop and looked at the cabin with dismay.

Only the frame stood. Black beams and posts burned and split littered the interior. He made out the crumpled table, the cabinets next to the sink, and the metal pump slouched over like a drunken man.

One word departed his mouth, past his clamped jaw. "Ahma."

24

ASHES

Cantor scrambled down the hill, the sound of his descent lost beneath the clatter of Bridger's lumbering behind him. Rocks dislodged by the dragon's big feet scattered around Cantor, who was too concerned to bother fussing at Bridger.

"Ahma!" he called, realizing as he did that no one was there. He jogged to the frame of the front door. The four by fours used to support the structure looked like coal.

Bridger came to look over his shoulder. Cantor carefully touched the surface. "Cold. This didn't happen today or yesterday or even the day before that." He examined the floor. "And it's rained since the cabin burned."

Bridger jostled his shoulder, trying to see what Cantor was doing. "How can you tell?"

Cantor pointed to a small patch of dirt showing through the rubble. "The rain washed the soot down, pooled, and then dried. You can see the pattern of a puddle there."

Cantor circled the cabin, then made consecutively larger

circles around the property until he was some distance from the house.

"Are we looking for something?" asked Bridger on the second round.

"I'm not sure what. It's just that I would expect Ahma to leave me some kind of sign if she's alive and went off with Odem or someone else." With his hands on his hips, he surveyed the surroundings. "Tom's not here. I wonder if Odem and Nahzy were here when this happened."

When they ended up in front of the cabin again, Cantor paused. "I'm going down to the village to see if anyone can tell me anything."

"Do you suppose they came running up to help when they saw the flames?"

He shook his head. "No, you can't see Ahma's place from the village. The path twists and turns and takes you to the other side of an outcropping. Though it's not far. They'd be more likely to have smelled the smoke if the wind was in the right direction."

Cantor swept a hand in front of him. "But I see no indication that someone tried to douse the flames. I don't think anyone came to her aid."

Again he peered through the collapsed walls at the debris on the floor of the cabin. He shook his head. "We're losing the light. I must go if I'm going to get back before full dark." He put a hand on the dragon's arm. "Stay here, Bridger, please. If anyone comes along, ask questions."

"As a dragon?"

Cantor let out a sigh and rubbed the back of his head. "No, the people of Dairine are not that familiar with dragons. That's why Tom held his dog shape for so long."

"Are they at all familiar with talking dogs? Ones that ask nosy questions?"

"No, I guess not." Cantor looked out across the valley. His body felt like it twitched and crawled under his skin. He wanted to know what had happened. Where was Ahma? Was she all right? She couldn't be under the burnt wood. He wouldn't think of that. He must be rational and do what could be done.

Cantor surveyed the ruins. The dragon still stood behind him. Depending on Bridger to ferret information from a stranger was a long shot.

He had to go. "Nobody comes by here except on very rare occasions. You probably won't get to ask even one question."

"Maybe someone will." Bridger's voice had changed timbre.

Cantor whirled around. An old man stood where Bridger had been. With a cane in one hand and a cat cradled in the crook of his arm, he looked like he belonged in this part of Dairine. He wore plain homespun, shabby boots, and a cloth hat. Bits of gray, stringy hair hung down to his shoulders, and deep wrinkles sketched age in his face.

"I'll wait here for you," said the old man form of Bridger. "You get on down to those people who might know something worth knowing. Don't worry about me."

Cantor stood for a moment, examining the shape-shifted dragon. The new form was astonishing.

"Bridger, you are an artist."

The dragon shook his human head and frowned at Cantor. "Go find out about Ahma. I'm worried."

"You're worried?"

"Yes! Get moving."

Cantor loped down the trail. He and Ahma used the uppermost part of the path to visit the fruit trees and the wild field of onions and greens. Constant traffic kept the dirt packed and free of plants. He noticed a few hardy weeds had poked up where they were not wanted. So Ahma hadn't been down this way for some time.

After he passed the orchard, the trail became steeper, the path rougher and more narrow. Undergrowth from the woods encroached liberally on this stretch. Where the trail leveled, he picked up speed, then slowed again where loose rocks or plants obstructed his way. One section ran along the base of a cliff. For years, one of his chores had been to clear debris from minor rockslides here. No one had done it since he left, but the course was still passable.

As he rounded the last bend, the village came in sight. Cantor heaved a sigh of relief. In the back of his mind, he had feared he would find the homes and shops leveled by fire as well. Whatever caused his home to be burnt must have been natural, perhaps lightning. No marauders had ravaged this corner of Dairine.

He could see people in their yards and walking on the lanes. Shops had closed for the day. The settlement took part in peaceful evening activities, such as chatting over a hedge with a neighbor, or women sitting on the porch with hand-work while the children played in the dimming light.

He'd known these people his whole life. Ahma insisted on living an isolated existence. She didn't fear the villagers, but had a great distrust of travelers. With scary stories about children carried away by strangers, she managed to tamp down some of Cantor's natural cordiality.

He raised his hand and waved at two old men sitting beneath a tree with a checkers game on the table between them. At the second house on the outskirts, a woman came barreling out her front door, carrying a package, and motioned for Cantor to come to her.

"Cantor, Cantor, wait up."

Mistress Golden was someone who might know about Ahma. He stopped at the gate of her white picket fence.

"Cantor, I have the last items Ahma had me sew for you." She handed him the package. "They're already paid for, but she never came back to get them. It's been quite some time. She said you needed them because you were going off to school in Gilead." The woman paused and looked him up and down. "You're already wearing fancy clothes. Have you been to Gilead already? Are you home for a visit? She's not ill, is she?"

Mistress Golden took a deep breath and grabbed Cantor's arm in a frantic grip. "I was just telling my Moseph that we should climb that trail and see if she's all right. We usually see her at least once a month, and I know it's been longer than that."

Cantor jumped in before she could get another breath. "That's why I'm here, Mistress Golden. I've been away, and I came by to check on her. She's not there. And the cabin is burned to the ground."

She clapped a hand over her mouth and stared at Cantor with horror in her eyes, then turned to the house and hollered. "Moseph, come out here. Moseph, right now!"

Her husband came out the front door and down the three steps from the porch. The two men abandoned their checkers and came too. Several people from down the lane and across the road hurried to find out what all the fuss was about.

Mistress Golden removed her pinching grip from Cantor's arm and transferred it to her husband's. "Cantor's been away, and he came back to the house burned and no Ahma."

"What about the livestock?" Moseph asked Cantor.

"Gone."

"Chickens as well as the donkey and cow?"

"Yes, sir."

"Then chances are she took them herself when she left."

Mistress Golden dug her fingers into her husband's arm. "Why didn't she come down to us? She knows the village would help her out, help her rebuild even, and of course, give her a place to stay."

Moseph winced and loosened her grip. He placed a finger on her lips, stopping the flow of words. When he removed the obstruction, she nodded, accepting his suggestion that she be quiet.

Moseph returned his attention to Cantor. "Did you see any fresh-turned earth on your land?"

Cantor closed his eyes and envisioned his walk around the cabin with Bridger. "No, no graves."

"And Ahma's cart?"

Ahma always left the cart at the head of the trail, right before the path turned off to the cabin. He'd passed that spot and didn't take notice of whether her cart with two big wheels had been there.

"I don't think it was there," he said.

"Then she's probably packed up what she could save and has gone somewhere. Maybe to a relative or a friend?"

"Odem."

"That's where I'd look first, son."

He nodded. That made sense. She would pack up, wait for a portal to open, and go straight to Gilead. Odem lived in a small town some five miles from the city.

"Thank you, Master Golden. I'll go first thing tomorrow."

"If you can get us word, we'd all like to know she's safe.

She's lived up there for fifty or more years. She's never been too sociable, but we've taken to her nonetheless."

Cantor nodded again. "I will."

He turned, and the village crowd that had gathered around to witness the excitement parted for him to leave. As he walked through, individuals gave him encouraging words, blessings for travel, and assurances that everything would turn out all right. He thanked them and waved good-bye with a lump in his throat. He trotted up the incline and slowed when the path became steep.

His climb back to the cabin took more time. He didn't anticipate finding new information when he reached his burnt-out home. Dusk hung in the air when he passed the spot where the cart was not parked. He could hear Bridger humming as he got closer to the cabin.

When the dragon came in sight, Cantor was surprised to see he'd strung a hammock between two trees. Still shaped like an old man, he lolled in comfort, with the cat on his stomach.

"Did you bring dinner?" Bridger asked.

"Dinner?" Cantor shook his head. "Never thought of it."

"My stomach has been thinking about it ever since you left."

"Don't you want to know what I found out?"

Bridger's face as a human was very expressive. "I've known since you left the village. They had no news for you. And you've decided to go on to Gilead."

"Then why didn't you know I was not bringing any food?"

Bridger stood up, and as he shape-shifted back into his dragon shape, the hammock gathered to become his tail. Cantor's eyes popped, and he had to consciously change his expression from astonishment to interest.

Bridger grinned, and Cantor knew he hadn't fooled the dragon. "Okay, I'm impressed. I'd be more impressed if you'd fixed dinner."

The dragon's grin grew wider, and he pointed to a spot closer to the cabin. On a spit over a bed of coals, a huge fish sizzled.

"And there are potatoes roasting in the coals."

"Bridger, I might get used to having you around."

Bridger stood straighter and nodded his head with slow deliberations. "Yes, I thought you might."

25

INTRODUCTION
TO GILEAD

Bixby had seen pictures of the Great Hall where members of the Realm Walkers Council had chambers. The mammoth structure did not have the refined lines of some of the palaces she had visited with her parents. However, the rich wood and dark colors lent the rather hefty-looking style a solid, unshakable impression. And the height of the walls, doors, and windows made Bixby feel mighty small indeed.

Totobee-Rodolow sashayed in with no obvious sign of hesitancy. She'd guided Bixby's choice of clothes and given her ample advice regarding holding her chin up, straightening her shoulders, and keeping her visage solemn until all the paperwork was done.

The colors Totobee-Rodolow had chosen to shine in her scales matched the burgundy, forest green, and somber gold of the rugs, drapes, and furniture in the entrance hall.

"Over here." The dragon approached a counter in the wall that revealed an office beyond.

Bixby followed closely and tried to keep from swiveling her head to see everything at once. If she tilted her head back far enough to see the painted ceiling, her crown slipped. She'd chosen the crown that calmed her and gave her self-confidence. She feared it was only working on half-power, since her knees felt weak and she constantly felt the need to clear her throat.

Totobee-Rodolow rapped her claws on the countertop, making a rhythmic call for attention. "Papers for a new realm walker, please. Let's do this quickly so I can take her to dinner at the Sky Realm and get her settled at the Moor."

Bixby stood on her tiptoes to see an older woman shuffle up to the counter. The clerk pulled her shawl tighter around her shoulders and adjusted the glasses that had slipped on her nose.

"Totobee-Rodolow! I can't believe my eyes. I thought you would never enter the world of realm walkers again."

"Yes, Penny Lunder, the last experience was tawdry, but I've found a young lady I can have faith in. I decided to give it a try and see if I still have the old touch."

Penny Lunder leaned across the counter and whispered. "Isn't that a bit dangerous, Totobee-Rodolow? The council won't look kindly on someone who doesn't fully commit. You could face fines and penalties, even social ostracism, if they think you've toyed with them."

"You need not worry. I know how to deal with their chicanery." Totobee-Rodolow patted Bixby on the shoulder. "This is Bixby D'Mazeline. I believe she's on your records. Give her the paperwork to fill out while you find her name. She's from Richra."

"Oh!" The woman put her hand to her heart. "I didn't

see you there. You gave me quite a start. I assumed Totobee-Rodolow and I were alone."

"Not to worry, Penny, dear. Bixby is discreet. She'll not repeat our conversation."

"Well, yes, if you say so. I've worked here too long to get sacked right before I can retire with my collected payback." The clerk handed over three sheets of vellum and a scratchy quill pen. An inkwell sat on the counter. All of this was beyond Bixby's reach.

Totobee-Rodolow scooped up the papers, ink, and pen and took them to a chair with a side table. "You'll be more at ease here, darling. I'm going to take a look through the registry book and see who's been in and out of the Great Hall recently."

She strolled over to a big open book where she signed her name and then searched the recent pages, flipping them slowly. Though an occasional smile lightened her expression, more often she frowned fiercely. Bixby's expectations of meeting delightful, interesting people plummeted with each scowl. She hoped the dragon would at least find a few pleasant acquaintances in the registry.

Totobee-Rodolow looked up at her and winked. *"There are many I would rather not meet again."*

A pleased shiver went up Bixby's spine. The dragon had heard her thoughts and answered. The chance of being constants with this elegant dragon grew with the strength of their friendship.

This time Totobee-Rodolow frowned at her. *"Don't assume this is a long-term arrangement. Remember what I told you to begin with."*

If Bixby didn't want the dragon reading all her thoughts, she would have to get out a different crown, one that guarded her mind. But she didn't really mind Totobee-Rodolow sifting through her mind. She trusted the dragon to have her best interest at heart.

Bixby finished filling in the information and took it to the counter. No one came to collect her paperwork, and she couldn't see over the ledge to the office. She cleared her throat, then cleared it again, only louder.

Finally, Penny Lunder noticed and came to the window. "Thank you, Princess Bixby."

She gasped. "Oh, please. Don't call me that. Bixby is good enough."

"As you wish. I'll make a note of that on the documents that are distributed to the faculty."

"Can't we just not mention it at all?"

"Well, that wouldn't accomplish much. Your mother is famous for her skills, and therefore you'll be easily identified. Child, your name has been on our books since you were born." Penny stood on tiptoe and leaned over the counter to peer down at Bixby. "Have you inherited her gifts?"

Bixby had the answer for this, a question as familiar to her as her own skin. "My mother says it will take maturity — in other words, time — before we can be sure what abilities I might develop."

"I see." Penny straightened and tapped the vellum papers against her chin.

Totobee-Rodolow walked over to look Penny in the eye. The gems implanted on the dragon's face flashed in the late-afternoon sunshine. No — they glowed. Bixby watched with fascination. The radiance came not from the sun but from behind each precious stone. And it increased.

Totobee-Rodolow spoke to Penny Lunder in a low tone,

with evenly spaced words. "You are not to gossip, Penny Lunder. The girl seems average, perhaps even a little lacking in possibilities. There is nothing of note to tell."

The glimmering gems faded until the flame behind each disappeared.

Penny Lunder looked at the dragon without expression, then startled as if she had just come out of a daydream. "Oh, yes, what was I saying?"

"You were about to hand Bixby a schedule for the next week's activities."

"Yes, I have it right here." She smiled without warmth, and her words sounded perfunctory. "I hope your initial week is pleasant."

"You are too kind. Good evening, Penny, dear."

Totobee-Rodolow guided Bixby out of the building.

Bixby barely waited until they cleared the massive doors before she started in with her questions. "Penny Lunder seemed much friendlier when we first went in. Did you do something?"

"Anyone who was after information would go interrogate Penny Lunder first. She keeps her eye on the comings and goings of the council members, and she has all the records at her disposal. Plus she likes to be the one in the know, and she relishes gossip." Totobee-Rodolow prodded Bixby to resume walking down the street. "Other than that, she's a very pleasant person."

"But you disarmed her. How?"

"Years and years and years ago, I knew a wizard."

"Really? Was it Chomountain?"

"No, but one of his commanders. He taught me the power of suggestion."

"Will you teach me?"

Totobee-Rodolow gave her a stern look. "Perhaps. It isn't as easy as it looks. And with some people, changing their thinking is impossible."

"And your gems had something to do with it, didn't they? I wonder if I have a crown that would substitute for your gems."

Totobee-Rodolow had picked up the pace. "Come along, darling. Our next stop will be so much more entertaining."

No longer strolling, but almost sprinting, Bixby worked to keep up. She had little time to inspect the houses, shops, people, and conveyances they passed. She did note that several dragons walked on the street beside important-looking people. She might look important as well if she weren't jogging to keep up with an elegant, dignified dragon.

Panting, she asked, "Where are we going?"

"To eat."

"Why must we hurry?"

"We are going to the Sky Realm, a very busy restaurant. We want to beat the crowd and get a good table."

Bixby had very little experience eating in places where one paid for the food. She imagined some tables being fancy and others being plain, but this didn't seem likely. "Are some tables better than others?"

"Of course not, darling. Some tables are situated so that one can see everyone else in the room. Some are tucked back a little along the side so one can eat without being on display. And some tables are next to the paths that waiters and customers traverse as they go about their business. It's annoying to be where the traffic is heavy, unless you want to waylay someone you expect to encounter at the Sky Realm."

Bixby gave up trying to keep up with Totobee-Rodolow and grabbed hold of her arm. The dragon hardly noticed. Bixby was able to float with her feet barely skimming the cobblestones. Her parents had not been favorably disposed toward her ability to float. Perhaps, since it was one of the talents her mother did not possess, they were prejudiced. She saw no harm in discreetly rising above the ground, but her mother thought it could draw undue attention to her daughter. And her father was all for being inconspicuous when not performing royal duties.

She knew if anyone wondered about the two racing down the street, that person would think the girl was unusually graceful. If she had time, Bixby could lengthen some of her skirts and float higher. But it wouldn't do for her to let anyone catch a glimpse of the space between her toes and the pavement.

Bixby caught her breath and was able to pepper Totobee-Rodolow with more questions. "There is no real sky realm, is there? I've never heard of one."

"No, just the nine planes in our planetary system. Our sun does have other sets of planes, but none are called sky realms."

This was one of the academic subjects Bixby had loved. "I studied those in school. Not that I actually went to a school. But my tutors provided those geography, astrology, and general science lessons."

"When you were two?"

Bixby heard the sarcasm in Totobee-Rodolow's voice. The dragon knew way more about Bixby's upbringing than Bixby had relayed. She wondered how much information the dragon pulled from her thoughts and how much she had learned from other sources. Keeping her secrets had become difficult, but Bixby trusted Totobee-Rodolow not to tell.

Bixby lowered her voice. "I was probably five when I finished those studies. I remember kicking up a fuss because my mother wouldn't take me to any planes but the ones in our stack."

226

"And you wanted to see them all."

"Exactly."

They turned a corner. The dragon pivoted so quickly, Bixby swung out like a ball on a string. Her collection of lace skirts fluttered like flags. She managed to get herself perpendicular to the sidewalk, but glanced around to make sure no one had seen the mishap.

When she looked straight ahead again, she felt her mouth drop open. "There must be a thousand people on this street. How far to the restaurant?"

"About twenty-two steps. And, darling, there are not more than two hundred as far as we can see. There might be more down in the shopping district."

"Shopping?"

"The best. Perhaps tomorrow." Totobee-Rodolow stopped in front of a beautifully carved entry. Tropical trees curved over an arch made by two glass doors. Bushes and birds embellished the sides. A huge frog sat under one of the leaves near the base of the carving. Rich green tones accentuated the depressed areas, while the figures were polished a honey gold. Extending from the top of the entry to a roof overlaid with glittery gold tiles, a thick blue paint textured the outside of the building. A few lighter areas suggested clouds, and birds in flight crossed between windows.

A doorman pulled open one glass door and gestured for the ladies to enter.

Suddenly, he held his hand up, palm toward them. "Excuse me," he said when they stopped. He looked carefully into the dragon's face. "Forgive my impudence, but could you be Totobee-Rodolow?"

26

SEEING
BUT UNSEEN

A quick glance at Totobee-Rodolow proved the dragon to have retained her composure. Bixby held her breath and tamped down the urge to flee.

Had someone from Effram sent spies to find them and prevent their reporting the injustices in that plane? The council could overturn a wicked ruler. History books told of earlier times when none of the ruling classes would dare ignore the council's mandates. Although, somewhere in ages past, the council had become the backbone of evil regimes, supporting instead of thwarting corruption.

Totobee-Rodolow smiled graciously and bobbed her head. "Yes, I am."

He stepped closer and spoke in hushed tones. "Madame, it is me, Clarart. Do you remember me?"

"Of course I do, darling." She put a hand on his arm. "You

are still dear to me. We must talk." She looked around, then patted his arm and let go. "We will be discreet. Are you on duty for the rest of the night?"

"Yes, Madame."

She beamed at him, and Bixby noted again that her toothy smile just didn't have the usual dragon fierceness. "You've advanced in positions since I saw you last. Marvelous. I'm so glad for you. I will slip you a note when we leave so that we can have a long chat tomorrow. You must fill me in on the things I should know."

"With pleasure, Madame."

Bixby trailed Totobee-Rodolow into the restaurant, now stepping on the polished wood floor instead of floating. The maitre d' also recognized her dragon friend and fussed over her long absence.

"We are so glad you have returned to us. Let me get you your favorite table, and perhaps some of the Dirogne valley wine."

"Thank you, Finnry, I haven't had a glass of that divine nectar for years. I think since the last time I was here."

A waiter appeared to guide them to a table, but it took ten minutes to cross the room. Many people stopped their progress to say a word to her temporary constant. Totobee-Rodolow smiled pleasantly, obviously remembered each person, and introduced Bixby D'Mazeline as her friend. She sidestepped every reference to whether she had returned for good or only for a visit.

Bixby swallowed often and offered only minimal comments. She'd attended social gatherings at home, but these strangers seemed to have an even higher standard of behavior than her mother. She wished she'd listened just a tad more attentively when her mother explained council town etiquette. It all seemed like so much posturing and the production of great walls of façade.

They finally took a seat, Totobee-Rodolow directing her to a chair on the back side partially in the shadow of a tall fern. Bixby hoisted herself up, with her legs tucked underneath her in order not to look like a child at the table. She hated to sit with her chin next to her plate.

The dragon eased her long body into a special chair on the same side, but in the light. Her scales glimmered in peacock colors. Her face bore slanted eyes with a thick fringe of eyelashes. Dragons didn't ordinarily have eyelashes or eyebrows. Totobee-Rodolow evidently felt that was a mistake, as she often shape-shifted lashes. For eyebrows, she simulated a ridge of darker scales above her eyes. Along with her fashionable form, she elongated her tail to gracefully wrap around the table's base.

The waiter bowed. "I will bring you the wine, Madame."

"Thank you."

As soon as he was beyond hearing them, Bixby whispered to Totobee-Rodolow. "I don't drink alcohol. It messes up my gifts."

"Neither do I, darling."

"But — "

"It's a code, darling. They will bring us a bubbly, clear beverage that tastes divine and has no alcohol whatsoever. This is a dangerous town, little one, and more dangerous if you do not have your wits about you." She patted Bixby's hand. "Now in that wonderful hamper of tiaras and crowns, do you have a circlet that obscures your presence?"

"Yes, I do."

"Well, dig it out and put it on, darling. I want you to see the people I point out to you and remember them, but I don't want them to take particular notice of you."

Bixby put on two circlets, one in gold and the other in silver. They were both simple with a minimum of fashioned leaves and tiny flowers. The silver tiara would help her remember everything Totobee-Rodolow said.

The waiter returned with two glasses and a bottle. He looked at the second glass when he placed it on the table as if it were there by mistake.

Totobee-Rodolow nodded toward Bixby. "My friend."

"Ah, yes." He did his little bow of acknowledgment.

Bixby thought the tight gesture possibly did wonders for his figure. His stomach muscles must be solid. To her, he looked unusually athletic in build, considering he carried bottles and dishes around for a living. She didn't have much muscle. Well, she did have some skinny flesh on her tiny bones, but to call them muscles was laughable.

She wondered if she should have tried food service. She knew how to cook, but serving might have given her another perspective. Ah well, there was still plenty of time to try something new after this adventure.

The waiter opened the bottle and poured the liquid into Totobee-Rodolow's glass. She sipped it and nodded. He almost left the table, but the dragon reminded him to pour the beverage for Bixby. That quickly, he had forgotten she was there.

Another waiter came by and recited a list of items being served that evening. When Totobee-Rodolow ordered two entrées he looked a bit concerned.

"Our dragon-size portions are ample, Madame. They tell

me that you were a frequent patron of the Sky Realm some years ago. Our quality and service are the same now as then."

Totobee-Rodolow laughed lightly, the sound almost like tiny bells. "Have you forgotten my friend?" Again she nodded toward Bixby.

Bixby smiled and waved at the astonished man.

"Oh, I am so sorry, miss. I can't think how I — I ..."

"We haven't taken offense," said the dragon. "Run along. We're starved, and I've promised Miss D'Mazeline a wonderful meal."

While they waited, Totobee-Rodolow pointed out different officials, diplomats, councilmen, and, with humorous antecdotes, some eccentric characters.

She waved to a female dragon draped in fluttery chiffon and took the moment to educate Bixby. "Mor dragons like Sallytime-Effinlow attend all the gala events and gather bits of information. They piece together scraps of gossip. Usually these society spies end up with a pretty clear picture of what goes on behind the propaganda issued by the authorities."

"Isn't that dangerous?"

"Indeed, very. But they've written their insurance policies in documents that would be released should they die unexpectedly."

"I don't follow."

"The mor dragons write out what they know and keep it hidden. As long as they're alive, the information isn't general knowledge. Should some reprobate want them dead in order to eliminate their intrusion, he's restrained by the knowledge that *all* his misdeeds will be put before *all* the citizens once the mor dragon is dead. It's in the villain's interest to keep the mor dragon alive, thus the hidden information is called 'insurance.'"

A gleam came to the dragon's eyes. "Look who just came in."

Bixby's head swiveled, and she rose up a little to get a clear view. "That man with the white coat and tan pants?"

"The light is tricky in here, darling. The coat is light yellow and the pants are darker yellow. The man is Krogerill Sandsyellow. He claims he is half mor dragon. Impossible, but I do believe he believes his lies after all these years. Don't worry your head about him. He's perfectly harmless, just needs attention."

Their meal arrived, delivered by a different waiter. Totobee-Rodolow had to point out that her friend sat beside her and would like her dishes to be placed accordingly.

Bixby smiled good-naturedly at the man's discomfort, hoping to ease his embarrassment. Previously, when she'd worn the obscuring tiara, she hadn't kept popping out of the background to be noticed.

The food reminded Bixby of the cuisine of her parents' home. Their talented cook assembled tender meats, steamed vegetables, luscious fruits, and delectable desserts. Totobee-Rodolow had kindly ordered food that Bixby had been missing, dishes popular in her homeland.

Three men and a lady in somber attire entered and sat on the stage. They pulled out large instruments from small hampers and played softly as the restaurant filled with patrons in high spirits. Totobee-Rodolow continued her identification of the people and dragons she recognized.

"It's a shame, darling, that I can't name everyone in the room. I've been away too long. But tomorrow, Clarart will give us up-to-date information." She paused, looking at the door. "Aha, at last, here is the person who knows how to reach Dukmee."

"Are you going to send for him? Will you wave him over if he looks this way? Perhaps I should go speak to him?"

Totobee-Rodolow hushed her. "No, no, no, darling. There is no need. He will see that we are here, and he will tell Dukmee. Tomorrow or the next day, Dukmee will contact us."

"But I have on the obscure tiara. He might not notice me."

"Not this one. No, this one will see you in spite of the shadow protecting you. He is a great one."

"His name?"

"At this time?" The dragon smiled, lips curved, head tilted, and a dreamy look in her eye. "I have no idea what his name is at this time."

"Since we aren't going to talk to him, can we leave now? I'm very tired."

"Oh no, darling, that would never do. If we left right after he arrived, people who notice things like that might assume there is a connection. We mustn't let them prattle." She gestured to the waiter. "We shall have our sweet and then depart."

Bixby sat in silence while nibbling on a dessert of hot chocolate sauce over a delicious mocha cake layered with pudding. Her stomach protested, and she put down her spoon. Totobee-Rodolow continued to savor her portion. For just a moment, Bixby marveled over the amount of food dragons consumed. Then she turned her attention to the crowd in the room.

The number of patrons entering diminished, and some of the early arrivals left. Bixby reviewed the names and information she'd acquired on each person who remained. She caught some people watching Totobee-Rodolow, but none who noticed her, until she came to the man with no name.

He wore fine clothing over a medium, stocky build. Bixby surmised that muscle made up his bulk, because his face showed no evidence of fat. His dark, straight hair parted in the middle and draped over his collar. Smooth eyebrows, a straight nose, planed cheeks, lips ready to smile, and a stubborn chin combined to make a very attractive man. Though she couldn't even see the color of his eyes, they claimed her attention.

He looked directly at her. Their eyes met, and she reached to connect with his mind. Just like with Dukmee, she encountered a wall.

He smiled, winked, then shifted his gaze away. She felt like she'd been politely dismissed. Her fatigue slipped away, replaced by energy to move and move quickly. Enthusiasm for being a walker and solving problems throughout the realms bubbled through her veins.

Totobee-Rodolow's hand rested on her arm.

"Calm down, darling. His effect will send you rushing from one good deed to another if you let it. Take deep breaths and restore quiet in your soul. You'll be a better walker if you work from a center of peace. Frenzied do-gooders do great harm."

"How do you know him?"

"He rescued me from my former life as a constant."

THE SUN RISES

Bridger slept well. Cantor knew because he observed the dragon ... all night. The great beast breathed slowly, resting deeply, with only an occasional snort, while Cantor tossed and turned all night. He had disturbed the gentle Jesha's rest several times. When he turned over and grunted, the cat had given him impatient looks. With obvious disdain for Cantor's lack of manners, she stood and stretched and settled herself again on Bridger's back just behind the dragon's folded wing.

He tried to engage his mind in a useful pastime, to make plans to search for Ahma, refusing to believe they would find her remains in the debris. But his attention flitted from mission to memory like a leaf in an autumn breeze.

From long experience, he knew the sunlight would bathe the house when it came up in the morning, giving them plenty of light to search for clues about Ahma's whereabouts. Those pleasant early rays had warmed the cabin after many a frigid night.

He thought of the hundreds of mornings when he had awakened to the bright light streaming in the windows, and to the smell of coffee and bacon. Ahma sometimes sang in the morning, and he would join her before he even rolled out of bed.

She told him that his name meant singer, a special singer. A cantor led others singing praises to Primen in houses of worship. He'd never seen such a house, but Ahma assured him that he would see them in Gilead.

This morning the sun did wake him, so he must have finally dozed off. He sat up and looked around the yard and buildings that had been home to him for many years. Without Ahma or the animals, and with the cabin a burnt and collapsed shell, no tender feelings urged him to stay.

Bridger made breakfast while Cantor examined the inside of the house. He looked for a clue that would tell him how the fire started. He looked again outside for a note or notice from Ahma. And most of all, he looked for bones.

He found nothing.

Relieved and frustrated at the same time, he went back inside. Perhaps he could find one of Ahma's lists still intact — anything that might give him a clue as to what she was doing the day of the fire. He stood quietly for a moment, allowing his aversion to instruments of writing to guide him to a fallen shelf, glad that for once the bizarre weakness could work to his advantage. A partially melted tin cup held the ashes of Ahma's writing tools. He examined the area, but the blackened paper he found crumbled in his grasp.

Next, he tromped among the ashes, using the toe of his boot to dislodge larger pieces of wood. He found a tin ladle massively warped by the heat. Several books bore a few unscathed paragraphs in the middle, surrounded by damaged pages. He looked in the cupboard where his bed resembled a huge campfire, long cold, with only bits of charcoaled wood evidence of the blaze.

Kicking aside several pieces of small beams, he smiled at a relatively unscathed square section of the floor.

Cantor raised his voice to call to his dragon friend. "Bridger, can you leave that for a few minutes and help me lift this beam?"

The dragon straightened from stooping by the pot on the fire. He had a wooden spoon in his hand.

"It depends on what's under there."

"A hole in the floor. It's where Ahma kept her valuables. The floorboards are scorched here, but it doesn't look like they burned through."

Bridger put down the spoon and came to the house. Puffs of ash marked each step he took. He trampled what looked like a piece of chair, and a dish cracked with an explosive pop when he flattened it. Jumping at the snapping sound, Bridger didn't carefully choose the next spot to put down his foot. His toes caught on a rafter, and he landed prostrate before Cantor.

A cloud of ash billowed up and encompassed them both. Coughing, Cantor reached a hand down to help his dragon friend up. When the air cleared a bit, he pointed to the square of flooring he'd found.

"I'll take this end." Cantor bent over the end of a blackened beam. "You take the other. If we can move it a few feet in your direction, I can uncover the trapdoor."

Bridger gasped. "Do you think Ahma's down there?"

"It's much too small for her to crawl into. I'm convinced she got out of the house. Then when it burned all the way down to the ground, she decided it was time to move."

"That's very reasonable. That's probably exactly what happened."

"Are you ready? On my count of three. One, two, three!"

They both grunted. With the beam out of the way, Cantor went back to push aside smaller chunks of wood. Bridger came closer to watch as Cantor felt around the edge of a plank until he found a fingerhold. He pulled off the cover to the hiding place and set it aside.

"It's here." He pulled out a limp sack and held it up. "Ahma's hamper."

He stood to pick his way through the rubble and out of the demolished cabin.

Bridger followed. "Do you know what's inside?"

"Our stash of gold and silver. She always collected way more than I did, but I never figured what she traded to acquire the wealth. Probably herbs and advice. Believe me, she had plenty of advice. I earned traps by doing odd jobs for people. A strong back and nimble fingers come in handy."

He fingered the material of the limp bag. "Ahma always took care of the money. Sometimes I thought the traps just multiplied like rabbits. I'm not sure how this hamper works. In theory, the traps will have been cozy in a dimensional void. The heat from the fire shouldn't have reached the gold. But if it did, all the traps will be melted together. That will make them awkward to use."

He knelt on the grass and opened the drawstring top. He sniffed and coughed. "Smells like smoke."

"Is it a vault? Can you stick your hand in there without getting hurt?"

"I never even knew about vaults until Bixby explained. Yes, I can remove the traps."

"Well, do it! I've never seen more than a couple of traps at a time."

Cantor looked up at the dragon, his hand shading his eyes from the sun. "You're not planning to rob me, are you?"

Bridger blustered. "What? Me? I'm your constant. What's yours is mine and what's mine is yours, so it's mine, and stealing it would be an unnecessary act."

Cantor laughed. "Calm down. I was just pulling your cork. And you're only *temporarily* my constant."

"Right. Let's see the gold."

Cantor put in his hand and pulled out his closed fist. Turning his hand over, he opened his fingers to display a mound of gold traps. The spheres were mostly the size of peas, but some were as large as marbles, and one the size of a walnut shell. He tilted his hand and let the gold pour back into the bag. He took out another handful and did the same.

"My, oh my." Bridger eyed the gold with a pleased glimmer in his eye. "It's beautiful, dazzling, so shiny, and such a lovely color." The dragon's long purple and black tongue slipped out between rows of jagged teeth and traveled over his top lip first and then the bottom. He slurped as his tongue withdrew, and he smacked his lips as if finding something tasty. "Does Ahma have any gems?"

"A few." Cantor sniffed again. "You know that smoky smell is getting stronger. I don't think it's coming from the cabin."

Bridger jumped. "Breakfast!" He tore off to rescue what was left of their meal.

Cantor stuffed the seemingly empty bag into the front of his shirt. He would find Ahma and deliver her savings. She couldn't have dug through the smoldering ruins. She had needed to go for some reason, and when he found her, she'd explain.

"Are you looking for the old man?"

Cantor turned toward the voice. A young man, dressed in fisherman togs, strolled up the narrow village street. The horizon cut the backdrop behind him in half. His head and shoulders stood out from the ocean, while the curving lane of houses blended with the man's tan trousers. He looked like he'd walked off a boat only moments before. Hair wild with the wind, young skin tanned like old leather, white teeth, blue eyes, and a cocky grin. He held a slicker by one crooked finger over his shoulder.

Cantor raised a hand in greeting. "I'm looking for Odem."

"That's his house. I live one house beyond. He's been gone for four months, but that's not unusual for him. I take care of things while he's venturing."

"Then you're Benrite Bassoon. He's mentioned you often." Cantor stuck out his hand to shake. "I'm Cantor D'Ahma."

Benrite nodded once as he took the offered hand. "And he's mentioned you more than once."

Cantor walled off the tide of disappointment rising to batter him. He had counted on Odem's help to find Ahma. Or even that Ahma would be here with him. "You haven't seen him or heard from him in four months?"

"That's right."

"Part of that time he was with us at our home. He left just before I went venturing myself."

241

"He never sends messages while he's away, so I never expect one. He returns the day he comes home and not a day before."

A rumble of laughter came from behind Cantor.

"What was that?" Benrite leaned to the side to peek behind him, eyeing the horse standing quietly.

He looked the animal over and then back at Cantor. "Your horse laughed?"

"No." Cantor glanced back at Bridger in his horse shape. "Of course not. His stomach rumbles. Probably gas."

The horse neighed and shook his head.

Benrite scratched his chin and lost interest in horses that laughed or had digestive problems. "Do you want to stay at Odem's house? He wouldn't mind. I've got a couple of repairs to make from the last storm, and I could use some extra hands and a strong back."

Cantor looked at the sky streaked with orange and purple over the dark ocean. Gilead was close, but not close enough to reach that night. Besides, he was tired and hungry. He could help Benrite with chores around Odem's place in the morning and plan how to approach the city tomorrow.

"Fine."

Benrite clapped him on the shoulder. "There's a shed out back where you can stable your horse. Then come to my place." He pointed to the next house in the lane. Lights shone through the windows. "You can meet the family and have supper with us."

"I'll need to feed my horse."

"I have some hay and oats meant for Odem's donkey. You're welcome to them."

"Sounds good. Thanks."

Benrite passed him and hurried up to his own front door.

Cantor took hold of Bridger's reins and started down the path between the houses.

"Sounds *good*?" Bridger blew air through his lips, making a horsey noise of disdain. "Hay? Oats? Not oatmeal with molasses, just oats? This sounds *good*?"

The shed was too small for Bridger, but an overhang at the side provided ample shelter. The extension of the roof came out more than eight feet. Two sides had half walls, and numerous poles supported the back and side. Cantor brought Bridger in through the front, an open space with not even a gate.

"I know you're hungry, Bridger. What do you want me to do?"

"You could buy me a chicken or two. I can fix them the way I like."

"Okay, I'll go see what I can find. Don't make trouble while I'm gone."

"How can I make trouble in this lean-to?"

"You could knock it down."

"That would draw attention to myself. I was thinking it would be better to keep a low profile."

"Exactly." Cantor left, jogging up the lane to a place he'd seen. A sign on the fence said they had eggs and chickens for sale. He purchased two stout hens, and the seller promptly rung their necks and handed the dead chickens to Canton by the feet. When Cantor brought them back to Odem's backyard, he hadn't been gone ten minutes.

Bridger had returned to his dragon shape. He took the hens and held them up for inspection. "Perfect."

"How are you going to cook them?"

"I'm going to revert to savage dragon ways and flame them

with my breath. The feathers and skin will fall off as ashes, and I'll eat the cooked meat on the bone."

Cantor made a face. "You aren't going to gut it? That's disgusting."

"Ah, but the innards are a great delicacy."

"I'm glad I won't be here to watch."

Bridger laughed. "I have now pulled your cork." He sniggered with a couple of snorts to emphasize how pleased he was with his own joke. His amusement built. His shoulders shook and he clasped his hands, still holding the dead chickens by their feet across his jiggling belly.

The limp chickens bounced and flopped in time with his laugher. The sight of lifeless hens flapping and shimmying broke through Cantor's solemn façade. It took time for the two to quit laughing. When they had controlled their outburst to mere snickering, they broke out again in loud guffaws. They both had to wipe tears from their eyes.

Cantor squeezed his face into a somber expression. "Weren't you going to tell me something about cooking chicken?"

"Oh, yes. Once the meat is cooked, I slice open the bird and clean out the cavity, which might contain impurities. I use my breath again to sear the inside. The only thing that would make it better is salt."

Cantor looked toward Benrite's house. "I think I have time. I'll get some from inside Odem's."

He went to the back door and tested the knob. The lock held. Rubbing his hands together, he created a stream of energy. He touched the sides of the lock in just the right places for the energy to kick the locking mechanism out of the way. Worried that Benrite might come and catch him accessing the house without a key, he dashed in and brought a salt shaker out to Bridger.

"Thank you, my friend." The dragon licked his lips.

"I best be going." Cantor backed up as he continued to talk. "I'll check on you before I turn in for the night. Would you rather sleep in the house?"

"I can't think on an empty stomach. Ask me when you come back."

"I left the back door open. You can go in if you want."

"Thanks. Now go away. You're delaying my feast."

Cantor chuckled and gave a perfunctory wave to the dragon. As soon as he turned around and started toward the front of Benrite's home, the smile fell from his face. The disappearance of Ahma and his inability to locate Odem knocked his confidence to a new low. His dreams of becoming a realm walker had always been infused with images of his two closest companions available with advice and tutelage. The prospect of going it alone did not generate any enthusiasm. Going it alone would be like eating his own cooking instead of Ahma's. His gut would be leaden instead of comfortably full.

Then again, so far, he'd not really been alone.

First he was waylaid by a crazy dragon, whose skilled shifting was matched by his inane clumsiness. But Bridger was no coward. Cantor had no doubt that the dragon embodied other noble traits, such as loyalty, persistence, and honesty. With the inept Bridger guarding his back, he felt strangely secure.

Then he'd run across Bixby hanging out in the trees. He didn't understand her, but she was good company. Her intellect obviously towered above his. Her talents seemed to multiply as the days went by. And comparing his upbringing on the side of a mountain, removed from civilization, to her cultured background and varied learning opportunities ... well, he came off as pathetic. She dressed strangely, but he found her peculiar clothing oddly attractive. She did look like she could unravel. Looked fragile. Acted tough. Looked silly. Acted wisely.

Dukmee! Who and what was Dukmee? A healer? Surely more. Dukmee had come to their aid.

No, Cantor concluded. He wasn't alone.

And the latest addition to the mix, Totobee-Rodolow. The older dragon played at life, with her ridiculous accent and dedication to exaggerated beauty. He'd never heard of a mor dragon shifting so that her body undulated colors or simulated jewels as part of her skin. She wore an ostentatious façade, but he believed her to be astute, knowledgeable, and clever. What an odd sister and brother she and Bridger made.

The evidence before him was that Primen would provide companions to aid his task of becoming a proficient realm walker. And the more immediate mission of finding Ahma and Odem would also be couched with ample help. He took a deep breath and blew it out, relaxing his muscles and determining to expect the best. Ahma had taught him not to drown his prospects in doubt.

Ahma wasn't here, but he'd follow her advice until he found her.

28

INTO THE CITY

Cantor had a pleasant morning with Benrite, Benrite's wife, and their three children. The wife and older girl went into Odem's home and did some cleaning as the men tackled a few areas of minor disrepair outside.

"Just to keep it spit-spot," she told Cantor. "It's not really messed up 'cause no one's here to muck about. But there's always dust, and I keep my eye out for varmints that might crawl in looking for a cozy stay."

Cantor hid a grin. Bridger had crawled in the night before looking for a cozy place to stay. He often thought of the persistent dragon in varmint-like terms.

Jesha sat up on the eves of the house, dividing her attention between the men hammering and the children playing.

Benrite wiped the sweat from his brow with the back of his forearm. "Where'd that cat come from?"

Cantor grinned at Bridger's cat. The animal had struck a

pose, sitting as still as a carving with her eyes closed against the bright sun. "He's not yours?"

Benrite shook his head. "Probably a neighbor's, but I've never seen it before.

"I've always heard that cats are good to have around the house."

"Don't tell the children. They'll set milk out for it and then we'll own a cat."

The two young boys spent the morning tormenting Bridger in his horse form. They brushed him and rode on his back all around the yard, down the lane, and back again. They brushed him some more and force-fed him oats. Every time Cantor mentally asked Bridger if he wanted him to haul the little nuisances away, the dragon nixed the idea. He informed Cantor that if the boys really annoyed him, he could always change back into a dragon and eat them.

Cantor responded with a chuckle that grew to a laugh as the dragon's ripple of humor augmented his own.

The rush of good feelings dwindled as Cantor realized the mental intimacy the shared laughter implied. Now he not only shared thoughts with the dragon, but emotions as well? He'd have to be careful with this tricky partner, or he'd end up with Bridger as his constant on a permanent basis.

Bridger tagged into his thinking. "*Yes, Cantor, our bond has strengthened. Do not be dismayed. We were meant to be constants. Our realm walking career will outshine the most noted heroes in the history books. The Tales of Bridger and Cantor shall be required reading for all school children.*"

Cantor groaned as Bridger bumbled into Benrite's squash patch and demolished a row of produce.

Benrite and Cantor did some roof repair. Cantor almost

asked Bridger to lend a hand, since most of the work involved toting shingles up a ladder. But even this close to Gilead, it was tricky to introduce a dragon to a rural neighborhood. On this plane, dragons rarely appeared on the streets of normal towns unless some disaster had occurred or was about to occur.

Odem had liked to whittle. As a boy, Cantor loved to sit at his feet, trying to guess what would come out of the piece of wood succumbing to Odem's sharp knife. The old realm walker talked as he whittled, and most of what he said stuck in Cantor's mind.

The tip of Odem's knife fashioned an eye in the side of the pinwood head. "Dragons are out of favor. The less people come into contact with real dragons, the more they believe superstitions blossoming out of fertile minds. There are old stories that are true enough. Storytellers serve a purpose when they stick to verified legends. But the new lot of minstrels and yarn spinners have no compunction at drenching the tales with fabrications. Makes you wonder what their motivation is in putting the creatures in a bad light. Embellishing tales to make them more horrific has become a profitable pastime. They get called to present at different functions by merit of their sensational stories. Each spinner attempts to outdo the others with preposterous but vastly entertaining fables."

Odem didn't often talk about things having to do with the council, but he was most likely to let a few truths slip in while he was whittling.

"The dragons are getting blamed for the things that should be laid at the council's door. And who's engineering that? Since things in general have deteriorated as the council becomes more falsehearted, it's safer to blame the dragons. Accusing the rulers could be hazardous."

Odem had shaken his knife in the air as if to cut down a few foe. "You see, boy. A dragon is there and you can fight it. But those responsible for evil deeds in the name of the council aren't so easy to identify. The people involved in corruption might be anybody. Your neighbor could be a traitor. It's not hard to understand when citizens grow wary of speaking out against the council. Too many people have disappeared when their voices got too loud."

Odem's wisdom had always proved true. Cantor would be careful in his dealing in Gilead.

After lunch, Cantor mounted Bridger and waved good-bye to his new friends. Once out of sight and closer to the actual city of Gilead, they ducked behind a large warehouse. Bridger returned to his dragon self. Jesha sat on the top of his head, between his two horns.

"Do you often change the cat when you shape-shift yourself?" asked Cantor.

Bridger reached up and took the cat into his hands, then snuggled her in the cradle of his arms. "No, she gets crotchety if I put her through a lot of shifts."

Cantor shook his head. "Doesn't it wear you out to keep changing?"

"Not at all. The more often I change, the suppler I remain. If I haven't shifted in a while, I get stiff. Sometimes, I shift three or four times a day, just experimenting with what I can do. It's entertaining when I'm bored."

Cantor glanced sideways at the dragon. He apparently had meant no sarcasm in his statement. He really did entertain himself when bored. And this habit had made him a most accomplished shape-shifter. Cantor found it odd that Bridger evidently didn't come from a family of elite mor dragons. He certainly had talents beyond the ordinary.

"But your sister doesn't have the same talent?"

"She spends all her talent on being beautiful. She shifts the shape of her scales, the colors, and the texture. Being something of an artist, she sculpts her body. Even the gems she adorns herself with are unique to her abilities."

Cantor thought back over all the styles he'd seen Totobee-Rodolow exhibit. Once she reminded him of a sleek racehorse. Once she looked like an elegant, colorful bird. And there was the time he had to look twice to determine she was a dragon and not a giant woman. Bridger's sister certainly was a puzzle.

"Where did she get her accent?"

"Our mother. Mother wasn't from Effram."

They came out of the alley and continued toward the center of town. With each block they passed, the streets became more crowded. Most of the people wore fashionable attire. Even the street cleaner had a decent pair of trousers, shoes, and a clean shirt. Cantor appreciated the clothes given to him by Bixby, Totobee-Rodolow, and Mistress Golden.

Soon they would be at the Realm Walkers Council. He felt a measure of surprise that he looked forward to seeing Bixby. Without the security of Ahma and Odem to drop back on, he accepted his more recent friends as valuable comrades.

The trip to the city was important. He also wanted to find out if anyone knew anything about Odem and Ahma. He fretted over not knowing where they were. A feeling of unease spread through him every time he thought of Ahma's burnt cabin and Odem's small, modest, and empty home.

Bridger stopped at a busy corner. Cantor stepped into the

street and started to cross before he realized the dragon was no longer by his side. He sprinted back to the curb.

"What's wrong?"

Bridger stared down the side street. "I think we should go that way."

"You said the council hall was the way we're going. Why make a detour?"

"Just a nudge or something that there's something down this road that we need to see."

"Do you get these nudges often?"

Bridger shook his head, his lips pressed in a line. "No, never." He stomped away from Cantor, not looking pleased with the detour.

Cantor followed, also unhappy. "It's late in the day. If we don't go to the hall now, the office may be closed by the time we get there."

Bridger nodded, showing he understood, but the dragon crossed another road, turned toward the east, and tramped down an even smaller side street.

If Cantor had been sure of the location of the realm walkers' hall, he would have left Bridger to his meandering. But he didn't know where it was, and he was loath to ask one of these bustling city-dwellers.

To arrive there for enrollment without a dragon was a major breach of protocol. The knowledge weighed heavily on his mind. He also fretted about turning up with Bridger. Would this dragon embarrass him? Would he somehow be stuck with Bridger as his constant? The choice between no dragon constant or Bridger filling in as his constant was clear. Bridger had to come along.

Cantor trotted to catch up. "Is someone in trouble?"

"No, I don't think so."

They marched another block and crossed a less busy street.

"Bridger, the clock on that building says it's ten minutes after four. We really should turn back toward the council office."

"Not much farther."

"What's not much farther?"

"Don't know."

Jesha walked up Bridger's chest and perched on his shoulder. She looked down at Cantor and mewed. The plaintive cry sounded like she sympathized with Cantor's concern.

At the next corner, Bridger stopped. They'd wandered far away from the busy part of town, and the streets were practically deserted. The afternoon wind chased crumpled paper and leaves down the gutter. A small empty can rattled as it joined the other trash.

Bridger looked around as if his new location surprised him.

"Why are we here?" he asked Cantor.

"You said there was something down here we had to see."

"Oh." Bridger again surveyed their surroundings. "I think it's gone now."

Cantor felt his muscles tighten, and a groan of aggravation cranked out of his throat. "Aargh! Bridger, we wasted a half hour going out of our way for nothing."

"Not quite nothing." A voice spoke from the alley.

Cantor whirled around to find a skinny young man leaning against the bricks of the building.

Bridger made a clumsy sort of bow. "Oh, it's you, sir. I'm glad to see you." He straightened and gestured to Cantor.

"This is Cantor D'Ahma, my constant. We're on our way to the hall."

"Yes." The man smiled pleasantly and tilted his head. "I'm sorry to have to detain you for a bit."

Jesha made an attempt to crawl down her dragon's arm to reach the stranger. The man came forward and took her. In his arms, she settled down to purr.

Bridger shuffled his feet. "Always willing to answer your call, um, sir." He glanced at Cantor and then back to the man. "Um ... what's your name this time?"

"Feymare, Bridger. I am currently a physician." He placed a hand on Bridger's upper arm. "I need to meet with your sister. Please ask her to be at the Conicaty Bridge at half past one tomorrow."

"Yes, sir."

"Thank you." He stroked Jesha's back, then handed her to Bridger. "You should be on your way." He looked into Cantor's eyes, with a smile in his own. "You won't be late."

A force of wind blasted dirt and debris into their faces. Cantor closed his eyes and leaned against Bridger. In only a few seconds, the air calmed. Cantor opened his eyes and found himself with the dragon and his cat on an entirely different street.

"We're here," said Bridger. He started up the broad steps that ran the entire length of the building. Columns held up a solid, flat roof that covered only the stairway.

"Wait." Cantor ran after Bridger and stopped him. "How did we get here?"

Bridger looked around at the people and dragons going up or down the stairs. He leaned closer to Cantor and whispered, "Dr. Feymare did it."

"How?"

Bridger shrugged. "Come on, let's go in and get the paper-work and our room assignment." He trudged up the steps. "We can find out where Totobee-Rodolow and Bixby are. Maybe we can see them tonight."

"How do you know all these details about the Realm Walkers Council?"

"Totobee-Rodolow sent letters while she was constant to Hilarill. She told us most of what happened on her adventures."

The magic word struck a note in Cantor's heart. Soon, very soon, he would be involved in adventures. Just one or two more bridges to cross, and he would be a fully accredited realm walker.

They opened the door and stepped into the dim light of an entry hall. A huge clock on the opposite wall dominated the room. One slanting stream of light from a window high on the west wall highlighted the round face, where two filigreed black hands pointed to the time.

Five minutes past four.

29

PENNY LUNDER

Cantor's attention scattered. The ceiling hung high over their heads. He'd never seen a room so tall. He thought half of his home village would fit in this space. All of it, if he could stack the houses on top of one another. The paintings on the walls depicted individuals and scenes. He wanted to read the plaques under each one and study them closely.

His eye kept returning to the clock. They'd stood in the entryway for three minutes. Eight minutes after four. All the time taken to follow Bridger's nudge had been absorbed somehow. He tried to identify his emotions as Ahma would have him do. Intrigued, but also wary. Suspicious of his own observance. Had he glanced quickly at the clock they'd passed? Did he read it wrong? Was that clock fast or slow or even stuck? He'd ask Bridger or Totobee-Rodolow or Bixby. Someone would have an answer.

An older woman behind a welcome desk studied Bridger

and Cantor. She signaled them to come closer, placing a stack of papers in front of her. They headed her way.

Bridger stood erect, looking a bit pompous as he took the lead in the conversation. "We are Cantor D'Ahma and Bridger-Bigelow, here to enroll in the first realm walker course. I believe you are Penny Lunder. My sister, Totobee-Rodolow has mentioned you."

"She arrived just this week. Would you like to know their building and room number?"

Cantor barely listened to the chatter between his temporary constant and the long-time guardian of the council filing room. He felt the uncomfortable twinge between his shoulders, indicating the existence of many writing instruments. He edged away from the desk as he realized the pencils and pens were stored in the office where the woman worked. A dozen pens set up enough clutter in his system to force him to distance himself. He guessed there might be over a hundred in the filing room. He felt his knees weaken and headed for a bench.

"Take these," said Penny Lunder, "to fill out and bring them back tomorrow. It's my duty, and most often my pleasure, to aid you during your training. I'll make sure you know what class to attend and where to go to attend that class. I'll keep record of each regimen you have completed. I'm also responsible for your needs. I can requisition anything but money." She chortled. Bridger laughed nervously.

Cantor pressed down the quivers from the writing tools and forced himself to act as if nothing bothered him. He could master this queasiness with effort. He reassured Bridger. *"It's all right. She meant the comment to be amusing."*

Bridger returned with a strong demand. *"You should be taking care of this. Come talk to Penny Lunder."*

Cantor sauntered back with his hands clenched in his pockets. At the counter, he folded his hands on the top and leaned forward. Penny Lunder took notice of his serious pose.

"Is there something I can do for you?"

"Ahma raised me. I'm sure you know her name."

"Certainly, she's one of the renowned."

"When I returned from Effram, our home had been burned to the ground. I inquired in the nearby village, but no one could give me any news."

Penny Lunder drew a sharp breath. "She's missing?"

Cantor nodded.

"I haven't heard any rumors." She glanced at the clock on the wall. "It's too late today, but tomorrow you must come back, and I'll send you up to the recorder's office. If anyone knows where she is, he will."

"Thank you." His hands began to shake again, and he wanted to bolt from the building.

She handed him a key and schedule and he tucked them quickly inside his tunic and thrust his hands back into his pockets. Penny Lunder reiterated they had rooms in the west wing of the Moor. Totobee-Rodolow's and Bixby's rooms were on the east wing of the same building.

"Shouldn't Bridger have a key as well?" asked Cantor as he backed away.

"We find that most mor dragons just shape-shift their finger into a key. It's something they learn at a very young age." Penny Lunder smiled at Bridger, who nodded.

After obtaining directions, the two left the building.

Cantor trotted down the many steps, glad to be out of the

hall and away from the nasty influence of pens and such. But he also regretted not having time to examine the artwork.

"That certainly didn't take long." The street was loud, and using his voice he might not have been heard. *"I think Penny Lunder was anxious to close up shop and go home."*

Bridger agreed. *"She took your inquiry about Ahma seriously."*

"Yes, she did."

"But ..." Bridger didn't finish his thought.

Cantor spoke aloud. "What?"

"I think Feymare would have a better chance of finding her."

"Why is that?"

Bridger reverted to thoughts. Cantor got the feeling that he didn't want anyone to overhear this conversation.

"Because he's not like us. He's not tied to one realm, one system of planes, or one universe. He's not even tied to the normal progression of time."

"That's why he could deliver us to the front of the council building five minutes earlier than it was when I last looked at the clock?"

"Exactly."

"What is he, then?"

"A Primen warrior."

Cantor continued to walk, but his mind no longer registered the street, the people, the noise, or the smells of dinner being prepared in a hundred places nearby. Bridger's revelation shook his beliefs.

Primen warriors were mentioned in the Volumes of Lore. These volumes were second only to the sacred word given by Primen himself. Some people believed the tales to be true.

Others regarded them as elaborate legends of things that might have happened. In the Volumes of Lore, Primen warriors were messengers from Primen himself. They instructed ordinary people, protected them, sheltered them, gave them temporary powers to withstand an enemy. Accounts of their activities had diminished over time and had completely disappeared at the same time Chomountain, the great wizard of Primen, had ceased functioning.

"Hey! Watch where you're going!"

Bridger pushed Cantor out of the way, just as a man with a heavy handcart struck the curb.

Cantor fell, and someone fell on top of him. The cart filled with ball squash and melons of all sizes tilted. Cantor covered his head just as produce bounced all around him, and a large melon cracked against his head. Juice ran down his cheeks.

Bridger fussed at the crowd. "Don't steal the man's fruit. Help him set up his cart and pick up what can be saved."

The weight of the person on top of him was lifted. He pushed up on his elbows. The red pulp of a squashed melon dropped from the back of his head to the sidewalk.

Bridger growled. "Now, I said put the stuff back in the cart. None of you are poor enough to have to steal food."

Cantor got up on his hands and knees.

"Put me down," someone complained.

Cantor stood. "Bridger, you still have that man in your hands."

The dragon took note of the squirming captive. "Oh! Sorry! I forgot I had you." He placed the man on his feet and went back to harassing the passersby. "There's lots here we can save."

A man sat on the curb, his head resting in his hands. Cantor approached him. "Are you all right, sir?"

He looked up and started when he saw who spoke to him. He jumped to his feet. He stammered a bit, and his voice trembled. "I'm all right. Are you? You would have been crushed by my cart if your constant hadn't given you that shove. A ruffian with a load of scrap metal passed me and his wagon clipped my cart. He just went on." The man put a hand on Cantor's sleeve. He still looked shaken. "Are you sure you're all right?"

"Yes, yes, you needn't be so worried."

The man wrung his hands. "You're not going to report me, are you, sir? I'd never do anything to disrespect a realm walker."

Cantor looked at him closely. The poor man was afraid. In fact, he was terrified.

Cantor shook his head. "No, no. This isn't worthy of a report."

"Oh, thank you, thank you. I have a stall in the Blinness Way Market." He gestured to his cart. The words *Blinness Way Market* decorated the side in bright orange outlined in green. "If you stop by, I'd be delighted to have you pick from my finest fruit to refresh yourself. Anytime, anytime. I'm a friend to the realm walkers, a real friend."

"Yes, I'm sure you are."

Bridger had organized urchins to clean up the broken fruit, and he'd given them permission to take the broken pieces home. People and dragons still had to pick their way through the sticky wreckage, but most of the fragments had been disposed of.

The cart owner took the opportunity to get back in the

flow of traffic. Cantor heard his loud sigh of relief as he left the disaster behind.

"That was odd, Bridger." Cantor still watched the man as he traveled through the crowd.

"What was?"

The man had been swallowed up by the traffic and could no longer be seen.

Cantor turned to look up at his friend. "That produce man was terrified because he recognized us as realm walkers."

Bridger shrugged and examined his sticky hands. "I need a bath. You do, too."

Cantor laughed. Melon juice dripped off his hair and down his neck, trickling under his collar and down his back.

"You're right."

They started walking again.

Cantor bumped Bridger's arm with his fist. "Thanks for saving my life back there."

"Oh, I don't think I exactly saved your life. Maybe saved you from being a cripple with crushed legs for the rest of your life. Or you could have been struck in the midriff and had crushed ribs and broken arms. Even if that heavy cart had broken your back, lots of people survive such an injury. You wouldn't have been much use as a realm walker, though."

"Well, I was going to tell you that you did a good job of keeping order and getting people to help clean up. But I'm afraid that would have you rambling again."

"Do you know the song about the rambling rose?"

"I think you sang it the other night."

"Yes, I probably did. We should work that out in parts. I'll take the bass, and you can have the tenor. Or we could reverse that if you like. But I get tired singing falsetto. And it isn't pleasing to the ear."

"Bridger, I think this is the Moor."

Bridger looked the long white building over and nodded. "Ah, home for a few weeks at least. I hope we find Bixby and Totobee-Rodolow."

Mentioning home and finding in the same bit of conversation slammed into Cantor's contented mood. Ahma. Home. Odem. Gone. But Odem and Ahma couldn't be dead. He felt sure he'd know if Ahma no longer lived. And he'd probably know if Odem was dead. He had to find them.

Tomorrow. Tomorrow he would know more.

30

MEETINGS
IN BEAUTIFUL
PLACES

Bixby sat cross-legged on her bed. The lighting in the barren room left a lot to be desired, so she sat on the end of the bed next to the window where the sun streamed in. With her hands, she worked at embellishing a piece of lace. When she was done, the small scrap of fabric would become a fancy cuff, one she could wear with many of her outfits. She'd fashioned flowers and leaves out of ribbon in shades that would go well with her quiet wardrobe.

She and Totobee-Rodolow had gone shopping for the third day in a row. Bixby couldn't believe the wonderful finds she had purchased in the marketplaces — fabric, beads, ribbons, and fine, thin metal she could mold easily in any way she chose. Totobee-Rodolow said there was only one more market to explore, and they would do that tomorrow. Imagine being in a city with four large markets.

Totobee-Rodolow usually came in so they could go through their purchases together and marvel at the wonderful finds a second time. She'd gone to the main building to check for messages, an errand that should have taken fifteen minutes. Concern edged around Bixby's thoughts. Her dragon was late.

Voices in the corridor brought her to her feet. She flew across the room and flung open the door. Totobee-Rodolow and her companions sauntered down the hall. With a squeal, Bixby dropped her cuff and ran down the richly patterned carpet to jump into Cantor's arms. Before the startled young man could object, she released him and grabbed Bridger around the neck.

"I'm so glad to see you." She kissed the dragon's scaly cheek, then turned to glare at Cantor. "What took you so long? We've been to some amazing places in the city. But you haven't missed anything that you would think important. We start our rounds on Monday. We haven't seen Dukmee yet. And I've eaten so much wonderful, fantastic, yummy food!" She looked down at her thin, waiflike body. "And still I could be mistaken for a fishing pole."

She released Bridger and hugged Cantor once more. She leaned away from him a bit and sniffed. "You smell good. Like soap and melon."

He sighed in relief when she stepped away, but she ignored his attitude. He cast a rueful look at Bridger before he answered.

"I almost collided with a market cart. Bridger pushed me out of the way, but I still got bombarded by falling fruit. I think my hair will smell for a while."

Jesha wound around Bixby's ankles, complaining in soft mews. Bixby bent over to pick her up, then cuddled her close.

"I missed you too. You are such a fine cat. Here, smell Cantor. Don't you think he smells good?"

Bixby stepped closer to Cantor and sniffed again. This time she breathed in slowly, relishing the fragrance.

She turned the cat to look directly in her face. "Oh, no. I don't think so at all. I much prefer he smell like melon and not fish."

Cantor's cheeks pinked, and he turned away from Bixby and the cat to concentrate on Totobee-Rodolow. "Bridger and I are starving. We came to ask where to eat and to see if you two could come with us."

"Marvelous, darling. Of course we will take you to the best restaurant nearby. Do you need to be economical?"

"No, I have plenty of traps with me." His tone lowered and so did his head.

Bixby frowned. "Why does having money make you sad?"

His solemn expression worried her. "The traps are from Ahma's cache. When we went to visit on our way here, we found her cabin burned to the ground with no sign of her or her livestock."

Bridger took over the narrative. "Cantor went to the village but no one knew anything. His Ahma stored the traps in a hamper under the floorboards. The fire hadn't reached them."

Bixby's heart twisted. "Did you ask at the registry for news?"

Cantor didn't speak, so Bridger continued. "He did, but Penny Lunder couldn't help. She recommended asking at the recorder's office tomorrow."

"We'll do that," said Totobee-Rodolow, "but I have additional resources we'll use."

Bixby raised her eyebrows, remembering all the people Totobee-Rodolow knew. Their second day in the city, they'd met Clarart the doorman and had lunch with him at a sidewalk café. He'd been funny and informative, joking about the doings of many of the people dominating Gilead's social life. In between humorous anecdotes, though, he'd soberly relayed more serious news of plots and intrigue.

Everywhere she and Totobee-Rodolow went, they ran into old acquaintances of the dragon. Bixby's admiration of Totobee-Rodolow grew as she watched the way everyone welcomed her warmly and eagerly imparted little bits of information they thought might interest her.

"Will we talk to Clarart again?" she asked.

Before his sister could answer, Bridger jumped in. "Oh, I forgot. We came across Feymare in one of the less busy streets, and he requests a meeting tomorrow. Half past one. Conicaty Bridge."

"Feymare?" Totobee-Rodolow cocked an eyebrow.

Bridger offered no answer but looked straight into his sister's eyes.

"Oh." A slow smile lifted her countenance. "That shall be most enlightening." She turned to the others. "Well, that is tomorrow and tonight we can do nothing. So let's eat and enjoy with light hearts. Tomorrow we may be required to be all too serious."

Conicaty Bridge crossed the Alletain River, which ran through the city. At this point, a lovely park with elaborate landscaping banked one side of the river. Mansions belonging to the well-to-do stood on the opposite side.

The bridge was designed to accommodate walkers. Small carts could cross, but were discouraged from doing so. Bixby found the views enchanting. Topiary animals populated one large area of the park, a maze of hedges blocked out another patch, and a cluster of statues dotted a large, neatly groomed meadow with a three-tiered fountain at the center.

Walking paths meandered in and out of all the garden exhibits. Attractive slatted benches provided patrons a place to stop and relieve their feet, or relieve their tension by just taking in the beauty of their surroundings. And in the trees, brightly feathered birds hopped from branch to branch and sang sweet songs.

Bridger and Cantor strode side by side down the groomed trail. Totobee-Rodolow strolled beside Bixby, who longed to skip and twirl as they followed. She restrained herself for the sake of decorum and also because Cantor's shoulders were tense. She could tell he wasn't up to boisterous behavior. He'd been to the recorder's office that morning and found out absolutely nothing about Ahma and Odem. She could sympathize. If her parents were missing, she'd be out of sorts, too.

Each time they came to an intersecting of paths, they followed the arrows on the quaint wooden signs. When the bridge came in sight, even from that distance, Bixby saw the man Totobee-Rodolow had pointed out as special in the restaurant. She wondered why all the people in the garden park did not stop and stare. He was obviously much more than a mere man.

"It's because they don't see who he truly is, darling." Totobee-Rodolow spoke aloud, interrupting her thoughts. "If they notice him at all, they merely think he's a somewhat attractive man."

"Does he wear an obscuring circlet?"

"No, he needs no artifice to manage illusion."

He turned and waved, then started toward them. Stopping at a bench, he spoke to a man and pointed in their direction. When this man unfolded his long body, Bixby recognized him.

"Dukmee! Look, Bridger, Cantor. It's Dukmee."

Dukmee wore his long, black healer's cloak. His hair was longer, looking like a black bush tussling with the wind. And he was so pale. Bixby wondered if he was sick or just didn't go out in the sun enough. A healer shouldn't be sick.

Cantor turned and walked backward as he addressed Bixby. "Did you bring the hamper filled with his things? Perhaps he can take them now."

She patted the right side of her skirt. "It's under the second lace overlay, which is under a long silk sheath." She turned to Totobee-Rodolow. "The bulky lace fits under the sheath because the sheath has splits in the seams to allow a peek at what's underneath. I've got on three more outfits, three of my favorites."

She noticed the look on Cantor's face. He tolerated her crazy fashion fascination. Her manner of dress gave him ample opportunities to tease. He looked more animated now than he had since he left for the recorder's office. She expected some smart comment, but he turned back around without another word.

As they met, a clamor of voices rose from the group. One of the many park patrolmen came by and asked them to move to the side of the path because they were blocking traffic. A picnic area with tables offered some solitude and enough seats for all.

When they'd settled, Totobee-Rodolow introduced the problem of Ahma and Odem first.

Feymare listened attentively. When she'd finished, he turned to Cantor. "I've met Ahma, of course. But I've had more to do with Odem. I hadn't heard that they were missing, but someone in our legion will have heard something. My first order of business will be to initiate an inquiry to get answers and send someone specifically to find them."

"Thank you." Cantor gave a slight bow as to one in authority.

Bixby studied Cantor's tense expression and wondered if he felt any relief. Did he doubt Feymare had the ability to actually get something accomplished? It was true that they didn't know Feymare — but Totobee-Rodolow and Bridger certainly seemed to trust him. Yet Cantor seemed to be too filled with dread to accept that there was now hope. A thought came to mind that made her tremble. Chomountain had been lost for eons. The Primen warriors had never found him.

"Now I have an assignment for you." Feymare nodded toward the healer. "Dukmee has told me about the situation in Effram. I want you to report the details to the recording office, but first I want you to drop the same information into the lap of a journalist."

Totobee-Rodolow took a short intake of air. "Simon Toolooknaut of the *Daily Journal*."

"Exactly." Feymare smiled. "Another friend of yours, I believe."

Totobee-Rodolow smiled and nodded. "It will be good to see him again."

Feymare looked Bixby in the eye, then Cantor, and last Bridger. "I want you three to begin your rounds at the realm walker training center. However, you'll need to keep your eyes and ears open. Only three councilmen have resisted the corruption. Three out of ninety-nine. Learn what you can, both in your rounds and by being observant. I'll come back for you."

"When?" asked Bridger.

Feymare shrugged his shoulders. "In a week perhaps, or possibly three months. Don't lose heart. I'll return." He clapped his hand on Cantor's shoulder. "My first priority is Ahma and Odem. I'll get word to you."

31

SHINE LIGHT
ON THE HIDDEN

Bixby stopped abruptly in the crowded street. "I forgot to give Dukmee his hampers."

Totobee-Rodolow took hold of her arm and tugged her forward. "Don't worry, darling. We shall see him again soon. Probably he'll be with Bridger and Cantor when we meet for dinner."

Bixby allowed herself to be pulled along by the dragon. Again, Totobee-Rodolow's pace was too quick for her to keep up, so she conveniently floated.

The dragon made odd choices in choosing which way to go. Each street seemed more off the beaten path than the last. "Did we take a wrong turn, Totobee-Rodolow?"

"Have faith, darling. I know just where we're going."

After a dozen more turns and twenty minutes of walking, the streets looked more squalid and the buildings more derelict than anything Bixby had seen in Gilead so far. The occupants stepped back to let Totobee-Rodolow and Bixby pass. But they stared, and Bixby grew nervous. "This neighborhood gives me skin shivers."

"Be patient, darling. We're almost there."

Totobee-Rodolow stopped at the opening of an alley. The buildings stood so close together, even in the daytime, darkness shrouded the narrow way.

"Oh no!" Bixby's feet slammed down on the pavement and she dug in her heels. "We can't be going in there."

"But this is where the man is that we want to see."

"If this is where he lives, maybe he's not the kind of man we should want to see."

"Oh, now what could be the problem, little one?"

"It's dark and there are puddles, dirty puddles, and thugs could be behind those boxes, ready to jump out at us. And it stinks."

"Darling, reach in your hamper and bring out a crown that will make you more comfortable."

Bixby grabbed her tiara hamper from the folds of her skirt.

"When you have on the proper head embellishment, you'll feel more confident. Then you need only remember to smile, and we shall lighten up this unfortunate corner of the world."

Bixby held up a twist of bronze flowers. "Maybe this one?"

"What does that one do, dear?"

"Heightens my hearing."

Totobee-Rodolow looked thoughtfully down the alley. "No, I really don't think that's necessary."

"This one? It gives me the ability to read the aura around a person so he or she can't hide his feelings from me. I'd know if someone was feeling hostile and edgy."

"Edgy?"

"Ready to attack."

"No, no, not quite right for this situation." Totobee-Rodolow studied her for a moment. "Do you have one that gives you courage?"

Bixby's shoulders slumped. "I always thought I had an adequate amount of courage."

"Of course, darling. I've noticed you generally tackle a situation with no qualms. What do you think the problem is here?"

"I'm not dressed for an unexpected event." She passed her hands over the lovely dress she wore over lace and hand-tatted skirts. "I wasn't expecting puddles."

"Well, now, we can fix that. I understand perfectly that it is easier to face a difficult situation when you know you're properly attired. It's a shame you aren't a shape-shifter, but you're well enough equipped. I shall become a little larger to block the view from the street, and I'll put a wing over you for a little added privacy. You rearrange your clothing to better suit our purpose."

Bixby stepped into the alley entrance as the mor dragon increased in size. "Oh, thank you, Totobee-Rodolow. It's so good to have a constant who understands."

Bixby noticed that her dragon friend didn't say she was only a temporary constant. She busied herself getting ready.

"I'm ready to shield you." Totobee-Rodolow extended her right wing.

Bixby began peeling off the layers. Her clothing used many ties and belts and other accoutrements to add to her style, so unfastening and shedding the superfluous doodads took a minute. She pulled out a hamper to store things as she undressed and dressed again. Some skirts and blouses she immediately tucked away in the hamper. Others she draped over the dragon's right knee, which was handy. When she got down to her thermea, she began dressing again, taking care to put the lighter clothing beneath and the darker bits and sturdier pieces on the outside. She tested her range of motion so that if trouble erupted, she would have ample ability to be swift and unrestrained.

She tucked the last two stray garments into the hamper and secured the bag under the first layer. "I'm done."

Totobee-Rodolow's wing moved, and she peeked under. "Are you feeling more confident, darling? You look exquisite as always."

Bixby curtseyed. "I feel much more prepared."

"And what tiara did you choose?"

"Discerning."

"Good job. Anything else we need to take care of?"

Bixby narrowed her eyes as she thought about problems that might arise from this visit. "Should I have weapons at the ready?"

"Darling, one should *always* have weapons at hand." She patted Bixby's shoulder. "But sometimes a sharp tongue parries an evil intent. A witty retort may stymie an enemy. And best of all, a kind and generous reply can take the wind out of the sails of a foe."

Bixby had been rearranging the placement of her small sword, knife, slingshot, and the little tube she used to blow darts as Totobee-Rodolow spoke. She twitched her clothing into order and smiled. "Ready again."

"Then off we go."

Totobee-Rodolow took the lead, and Bixby trailed behind, keeping her eyes open. She floated over puddles to keep her feet dry and took extra caution when passing anything that might be used as cover for an ambush.

At the back of the alley, just before the dirty lane turned a corner, the dragon stopped before a gray door adorned with scribbling. She leaned closer and listened. Then she used a hard knuckle to tap loudly on the door. The rhythm seemed elaborate to Bixby. When Totobee-Rodolow repeated it, she realized it must be a code.

"An old code, darling," Totobee-Rodolow reassured her. *"I'm sure they've had a score or more since I last used one. But old Simon Toolooknaut will recognize me."*

The door protested with scraping of metal against metal and a screech of stiff hinges. A small, nervous man poked his head out, swiveled his neck around to survey the alley, then waved Totobee-Rodolow and Bixby to enter. The door repeated its complaints as it shut. The man bolted and locked it. He wrung his hands and muttered before he gestured for the guests to follow.

"I am Ponack. Toolooknaut is expecting you. You know this is dangerous, don't you?" He didn't allow them time to answer. "Oh, oh, oh. What we do every day is dangerous, but this? This goes beyond. This is perilous. That's what it is. Risky business. Treacherous people. Precarious times. Hazardous to be coming and going. And still Toolooknaut persists."

They turned a corner and followed the fussing man up a long flight of metal stairs. Their shoes clanked against the steps, and the rails rattled as they progressed.

The man looked back over his shoulder. "No need to hold on so tight, missy. If the stairs collapse, the rail will collapse along with it. It'll all come down, so you needn't think that holding on tight will save you. You can cling to the rail with all your might, but you'll be clinging to something that's falling just as fast as you are. Don't put your trust in rusty metal."

Bixby exchanged a look with Totobee-Rodolow. Both ladies had their eyebrows raised. Bixby almost laughed. The dragon's manufactured brows rose to great heights, looking like they might just disappear over her forehead, across her scalp, and down her back.

The stairs led to a platform circling the outer wall. Made out of the same metal, rusty and shaky, the whole thing felt like a catwalk. Bixby looked down at her feet, and through the slats she could see the floor far below.

As they followed the twittering and twitching escort, Bixby realized that they were not at the outer wall. Doors they passed evidently opened to offices. A few were open, but Bixby's quick peeks inside revealed only dirty, dusty, unused desks and office furniture. Glancing ahead and to the left, she saw the rickety walkway had given way. Several sections clung together and dangled one after the other to the floor below. Bixby hoped Ponack would open one of the few doors left.

As if understanding her impatience, the nervous man stopped abruptly. He pushed at the door as he softly knocked. "Toolooknaut, they're here."

Bixby couldn't distinguish the reply, but Ponack swung the door open, bowed to Totobee-Rodolow, and motioned for the ladies to enter. The dragon entered first, and as soon as Bixby went through the door, Ponack reached in, grabbed the doorknob, and pulled it shut. The breeze caused by the brisk motion fanned her dress, causing her ribbons to flutter.

An old man jumped up from his desk and came forward, a grin on his face and his arms stretched out to embrace

Totobee-Rodolow. "It's so good to see you, and to see you looking as beautiful as ever."

Bixby blinked as she realized Totobee-Rodolow had drawn herself in so that she was basically the same size as Toolooknaut. The dragon allowed the man to grasp her arms and kiss her on both cheeks. She, of course, looked glamorous, especially beside the gentleman dressed in wrinkled clothing, two sizes too big.

"Yes, darling, of course, I've kept up my style. It's this that has paved my way in society." She shook her head and tsked. "But it is *not* good to be back. I enjoy seeing my friends, but the state of our council is most distressing." She turned slightly and indicated Bixby with a gesture. "This is Bixby D'Mazeline. I'm willing to let this next generation take up the cause."

Toolooknaut nodded, acknowledging the introduction. But his attention riveted on the dragon. "You must not hide from your duty, Totobee-Rodolow. Surely you see that although the youngsters give us new energy, they need the wisdom of the older to make sure that the energy isn't wasted."

"Darling, today I am here, so let us deal with the business at hand."

"Yes, of course." Toolooknaut pulled two chairs closer to his desk and offered his company seats. "May I get you something? I have stale water from old pipes. We have tea made from reused teabags, and ... well, I don't think there are any other choices."

Totobee-Rodolow raised an eyebrow Bixby's way.

"Oh." Bixby jumped to interpret the dragon's thoughts. "I can provide refreshments. Forgive me for being so slow." She faced Toolooknaut. "Do you prefer a hot beverage or cold?"

"Hot. Thank you, Princess Bixby."

"I'm not a princess here."

He steepled his hands in front of him and slowly nodded. "I see."

Bixby wasn't sure what he saw. "Would you like cakes? Cookies? Pastry?"

"Do you have something with cinnamon?"

"Yes, both pastry and cookies."

Totobee-Rodolow waved her hand. "Bixby, really! Just serve whatever you have and be quick about it."

When Bixby started at the tone of voice, Totobee-Rodolow's words entered her mind. *I suspect we could be rudely interrupted at any time by those who would not like us giving information to Toolooknaut.*

Bixby nodded and went about pulling hampers out of hidden pockets in her skirts. She then rummaged through the hampers to produce plates and cups and napkins. In only a few moments, she had a kettle on a self-heating stone. After spooning into the cups a tea powder blend that would dissolve in hot water, she arranged cakes, cookies, and pastries on a serving platter.

Toolooknaut nodded when Bixby offered him tea. From his expression as he looked at the treats, she assumed it had been quite a while since he'd had a proper tea. Totobee-Rodolow continued to provide information about Effram as Toolooknaut juggled his cup, a plate of sugary tidbits, and a pad of paper on which he took notes.

Bixby took pity on the poor man and cleared some of the clutter off his desk so he could put things down. Again he just nodded to her, indicating he appreciated her help. His pencil moved much faster now. She refilled his cup once and his plate twice while Totobee-Rodolow covered all the situations in Effram that warranted action by the Realm Walkers Council.

The list was long. Toolooknaut's expression alternated between sincere concern and outrage, with brief flashes of glee. Undoubtedly, he relished the writing of this article, its publication, and the stir of excitement it would cause.

Totobee-Rodolow came to the end of her information and sipped her tea. Toolooknaut riffled through his pages of notes, ignoring his guests as he checked for clarity.

"I've got it." He closed the pad of paper and patted the top page. "This is going to cause a stir." His eyes blazed with the challenge of a good cause. "Here in Gilead, the realm walkers act pretty much as they're supposed to. But when problems are considered on the floor of the forum, the doors are shut. I find it almost impossible to report on actions they're taking."

The fiery zeal in his eyes slipped away, replaced by sadness. "We constantly hear rumors of outrageous behavior where realm walkers were sent to secure peace. Corruption. Fraud. Duplicity. Treachery. Citizens are suffering. It's high time the council received a cleansing."

Bixby knew something of court intrigue, given her parents were king and queen of her homeland. "How can evil be rooted out if all are corrupt?"

Toolooknaut held up a finger. "Not all, girl. There are three out of the ninety-nine who still have some semblance of decency."

"Perhaps we should go to them and tell them we're available to help."

The old man shook his head and snatched another cookie. "We have no names of the three."

Bixby furrowed her brow. "Then how do you know there are three and not thirty-three?"

"Because whenever they have a closed vote — that means secret ballots — only three, and always three, vote against the core of corrupt officials."

A scratch at the door announced Ponack's entrance. "A runner, sir, with news. The council police are on the move. They're searching for the printing press."

"Well, they won't find it." Toolooknaut stood. "They're more likely to find me. We must go to ground."

He stuffed the pad of notes and a few other papers in his large pockets. With a look of regret at the tray of treats, he started toward the door.

He dashed back to bow over Totobee-Rodolow's hand. "You must depart as well."

"We will. We will, darling. Don't worry for us."

Toolooknaut nodded again to Bixby. Since he was back beside his desk again, he scooped a number of cookies into his hand and deposited them in a pocket as he headed for the door.

"Take care," he called over his shoulder. "As Ponack no doubt told you, this is a dangerous affair."

32

ROUNDS

Holding a crumpled paper in his fist, Cantor knocked on Bixby's door. Today life looked more doable. Obstacles of yesterday melted under the warm attention of Feymare, Dukmee, and Totobee-Rodolow. The first half of his night had been wrought with heavy thinking. Thinking? Ha! It was worrying, not thinking. Finally, Ahma's teaching soothed his mind and helped him to reclaim his sanity. She'd said it often enough. "Worrying is a circle. Just like a dog chasing his tail, you get nowhere. Even if the dog catches the tip of its tail, it's no better off than before it started its endeavor. Thinking leads to something other than your own backside."

Now he had proof in his hand that Primen worked where no man could see. And today they would attend the biggest sanctuary on Plane Dairine.

"Bixby, you're going to have to get up if you want time for breakfast before Sanctuary."

The door opened, and Bixby greeted him with a smile.

"Totobee-Rodolow doesn't do mornings until eleven o'clock." She leaned back and reached, snagging her purse from someplace out of his line of vision. She quietly pulled the door closed.

"What's that you have in your hand?"

Cantor straightened the page and handed it to her. He enjoyed her reaction to the printed news of happenings in Effram.

Her large blue eyes grew larger and her mouth stretched in an incredulous grin. "He did it. Toolooknaut did it."

Impatient at her lagging pace as she read, Cantor took hold of her elbow, then slid his hand down to clasp hers. He sprinted down the hall, dragging her along. She tried to read the paper as she hustled along beside him.

As they came to the stairs, Cantor slowed down. He didn't want her to fall while reading Toolooknaut's article. He opened the door and guided her into the stairwell. "We need to meet Dukmee for breakfast."

That caught her attention. "Dukmee? Wonderful! You got to go with him yesterday."

They ran down the stairwell. Their footsteps echoed off the walls.

Bixby kept up with him. "Why?"

"Why what?"

"Why are we meeting Dukmee?"

Cantor put a finger to his lips and shushed her, adding a wink to soften the command. Once they opened the door to the outside, Cantor put his arm around her shoulders and pulled her close.

His whisper blew corkscrew blonde tendrils away from her ear. "We're going to sit at a sidewalk café and listen to the chatter from those who've read this." He tapped the paper Bixby held.

Five minutes' walk took them to a busy street where the clientele of small eateries provided the foot traffic. The aroma of coffee and baked bread tinged the air with an enticing lure.

Bixby handed the paper back to Cantor, and he stuffed it inside his tunic. "You're awfully chipper this morning."

He grinned, reaching over to pinch one of her wild curls and giving it a tiny tug. "I started counting all the things that are going right for us, instead of those things still off kilter. Feymare is going to help find Ahma and Odem. People are waiting to help whoever steps forward to bring Primen's principles back to the front of our council. And Totobee-Rodolow knows who they are and how to reach them. And" — he paused for a moment with his finger in the air — "We are the ones these helpers will help."

Cantor looked ahead of them, through the crowd of people enjoying the Sunday morning social scene. He didn't yet see the café Dukmee had described. "And Dukmee, Bixby. Dukmee takes us seriously. We're not tagging along. We're part of the big picture."

She stretched to see over the taller people all around her. "Do you see him?"

"No, but Bridger came here while I fetched you. We'll find them."

A clatter of dishes breaking reached their ears. Men shouted and a dog barked. Female squeals and protests added to the hullabaloo.

Bixby and Cantor exchanged a look.

Bixby grinned. "I bet Bridger is in the middle of that."

"Should we go restore order, or shall we slink away and pretend we don't know him?"

"I'm sure Dukmee can handle whatever it is."

Cantor pinched his lips together, then shook his head. "No, that's the coward's way. And we aren't cowards, right?"

Bixby laughed. "No, 'coward' is not listed among our credentials."

"Right." Cantor took her hand again and shouldered his way through a crowd of people and dragons gawking at a scene ahead. When they passed through the inner circle, they saw Bridger mopping the face of a disheveled man. His limp victim sat in a wrought iron chair with what looked like a bucket of whipped cream spilled over his head and chest. Jesha sat at his feet catching drips with her tongue. Dukmee stood back against the outside wall of the café, watching.

Employees streamed out of the door, bringing mops, dishtowels, and brooms. Cantor glanced down at the floor and saw a pink, foamy liquid spreading under the tables. The occupants at the tables stood and scattered as the flood grew near.

Bixby tapped on his shoulder and pointed to the source of the chaos. Shattered glasses surrounded an overturned serving cart. A huge cylinder with a spigot at the bottom lay on its side, with the top popped and the last of the pink beverage trickling out on the pavement. A stack of paper napkins fluttered in the breeze. With each gust, another pulled loose and lifted on the wind to fly away.

The manager of the restaurant took over for Bridger. He patted the man with a larger cloth and spoke soothing words as other staff set to work mopping and tidying.

The man's eyes opened, and he whispered, "Is he gone?"

"No," said the manager. He looked around and nodded

approval to his team of cleaners. The sidewalk café now looked more like a place to eat than an establishment devastated by a tidal wave. When his gaze settled on Bridger, he scowled. Dukmee scuttled over to the dragon and dragged him away from the calamity. Cantor and Bixby followed.

Bixby pulled her hand loose from Cantor's. "Just a minute."

She pivoted and dove back into the crowd. Moments later she reappeared with Jesha in her arms. "I didn't think she would follow us until there wasn't a lick of whipped cream left."

She sniffed. "Doesn't that drink smell wonderful? I bet it's fruit with a high concentration of starflower pulp."

Cantor grinned. "Do you want to stay and buy one?"

"Oh, no! Some other day." She glanced back at the disapproving manager and a smile touched her voice. "Many days from now. Right now I want to catch up with Dukmee and Bridger and find out what happened."

A few more paces took them out of the thick crowd to where they could see ahead. The healer and the dragon stood talking at a corner. Cantor picked up the pace. He glanced back, ready to pull Bixby along as he had before, but her arms were full of cat and her hands unavailable. A twinge of disappointment surprised him, but he dismissed it with a rueful chuckle. Perhaps it was because he could tow her where he wanted. He'd take whatever power he could. She often made him feel powerless.

"Why are you laughing?"

He looked over his shoulder. She was only a step behind him.

"I was ruing my sinister self, which rises to the surface at odd times."

She caught up to walk beside him. "You aren't going to scold Bridger, are you? I'm sure he feels terrible about what happened."

Cantor humphed. He hadn't even thought about Bridger's role in the instigation of such pandemonium. "Aren't you a bit hasty in assuming he's guilty? Someone else might have started the chain of events."

Bixby studied him for a moment, then grinned. "Nah, it was Bridger."

Cantor smiled back. "Probably."

Ahead, Dukmee and Bridger disappeared around the corner. When Cantor, Bixby, and Jesha caught up, they were seated at another sidewalk café.

Cantor pulled out a chair for Bixby next to Bridger, then took the last chair. "What is it with the people in Gilead and eating outdoors?"

Dukmee laughed. "The weather is always balmy. Rain once in a while, but otherwise mostly sunny with moderate temperatures. I imagine this is why the councilors decided to center their operations here."

Bridger studied the edge of the table. Cantor noticed his form shrinking bit by bit. Bixby reached over and put a hand on his arm. The dragon didn't look at her.

"What happened?" she asked.

"I stood up. Jesha had put herself in a spot of sun, intending to take a nap. But it was right where people walked, and I thought she'd get stepped on or would cause someone to trip. I got up. A man stepped on her. He tripped. A waiter pushed the beverage cart into the walkway. The man fell against it. A bucket of whipped cream catapulted into the air. The man and cart went down. The bucket came down."

Cantor didn't like the choppy sentences coming out of Bridger's mouth. He'd lost his eloquence, surely a sign of despair. The dragon probably thought he was too clumsy to be a realm walker's constant. He was inept.

Bixby patted Bridger's arm. "I'm so sorry, but it could have happened to anyone."

Cantor had never seen Bridger so contrite over one of his mishaps.

Dukmee spoke up, his eyes sparkling with good humor. "Like I've been telling you, Bridger, it's all right. No one was hurt. And that pink fluffy stuff rather made the whole place a bit more inviting and boosted the ambiance. The café's whole tone softened from iron, brick, and concrete to an impression of understated gaiety."

They didn't seem to be reaching beyond Bridger's remorse. Cantor hated to see him looking so glum.

"Hey, Bridge."

Bridger's eyes came up to meet Cantor's.

Cantor pressed his lips together, trying not to say something that would pin him to this dragon for the rest of his life. "We start rounds tomorrow. And we don't want anyone looking at us as if we're not a normal partnership. You'll have to pretend there is no friction between us. I won't say anything about going back to Effram sometime in the future. You know, looking for my real constant. And you have to remember not to say the stuff you say, trying to get me to commit. Training is going to be tough all by itself. We don't want to worry about the authorities realizing we are just pretending to be constants. We're going to do such a good job of pretending to be a team that we will actually be a good team—for now."

The sorrow in Bridger's eyes lifted. He didn't quite have the eagerness for life that usually twinkled there, but he looked better. Cantor smiled at him and was rewarded with the huge toothy grin that always made the dragon look happily vicious.

The waiter came to take their orders. Once they'd gotten that business out of the way, Dukmee looked around the circle as if sizing up each of his companions.

"Speaking of rounds." Dukmee put his palms together and steepled his forefingers. "I have some news."

Cantor and the others gave him their attention.

"I've been told who your mentor will be."

Bixby bounced in her chair. "Cantor and I are going to have the same mentor?"

"That's true."

"Why?" asked Cantor. "The Moor is mostly vacant. Surely there are enough mentors to handle two more initiates."

"I don't think it has anything to do with numbers."

Bixby bounced again. Her ribbons and lace danced on her tiny form. "Who is it?"

Dukmee took a moment to look each of them in the eye. "Me."

If he'd wanted a gasp of astonishment, he got it times three.

Cantor emerged from a stunned state first. "How can that be? You aren't a council member, are you? And I got the distinct impression at the recorder's office yesterday that they didn't appreciate our presenting the case for Effram."

Dukmee nodded. "I got an inkling of their disdain." He smiled. "That may be one of the reasons they've assigned me to you. They hope to keep me so busy I won't be able to further investigate the conspiracy in the guild. Plus, we'll be forced to use facilities outside of the main hall."

He held up a finger to make a point. "That I lay at your

door. I believe they don't want you two constantly under foot. And Totobee-Rodolow is known for being clever and honest. They can't want her around with her keen observing and deductive prowess."

Bridger looked like he was going to say something, but his eyes shifted. "Here's our breakfast."

The waiter distributed eggs, bacon, muffins, and juice to his customers. After asking if there was anything else the party required, he went off to take care of others.

Dukmee leaned toward Bixby and whispered, "It's time you put on your hearing tiara, Bixby. You can listen while we remain silent and eat. Find out what others are saying about Toolooknaut's Effram article."

As she searched for the right hamper, she looked worried. "You can hear them too, can't you?"

"Yes, I can. We'll compare our discoveries later."

She pulled out a hamper and soon wore an attractive and unobtrusive bronze crown. She put a finger to her lips and giggled.

33

SANCTUARY

From breakfast, the friends had to hustle to get to Sanctuary on time. Bixby slipped into a ladies' room to change. She'd been wearing a quiet mix of clothing, but she almost always wore her joyful outfits to attend Primen Worship. She came out wrapped in reds, oranges, greens, and a bit of black for contrast. She wore her most elaborate crown bedecked with brilliant gems, which did very little but reminded her to be humble and respectful during the service.

She found Cantor and Bridger next to the entry. Jesha hid under one of her dragon's wings. Bixby heard her purring.

"Where's Dukmee?"

Cantor used his thumb to indicate the sanctuary. "Totobee-Rodolow came, and he's sitting with her."

"Oh, I hope we can squeeze into their pew. I'd like to sit with them."

Cantor raised his eyebrows. "I don't think that will be a problem."

As soon as they stepped through the doors, Bixby understood. In a sanctuary that could have held a thousand worshipers, less than a hundred sat scattered around in the beautiful carved and polished pews.

Cantor leaned toward her. "I believe we had more in attendance in the wee sanctuary at home."

Bixby saw movement out of the corner of her eye. She glanced that way and saw Feymare standing between two pillars. When she blinked, he was gone, replaced by a lifelike bronzed statue of one of the peacemakers mentioned in Primen's Book. Blaming the dim light, she turned to study the walls on either side of the pews. Many life-size statues filled the alcoves. Some were easily recognizable, but she didn't know the names of all of the people depicted.

Cantor offered his arm in a gentleman's gesture. She laughed to herself that the country boy so quickly picked up city manners. Bridger followed them to the pew where Totobee-Rodolow and Dukmee sat. A flute and violin played the *Contemplative Moment* arrangements. Bixby recognized some of the bits from the pieces played at the *Contemplative Moment* in the sanctuary next to the palace. They sounded different — more melancholy — when only two instruments joined forces.

Two cantors in robes came out on the dais. Turning to face the congregation, they opened their books. In clear voices, they intoned a chant. After the first stanza, twenty more cantors joined them. When this group sang, Bixby grew goose bumps. She rubbed her arms and glanced at Cantor, whose expression showed his fascination with the music. She remembered then that Ahma had said it was a sign of his realm walker gift to be named for a contributor in this sacred form of worship.

The beginning of their time in Sanctuary brought memories of her childhood. All of her mentors had taken her to services, but the depth of worship fluctuated. As the hour proceeded, her disappointment grew. The homily given by a man in elaborate robes said little other than to try to think good thoughts. According to the speaker, this practice of thinking good thoughts would order the rest of your life. As if thinking about daisies would eradicate sewer problems.

Disgusted, she let her mind and her eyes wander. The light of candles and sun did nothing to warm the large room. Bixby peered upward at a ceiling boasting twelve skylights. Even though the sun beamed outdoors, little came through the rooftop domes. She puzzled at this for a while — it wasn't logical. The noonday sun should be flooding the sanctuary with a golden glow.

Unable to come up with an explanation, she soon gave up and tried to interest herself in the artwork surrounding her. Shadows hid most of the statues lining the walls. She wondered who mistakenly put the sculpture art against the wall and the columns between the statues two feet in front. Of course, the ornate carvings in the tall wooden columns could be seen and inspected. At first she thought they were pictographs of stories she knew. But as she studied the ones closest to her, she realized that none of them fit with tales in the Book.

The strain on her eyes responded to the simple remedy of closing them. Praying that she wouldn't go to sleep, she bowed her head so that no one could see her lack of interest.

She gladly stood when the cantors sang out the blessings that ended the service. While the cantors held the note of the last word of each line, the people answered.

Truth is in Primen's heart
And so are we
Primen's heart is strong
And will contain me
Primen's heart is great
And will sustain me
Primen's heart is gentle
And will hold me
Primen's heart is wise
And will quiet me
Primen's heart is aware
And will prepare me
Primen's heart is artful
And will form me
Primen's heart is faithful
And will renew me
Primen's heart is careful
And will comfort me
Primen's heart that shelters you will never let you down
Primen's heart that shelters me will never let me down
So believe
So believe
Carry Truth
Carry Truth
So be it
So be it forevermore

The next exercise included the cantors' solemn plea for righteousness and the slightly reworded response by the congregation.

Bixby had always loved responsive singing. Vocalizing the

blessings made her feel purposeful. She and the others in the congregation agreed to live up to the call just given.

The cantors' voices rang true, and the unity of tone imbued the air with a rich heady quality. Cantor and Bridger both had strong voices, and they stood out as leaders in the responses from the congregation.

As the last note faded away, a snort and resounding snores echoed in the chamber.

Perhaps all the others hadn't answered the call.

Dukmee took Bixby's hand and tucked it into the crook of his arm. The friends walked to the doors.

Bridger's head swung back and forth as he looked for something. "Isn't someone supposed to be standing at the door? You know, the man who shakes our hands and says how glad he is to see us."

Cantor shook his head. "I suppose some sanctuaries don't have that person."

Bixby squinted in the bright light of noon. Her eyes adjusted rapidly, and she noticed more citizens ambled on the street than an hour before.

Dukmee bowed to the friends. "Come to my vilta. I've told Minka Naf to have a cold lunch prepared for us. It's quite a walk, and your appetites will be ready for her wonderful cooking."

They passed the cafés they had visited that morning. Bixby didn't recognize any of the people seated at the open air tables. The waiters now served a luncheon.

When they came to streets less crowded, Bixby asked the questions that had troubled her. "Why did they put the statues behind the wooden columns? What stories do the carvings represent?"

Dukmee turned, gazed at her intently, and then responded. "You're very observant, but you've made an error. The statues are a part of the original architecture. Each serves as a support beam as well as adding to the depiction of Primen's creation of and dealings with our world. The columns were added only a hundred and sixty years ago. They serve no function. The pictographs are of the glorious achievements of men and dragons. Every event of note from the beginning of recorded history has been commemorated in polished wood."

Bixby felt a chill, and not from a cold breeze. She had learned at her mother's knee to revere Primen and keep him as the prime priority in her life. The carved columns disregarded the order of righteousness and bloated the role of men and dragons.

Her father had laughed at some example her mother had given of men who thought too highly of themselves. She hopped around her father's throne and danced between her parents as they talked.

He said, "They have bloated egos, and we all know the fate of things that are bloated."

Bixby came to a sudden stop, and she stared at her father.

He laid a hand on her shoulder. "Why the worried face, Princess? What troubles you?"

"Do they really pop, Papa? Is it a mess and a stink and a horrid thing to get on your shoes?"

"Ah, child, we wouldn't be able to see what has burst. Their bodies would probably look much as they have always looked. But inside, the damage would be great. And without a touch from Primen himself, the putrid soul would never be refreshed."

At the time, Bixby had been appalled that people could

be walking around with their egos bloated. Who knew when these poor people would have that something that was inside explode? She'd watched those in the palace very carefully and made a mental list of those who were in danger. Now, she recognized self-centered individuals quite easily, but she no longer had a list.

As the friends walked through the city streets toward the closest rural area, Bixby and Dukmee told the others what they had overheard at breakfast.

Bixby pulled her shoulders in and looked up and down the street first. Seeing that no one was close enough to hear, she still lowered her voice. "Everyone is saying things without saying things."

"Ah, yes, darling. That is just as it always is in political circles. Did you understand any of the messages behind the words?"

Bixby nodded vigorously. Her crown slipped, and they all stopped while she switched the ornate headdress for a simpler style.

Cantor sidled up to her. "What does that one do?"

"Its ability is directions. If I wear it now, as we're just strolling through the city, the crown will register more details of the street layout."

"Very useful, darling, but tell us about the table talk in the café."

"Right. One man said that news traveled slowly from plane to plane." She lowered her voice. "But once a tidbit arrived, it could zip around a country faster than a bee in a daisy patch."

Cantor agreed, nodding his head. "That's true of any type of news. So that wouldn't get the speaker in trouble."

"Then his companion, a woman wearing a business dress—"

Totobee-Rodolow arched an eyebrow. "On the weekend? Surely she knows to allow herself a day of rest."

Bridger was a step behind but could hear what they were saying. "Maybe she rests on Tuesday, Totobee-Rodolow. Not everyone adheres to the Sunday tradition."

"True," said the dragon with disapproval in her tone. "Go on, Bixby."

"His companion said, 'You know what happens to the bee after she's stung someone. And it isn't the fault of the bee.'"

She paused to visualize the man as she thought of the underlying rebellion in his words. "He said, 'Sure, the bee dies, but think what a good job she's done in pollination. She's done all she can to promote new life.'"

Bixby looked around at her audience. Dukmee held Jesha and walked a bit ahead of the others. Of course, he'd heard what the citizens at the restaurant had said.

"Then the woman said it was a shame the bee died. But if you chose to do dangerous things, then dying should be expected."

Cantor scowled. "So she's against bees flying around and delivering pollen?"

Bixby nodded. "But the man said that the bee doesn't die from delivering the pollen. She dies when someone tries to stop her, and she has to defend herself.

"The woman was eating and she said this with her mouth full. 'I'd rather be a flower than a bee.' That really made the man fume."

Bridger leaned closer. "Because her mouth was full? Was

the man her father? Had she disgraced her family with bad table manners?"

Bixby exchanged a look with Cantor. Cantor looked annoyed, but she thought Bridger's questions followed a skewed logic and his way of thinking was funny.

Again Totobee-Rodolow prodded them back to the subject. "What did he say?"

"He said that it wasn't much good being a flower in a garden if you died from lack of fresh air."

"What does that mean?" asked Bridger.

Totobee-Rodolow tsked. "It means he mixed the metaphor."

Bixby clapped her hands together. "That's exactly what she said. She said that he *should* have said that the garden would wither and die without the bees' help exchanging pollen. She said that the flowers needed to know about what was happening on the other flowers, and they learned that through the pollen."

Bixby paused and glanced around. They were still safe from being overheard. "The man said, 'I'm glad you agree with me. You put my argument into words very well. In fact, I couldn't have said it better.' Then he started laughing, and she bristled. And the last thing I heard her say was, 'The bees still die.'"

Totobee-Rodolow turned to Dukmee. "And what did you hear, sir?"

"The same sort of thing. The upshot is that everyone wants to hear what's going on. Everyone's outraged by the news. Everyone's very aware that spreading the news is dangerous. And very few people think that anything can be done about it."

"Are they right?" Bixby asked.

"No, darling. As long as there are citizens who love, there is hope."

Bixby let that thought sink into her heart and gently stir her conceptions of relationships, then said, "Everyone loves."

"Exactly, my dear. Even the meanest of mean loves, even if it is only himself."

"Then how is it that if everyone loves, our worlds aren't at peace?"

"Because we are narrow-minded, darling."

Bridger quickened his pace to come next to Dukmee. Jesha jumped from his arms to Bridger's shoulder. The dragon smiled and stroked the cat. "I think the problem isn't that we're narrow-minded, but that we all suffer from narrow hearts."

34

A HILL TO CLIMB

The first morning of their training, Bixby and Totobee-Rodolow, Cantor and Bridger followed the long route out of town to Dukmee's vilta. They had been told they couldn't fly until they'd satisfied their mentor and passed the flying round.

Cantor fought down the urge to fly anyway. Dukmee knew they'd flown before. Signing a paper wouldn't make them more proficient. He decided to ask Dukmee to do the flying round first, so they wouldn't have to waste so much time just getting to their courses.

On the long list of rounds they must pass before reaching the second level of realm walkers, Cantor figured he and his friends already were proficient in quite a few of them. They'd pass quickly. Of course, there were some he knew would be hard for him, because Odem and Ahma had not already covered them.

A moment of unease shattered his happy contemplation of training. He wanted to drop everything and continue his search for his mentors. He'd have to trust Feymare, and he forced his attention back to the upcoming rounds.

Anything written would cause a problem. All through his school years, pencils and pens had made him uncomfortable. Neither Odem nor Ahma had had any success in ridding him of the nervous, skin-crawling willies that plagued him when he was around writing instruments. He avoided them and avoided allowing anyone to know how bothered he could be. Why would a grown man run from a pencil?

Dukmee greeted them at the door and invited them into his study. "The council has sent your papers. I know Totobee-Rodolow knows what they are, but Bixby, Cantor, and Bridger will want to examine them."

He gave them each a small book with their names engraved on the leather cover along with the official seal of the Realm Walkers Guild. Inside, each page had a round named at the top, with a list of goals that would lead to their mastering the skill. In order to move to the next level of the guild, they had to become proficient in thirty-five of the thirty-six abilities.

Dukmee only gave them a moment to flip the pages to see what was before them. Raised as a future realm walker, Cantor had a good idea of what would be listed. Many of the tasks he believed he could be tested on that very day and prove his competence.

Dukmee explained, "On each page, there's a list of steps that will lead to your expertise in that area. I initial each phase, and when all are accomplished, I circle the entire page. I believe that's why this procedure came to be known as rounds."

He approached each of them with his hand out. "I'll keep them for you. You may look at them at any time. You'll plan your strategy to tackle the program. I suggest that you do a physical and mental category side by side. Two physicals or two mentals can be devastating."

He put the small stack of books on the desk. "Aside from the attributes that you must complete, there's the matter of overall stamina. Should you pass all thirty-six of the rounds, but fail the tests of strength and endurance, you'll have forfeited the final prize."

His eyes met those of first one initiate and then the other. Cantor felt like he spent more time on him. The steady gaze became uncomfortable, but he forced himself not to squirm. Did the healer read minds? Could he judge the state of his pupil by the tone of skin, quality of breath, or even by the heartbeat? He hoped not, because by the time Dukmee quit staring at him, he was flushed with sweat on his brow, breathing swift, shallow breaths, and his heart raced.

"Now for my last bit of business dictated by the guild." Dukmee looked apologetic as he spoke. "You're to live here in the vilta instead of the Moor."

Bixby stood straighter and her eyes narrowed. "Why is that? I understood living in the Moor was essential. How will we become acquainted with other initiates? How will we forge friendships that last a hundred years? How can we do research without the guild library?"

Totobee-Rodolow patted Bixby on the shoulder. "Do not distress yourself, my dear. They're already afraid of us. We're exiled to this beautiful home because we're a threat. They don't want us underfoot, perhaps spying on their illicit activities." She paused as if considering. "And perhaps they think that we won't pass our rounds because we have inferior resources and a mentor who isn't even a guild member."

"I agree," Dukmee said.

Bridger huffed, emitting a tiny flame and black smoke. "We can still make our rounds."

"I agree," Dukmee repeated. "Totobee-Rodolow and Bridger-Bigelow, you will begin a regimen to increase your flying stamina."

Bridger saluted. "Yes, sir."

"And your first task, Bixby and Cantor, is to run up the hill. You'll find a footpath around its crown. Traverse that path three times, then run down the hill."

The door slammed against the corridor wall, announcing Bixby's departure. Cantor took off after her and caught her struggling to get the front door open. He reached over her shoulder, grabbed the knob, and wrenched the door toward them.

Bixby squealed. "Don't hit me in the face with it."

Cantor laughed, picked her up, and put her down behind him, then ran. He could hear her feet scrabbling on the crushed shell driveway. He'd have to run all out to beat her.

The walking path just below the top identified which hill they were to use. Cantor noted that it was not at all a mountain, but still a very tall hill.

The path from the base wandered back and forth rather than going straight up, making the route longer but less steep. Someone had made an effort to smooth the track, which was largely clear of rocks and tree roots. Trimmed bushes lined part of the course. Benches perched on the edge so that one could sit and enjoy the view. Cantor raced by the resting spots without a second glance.

When he came to a place where he could see the crest of the hill and the intersection with the circular walk, he slowed enough to glance over his shoulder. Abruptly he stopped. Bixby wasn't following. He trotted back to the last curve and peered over the edge. Several bends below, she sat on one of the benches. Bushes and small trees partially blocked his view.

"Bixby! What are you doing?"

She didn't respond to his call. Without another thought, he plunged down the trail to see what was wrong. When he made the last turn, he saw she had her shoes off, one foot rested on the opposite knee, and she was wiping tears from her cheeks.

What could be the matter? A sprained ankle? He dropped to his knees in front of her and reached for her foot. She jerked it back and tucked her skirt around it. "What happened? Did you fall?"

"I never fall."

He looked up at her face. She sniffed and looked away.

"All right. So what happened to your foot?"

"I twisted it because I'm wearing the wrong shoes, and I've got big blisters starting. Stupid, stupid, stupid."

"You're definitely not stupid, Bix."

"What good is intelligence if you rush off without using it?"

He shrugged. He didn't have any words to say, because he honestly didn't see why she was all in a dither. When Ahma overreacted, he found the best thing to do was wait. Wait and say nothing. Especially say nothing. So he waited, and said nothing.

She looked down at her hands. "Cantor, I might not be able to train as a realm walker."

"Why?"

"I looked at those lists. I knew what to expect, but I thought maybe I could get by without actually having to do everything. I think Dukmee is going to make us do everything and do everything well. There are things I just can't do."

"Good."

"Good?"

"Yeah, I was beginning to think there was nothing you couldn't do, and in fact, you had already done almost everything."

"Don't be ridiculous." She looked away for a few moments.

Cantor waited. He figured it wasn't safe yet to talk.

"I'm not even sure I want to be a realm walker. But since I can see the portals, then I guess I should try."

"That makes sense."

"My father would be very pleased if I became a realm walker, but only if I were a very good realm walker."

"Does he know about the state of the council? About the graft and corruption?"

"Yes, but I don't think he realizes how rampant it is."

"It has occurred to me that we may end up being rebels."

Her eyes grew big. "Rebels?"

"If it's true that there are only three council members who aren't dishonest, then we don't have much chance of making things better within the system. We may have to organize a second guild."

Her eyes widened. She opened her mouth, then slammed it shut. A moment later she shook her head so vigorously her hair shed the few pins supposedly taming the mop. "That's crazy."

"Yes, I know it is. I sure would like to talk to Odem and Ahma." He picked up her shoes and handed them to her, then lifted her into his arms. "Well, we messed up our first challenge. Let's go back to Dukmee and get your feet taken care of. And don't say a word about my radical ideas. I don't want to be thrown out on my first day."

35

A SMALL THING

I f you did it by accident, you can do it on purpose."

Bixby groaned. If Dukmee used that reasoning one more time, she'd explode. Why did she ever think he was interesting? Had she really wanted to study under him when they first met at his healer's shop?

"Quit wasting your time complaining and put your mind to the task."

Great! He was reading her mind. She forced herself to sit straighter on the padded bench across from his desk. The library fireplace lay cold and so did the rest of the room. She shivered, wishing she had another layer of warmer clothing over her assortment of quiet colors. If she'd known she would be trapped in this mausoleum, she would have turned her thermea skin inside out.

Her conscience smote her. The vilta given to Dukmee for his use was a lovely, luxurious home. Servants kept up the house and the grounds efficiently and, for the most part, quietly. Sometimes she'd look up and see one working and wonder when the man or woman had come into the room. Their quarters here outshone the Moor at every level. The vilta was luxurious, certainly not a mausoleum, but even her parents' palace felt more like a home.

Bixby made a conscious effort to control her tone of voice. She didn't want to sound like whining royalty. "Perhaps if I used one of my tiaras, I could focus on a portal and open it."

"Not everyone has been gifted with a hamper full of crowns. Everything you do with the crowns, you can do on your own."

Now that can't be right. Mother still uses tiaras from time to time.

"Your mother uses them as a fashion accessory."

"How do you know that? Have you ever met my mother? And quit reading my mind."

Dukmee grinned at her, but instead of the expression being pleasant, he looked maniacal. She leaned away from him, half expecting his eyes to glow red.

He relaxed. The menacing persona faded. "You really do have an imagination." He came to sit next to her. "If it bothers you that I'm reading your mind, all you have to do is shield it."

Bixby sighed. "But not with a crown."

"All right. We'll try a different approach. Get out your mind-shielding tiara."

Bixby quickly pulled out the hamper holding her crowns, circlets, and tiaras. With the right headdress resting on her billowy blonde curls, she turned a confident smile toward her mentor.

"Now, I want you to concentrate. Close your eyes and feel the hedge that has been put around your thoughts. Try to visualize what it looks like."

Bixby closed her eyes and, after a few moments, nodded.

"Fine. Now I'm going to try to get through the barrier. I want you to feel the pushes against the hedge."

They sat in silence, but Bixby worked hard to pinpoint exactly where Dukmee's energy prodded her defense. The mental exercise was enough to warm her so that she no longer felt the chill in the air.

"Nod each time you feel my intrusion."

Again she concentrated.

"I want you to feel the guarding wall and nothing else. Ignore everything but the problem at hand."

Bixby's awareness of the hedge and the probes grew. This lesson was the most pleasant she'd had since their rounds had begun. She smiled a bit, realizing that her thought had not been read by her mentor.

"Good, good. Your nods are matching the timing of my probes."

Dukmee touched her shoulder. "You've done well. You can open your eyes now."

She grinned as she obeyed the command, but the smile slipped from her face as her mouth dropped open. Dukmee sat before her with the tiara in his hands. She reached up and felt the top of her head. Nothing but hair, an abundance of curly, unruly hair.

"When did you take the tiara off my head?"

"About fifteen minutes ago."

"I've been guarding my thoughts on my own?"

Dukmee's eyes twinkled as he nodded. "Now jog up the mountain and back, then swim across the river, pulling the rowboat."

She scrunched up her face at him, but she couldn't really

be mad. She'd done something new. In all her years with various mentors, most of her achievements had been memorizing or absorbing knowledge. She also did handiwork type projects with dexterity. But weaving a piece of material, creating a ruffle in a skirt, or mending socks without a needle didn't make her feel like crowing.

As he went through the ancient rituals of the warriors' Aray Anona Yara, Cantor listed the planes, their countries, their capitals, the type of government, industries, and form of worship. He'd found that if he timed it right, he'd finish the memorized geography one set before the end of his regimen. Then if he'd succeeded in the mental task, he'd throw extra enthusiasm into the final set of Aray Anona Yara.

Most days, Bridger joined him for this training. Today the dragon had been given a treasure hunt-type list and ordered off to find each item.

Dukmee waited for Cantor after he came back from the river.

"How was your swim?"

Cantor talked from under a towel he used to rub his hair dry. "I think I'm ready to pass all the proficiencies on that page. I'll have another round marked off."

"We'll have to go to the falls for your high dive. We'll make a day of it. We can ask the dragons to transport us, and Bixby to provide the food. She should be working on her animal, vegetable, and fruit requirement."

"She's already a good cook."

"As you know, that page is a bit more inclusive than people

generally think." Dukmee pointed toward the main building of the vilta. "Meet me in my office, and we'll test your geography. I feel confident you can pass." He paused. "Now, why do I get that response from you?"

Cantor hung the towel around his shoulders. "What do you mean?"

Dukmee shook his head and sighed. "Why do you ask that question when you know what I mean and you know that I know what you mean? It's a waste of time." The healer's face lost all friendliness and he glared at Cantor. "Just answer."

"I'd like to do the questions orally. You'll ask and I'll answer."

"Part of the test is spelling."

"I can spell the names and words, and I could even spell the numbers if you wish."

"No. Don't take too long getting into dry clothes. I want this done before we eat our evening meal."

Cantor fumed as he went to his quarters, and he realized that as long as he was in the same compound as Dukmee, his mentor would know he chafed at the order. But he'd obey. He thought of Ahma and her herb tea that helped him relax. As he stepped into the bath, he hoped he could make himself pick up the pencil.

To take his mind off the actual test, he ran through the litany of planes and their pertinent facts. He kept his mind occupied until he stood before Dukmee's office door.

He lifted his hand to knock, and his mentor called, "Come in."

Dukmee spoke without looking up. "I'm in the middle of something. Have a seat and I'll be right with you."

Cantor sighed in relief. "I'll not disturb you. I can wait outside."

"Sit down."

Cantor took the chair positioned across the room. He sat on his hands and willed his mind to recite the facts he needed for the test.

The nearness of the writing instruments broke through. He took slow, deep breaths to counter the panic rising in his throat. His discomfort increased. Dukmee must have had a hundred pencils and pens in that desk.

He closed his eyes and pulled up images of his home with Ahma. The picture detailed every tree, every large rock, and each log in the walls. He concentrated on the smell of her baked bread and the stews she simmered at the hearth, and the odor of wet dog. Tom had loved to jump in the lake and swim, then return home to dry in front of the fire.

The scene blurred. His skin tingled as the pencils and pens demanded attention. He realized he'd pulled his hands out from under his thighs and placed them on his knees. He clenched them into fists, and the strength of his effort made his muscles sore. He really could not stay in this room any longer.

He stood. Dukmee also rose behind his desk, his eyes on Cantor.

Cantor tried to speak. His voice caught, and he tried again. "I have to go out."

Dukmee nodded solemnly and pointed to the double glass doors that led to the veranda. "We'll talk out there."

Cantor bolted for the doors. He flung them open and raced across the broad surface made from blocks of stone, not stopping until he hit the balustrade on the outer edge.

Embarrassed, he tried to get his breathing under control. Too soon, Dukmee rested his hip against the stone railing, and he watched Cantor's face.

"So," Cantor said, trying to sound normal, "did you finish whatever you were in the middle of?"

"Yes." Dukmee put his hand on Cantor's shoulder. "I've ordered a drink for you. It will help you recover."

Cantor turned to look at the other man. Instead of the stern mentor façade, Dukmee looked concerned and compassionate, a healer at the bedside of a patient.

"The something I was in the middle of was figuring out what causes you such distress. And yes, I now know."

Cantor gritted his teeth. "A stupid fear."

"The fear has come about because no one understood what happens when you're near a pencil."

"And you do?"

Dukmee nodded with a confident smile warming his expression.

"Here's your drink." He motioned to a servant who carried a tray, then offered a tall glass of a bubbling, clear liquid to Cantor.

Cantor took the glass and sipped as he watched the servant depart. "It's good," he commented after the man had reentered the house.

"Yes, and it will soothe your nerves. Let's sit."

Several tables with chairs provided comfort. The initiates often studied here, and sometimes ate the noon meal outdoors.

Dukmee waited patiently as Cantor slowly drank and regained his composure. When the glass was empty, Cantor put it on the table, folded his hands in his lap, and turned to concentrate on his mentor. He hoped the man's healing would touch him and he'd be rid of this annoying reaction.

"What is it?" he asked.

"It's a gift. Writing instruments ... well, for the lack of a better term, they whisper to you."

Cantor jerked. This was harebrained. He'd never heard words from a pencil. No pen had ever spoken.

Dukmee held up his hand to stop any objections.

"You haven't learned to listen, so you don't hear what they say. You've been tormented by the feeling and done your best to block their influence, and thereby, unwittingly prolonged your distress." He nodded toward the house. "I'll bring a pencil and paper out here, and you can experiment with your gift. Once you understand, you will no longer be besieged by fear."

36

WHISPERING PENS AND WHISTLING ARROWS

antor paced while he waited for Dukmee to return. After his twentieth or so walk back and forth, he stopped and surveyed the area. A gardener worked on the far edge of the lawn, but Cantor spotted no one else. Good. He didn't want any witnesses to this experiment. Part of him longed to hide in a dark room in the vilta. But from experience, he knew that confronting a writing implement within four walls made him wild to get out. Being outside was a better option.

The doors to Dukmee's office opened, and the healer appeared with paper and pencil in hand. Cantor steeled himself.

Dukmee took a seat at the table and laid down the writing

implements. A slight breeze lifted the paper, so he rested one hand on it. "Do you want to stand or sit for the first try?"

"Stand."

"Understood. Stay where you are until I've explained."

Cantor licked his dry lips and nodded.

"I wrote a sentence while I was inside. The energy of my movements has impressed upon this pencil. When you take the pencil in your hand, your gift will interpret the energy. You only need to place the tip on the paper and allow that energy to guide your hand." Dukmee held out the pencil for him to take. "Hold it normally."

Cantor wiped his palms on his trousers and stepped forward. He felt the zing of energy, but it was controlled, a single pulse without others twining through the main stream. Taking the pencil from Dukmee, he moved closer to the paper.

Dukmee spoke softly. "Take big, relaxing breaths."

Cantor complied.

"Good. Now loosen your grip."

He did. He continued to breathe in the relaxation technique used when they did Aray Anona Yara.

"Good. Focus on the stream of energy, but don't try to hold it or bend it or change it in any way."

Cantor tried, but with the first movement, he froze, strangling the pencil then dropping it as he felt the pulse within. He likened it to feeling the flexing muscles of a snake as he held the inoffensive reptile.

Dukmee cleared his throat. "Did you feel the difference? Did knowing that you are supposed to feel something take away some of your apprehension?"

His mood of discovery left him like bees swarming from a hive. Surrounded by a zillion energy blasts like being caught in a hailstorm, he didn't want to cooperate. Leaving this for the last of the things he had to conquer sounded like a great idea.

"Let's try again." Dukmee picked up the pencil and held it out to Cantor.

Perhaps he'd been too slow the first time. Maybe the apprehension had time to grab hold of him, so that the task overwhelmed him before he began. Snatching the pencil, he swung his arm toward the table. He aimed the lead at the blank paper and overshot his target. The pencil screeched across the table top, and Cantor let loose as he pushed the stupid stick to the opposite side of the table.

Dukmee calmly stood and walked around to retrieve the pencil. "Well, now we know two methods of attack that don't work."

He sat on the chair facing that side of the table. "What manipulations of matter can you do with your energy flow?"

Cantor put his fidgety hands in his pockets, willing them to be still. "The usual. Unlock locks, move objects horizontally quite efficiently, move small objects vertically with some precision, adjust the speed and accuracy of a propelled stick, rock, arrow, dart, and the like. Odem said my good aim is innate, not something I can claim as a learned skill. However, if I'm keen on using my talents, I rarely miss."

"I see," said Dukmee. "And when you use your energy in these ways, does it unsettle you? Do you experience nausea, the adrenaline rush, or discomfort of any kind?"

"No. I get tired, of course, as anyone would who exercises."

Dukmee put the pencil on the table, and with a flick of a finger sent it rolling toward Cantor. "The energy you use for these commonplace talents of a realm walker is exactly the same as the energy used to interpret the writing instruments' messages. If you can do one without unpleasant side effects, you can do the other." He smiled encouragement. "Try it again and expect it to be no more of a trial than opening a locked door."

Cantor approached the pencil with a different perspective. Now he recognized that the energy felt much like the charge he would create to unlock a door, or nudge a pan away from the hottest part of the fire, or pull a dropped coin back to his hand. He'd developed those skills at an early age. This ability to sense something hanging on to the writing tool dovetailed with the more familiar talent. He felt the pencil move across the paper. He could see the lines and loops in his mind just before the marks appeared on the page.

The pencil stopped, and he drew back his hand to read the sentence. "One who is called must call out to the caller."

Dukmee slapped his back. "Congratulations! Do you want to do another one?"

Cantor didn't have to think about it. "Yes!"

Dukmee stood and started toward the house.

"Wait," Cantor called.

The healer turned. "Something wrong?"

"No." Cantor waved his hand to indicate the paper. "That's from the Primen Book, isn't it?"

"Yes. You should be able to tell me the reference number for that verse."

"We didn't have a Book at Ahma's. Odem would bring his when he visited. He always said if he found one, he'd bring it to us."

"I'll see what I can do. We'll ask Feymare." He stood for a moment with his eye on Cantor.

What did he want? Was he judging Cantor's reaction? Was he reading his mind? Cantor shifted from one foot to the other. A breeze teased the paper, and he slammed his hand down to keep it from blowing away. Even with his excitement over the progress he'd just made, the mention of Feymare's name brought a longing to find Ahma. To show her and her lifelong friend the discovery of using pencils instead of shunning them—

"Was there something else, Cantor?"

"Yes, yes. I wanted to say thank you."

Dukmee smiled. "You're welcome. We still have a lot of work to do. You need to be able to work with many writing instruments around you. You'll have to discern which has a message of import. I used this pencil right before I came out. You'll have to be able to work with a tool that hasn't been used in a long time."

Cantor nodded with enthusiasm. Anything. He'd practice until his fingers grew calloused now that he was free of the crippling fear.

Dukmee held up a finger. "And we'll try to hone your skill to the point that you'll know what a pen would say without going through having it rewrite the message." The healer's eyes twinkled. "*Before* you set it to paper. And after that ... "

Cantor could not imagine what could be after that. Dukmee laughed out loud. "We shall see if you can read a message that's no longer there."

He watched Dukmee return to his office. He looked down at the pencil he'd been using and picked it up.

"All the years I've wasted."

Bixby pulled the last arrow out of the tall bucket and nocked it to her bowstring. Her previous forty-nine shots limited the space left in the bull's-eye. She reached up to adjust the crown that increased her target skills, found her head bare, and remembered she'd removed the crown halfway through her practice.

Cantor lay on the grass, his hands behind his neck, his eyes on the two dragons flying above them. His bucket was empty. His skill in archery was quite a bit farther along than hers. But she was catching up. At this point he was quicker at firing off his shots, but she was just as accurate.

She aimed again. A small spot next to the right outer rim of the red circle provided the only possible place to target. She let go of the bowstring and sighed with satisfaction when the arrow struck true.

She nudged Cantor with the toe of her boot. "Come on, lazybones. I've given you time to rest. On this next set, I'm going to speed up so you don't get ten minutes to relax." Slinging the bow over her shoulder and grabbing the bucket, she headed across the field toward the target.

Cantor sprang up and marched beside her through the knee-high grass.

She came to an abrupt halt and muttered, "Just what am I going to use this skill for? Food? Shooting a bunny?"

Cantor had stopped as well, and looked at her with his head tilted to one side. She thought of the nest of cute, cuddly baby rabbits she'd once come across in the wild and projected the image into his mind. He grinned, shook his head, and tramped off toward the targets.

She scurried to catch up. "I can eat a rabbit if someone else traps it. I can cook it if it comes to me without head, skin, or innards. But, Cantor, I cannot imagine shooting a rabbit. Ditto on shooting deer, with those big eyes."

She swung the bucket in front of her to knock down some of the taller grass. "I don't think I could even shoot wild turkeys!"

"Wild turkeys are obnoxious, Bixby. You could probably shoot one after you've known it for a while."

"Know one? It would be harder if I was personally acquainted with the bird!"

She'd seen the grin he'd been trying to hide. Now he lost all control and was laughing like a boy juiced on mindmash.

The next thought stopped her in her tracks. And even though she had not consciously sent it to Cantor, he sobered, his laughter broken off abruptly.

She looked at him with eyes too close to weeping. "Could I shoot a person?" Indignation straightened her shoulders. She slammed her hand against the bottom of the empty bucket. "No! I could not." Satisfaction briefly filled her. She'd made a decision. Just as quickly, the surety of her stance sunk into shifting sand.

When they reached the target, she put the bucket at her feet and began the arduous task of pulling the arrows out. Cantor slipped them out with ease, but he had a great deal more muscle to work with. Even with her small fingers, placing them around the arrow where it had entered the target was difficult. She really needed to come fetch her arrows when the bull's-eye wasn't this full.

The first arrow she freed reminded her of watching a physician doctoring a soldier. The memory of the flesh around the wound starkly contrasted against the bit of hay coming out with the shaft.

"Ugh, Bixby. Stop thinking about blood and guts. No wonder you get sick to your stomach." Cantor had all his arrows in his bucket. He pushed her aside and neatly plucked hers from the target.

She stood back, not affronted that he took over her job and handed her one arrow after another. "Shoot a human? Shoot a dragon? I couldn't do it, Cantor."

The arrows plunked in the tin bucket as she dropped them.

"Bixby, you have to think in context. What if you were in a desperate battle? Could you shoot to kill? Maybe you could shoot to wound."

She ran this scenario through her mind and saw Cantor grimace.

He pulled out the last few arrows and shrugged. "Maybe not." He examined the pulverized red circle. "These two targets are ruined. We'll have to use the next two in line."

She heaved a big sigh and picked up her bucket. "All right. I could probably shoot to wound someone who's hurting a child."

They walked back to the line they had shot from during the first set.

"We need a challenge," said Cantor, and led Bixby to the next line that added nine yards to the distance. He grinned as he dropped his bucket and restrung his bow.

The dragons above them had ceased any pretense of battle maneuvers, but they made pass after pass so their wingtips seemed to touch. Then they circled and repeated the strange aerobics.

"What are they doing?" asked Bixby. *"Totobee-Rodolow, what are you doing?"*

Cantor's wide smile showed his white teeth against

sun-darkened skin. "They're passing small objects back and forth. They won't have to land to give each other something little."

Totobee-Rodolow flew in a lazy circle, away from her little brother. But she spoke to Bixby. *"I'm exhausted, darling, and sore. I'd forgotten how rigorous the physical training is. Do tell me, sweet child, that you have salve for overworked muscles in your healing hamper."*

"I do. Why are you so sore? What have you been doing all day?"

Totobee-Rodolow moaned. *"We did long-distance transport. It's easier to carry passengers than bulky, heavy canvas bags. At least a person, you can talk to. Then Dukmee 'suggested' we practice battle maneuvers. Now we are passing various objects back and forth. I believe I shall indulge in some therapeutic shopping tomorrow."*

Bixby eyed Cantor, who had lain stretched out on the grass. His eyes followed the dragons' movements and his mouth remained still. But she knew a conversation was going on between realm walker and dragon even if she couldn't make out the words. In order to tap into their chat, she would have to concentrate and at the same time block out Totobee-Rodolow's comments.

Bixby sank to the ground and took up a similar comfortable position, flat on her back with her hands behind her head. She'd much rather natter with her dragon than fire off fifty more arrows.

"How are you doing on your rounds?" she asked.

"Don't ask. I thought they'd give me credit for the ones I passed last time."

"They didn't?"

"Not a one."

"That's horrid."

Totobee-Rodolow did a graceful backward roll, more of a dance move than a military exercise. *"I think perhaps these sitting-behind-desks councilmen are trying to encourage me to continue my retirement instead of returning to active duty."*

"And that means they're afraid to have you where you can uncover their criminal deeds."

"I'm not very interested in their greed, immorality, and vile cruelty."

"Oh, Totobee, you can't mean that. Surely you don't want them to continue taking advantage of people, cheating them, and causing harm, even death, to those who thwart their efforts."

"Darling, I don't care what atrocities these evil men commit. But I do care about the citizens who suffer. The councilmen can be as malevolent as they please as long as they hurt no innocent bystanders. But that is not possible. Therefore they must be stopped."

"I agree. But, Totobee-Rodolow, I don't know if I could fight someone for real. I'm getting very good when we practice. But actually hurt someone? I don't know that I could."

"It's instinct, dear girl. Someone swings at you, you duck. They swing again, and you look for a way to stop them. Your instinct will bring your fighting skills into play."

Bixby started to speak, but her dragon continued. *"And anger, rage, moral indignation hyped up to its maximum caliber. Someone kicks a child, and you do something to stop it. That's where the training is a double blessing. Not only can you rescue the child, but you can control the anger. You'll use it to defuse a situation. You won't cross over to be the same kind of brute you are fighting."*

"I think I'm afraid of that. Of hurting someone because it feels good to hurt someone. Avenging the child."

Bixby had the sensation of leaning against Totobee-Rodolow's chest with her wings folded around her. She could still see the beautiful dragon gracefully flying in loops above. But she felt warmed as if Totobee-Rodolow held her in an embrace and murmured soothing words in her ear.

"You need not fear, darling. Someone watches your heart and will pull you back if that's what is needed."

"Primen?"

"Yes."

"How?"

"Through loyalty and faithfulness. Your loyalty. His faithfulness."

37

TOTOBEE-RODOLOW

Bridger came to the dinner table with a gloomy expression. Cantor regarded him with concern. His dragon friend rarely frowned quietly. He often complained loudly, but he wasn't known for stoic displeasure.

"What's wrong?"

"Have you seen my sister today?"

Cantor shook his head. "No, I haven't."

Bridger turned to Bixby. "Have you?"

"Not since early this morning."

The dragon sat down in one of the special dragon chairs and settled Jesha across his chest. He forgot to tuck in his tail, and the servant coming to place a bowl in front of him tripped. Luckily, the man had superb coordination. He saved the stew and served it with aplomb.

Once the man left the table, Bixby leaned forward and

whispered, "Last night she said she needed a recreational shopping spree."

Bridger's face brightened. He stabbed a piece of meat with a claw and stuck it in his mouth. As he chewed, he said, "She must've gone to the markets."

Bixby wrinkled her nose. "Mind your table manners, Bridge. You never know when someone might be scoring you for the etiquette round."

"Bother!"

An alarm registered in Cantor's brain. He didn't like people or dragons to disappear.

"Bridger, can't you locate her with the connection you have as siblings?"

"I've tried, but she's always been pretty clever at shielding herself when she wants to do something she shouldn't."

Cantor turned to Bixby. "How about you? You two had the thought-reading connection down even before we got to the vilta."

She shook her head and finished chewing before speaking. "No, she's out of range or something."

"Use one of your tiaras. Surely you have one to help you locate people."

Bixby huffed as she pulled out her tiara hamper. "Why are you so upset? She's probably gone shopping. We've all been pushed until we're ready to snap. And she's done all this memorizing and stamina building before. It really isn't fair that they're making her do it all again."

Bridger stopped eating to comment. "Dukmee told me they want her to be a part of the team. If she didn't go through the program with us, we wouldn't have the shared experiences in exactly the same way. Besides ..."

The brother's grin reminded Cantor of the expressions he'd seen on human siblings' faces. Ornery and smug. "Go on. Besides …?"

"Training is supposed to make you humble. My sister could use a dose of humility." Once the words were out, he looked embarrassed to have spoken them. He hurried to explain. "Well, you have to understand. I'm proud of her. She's amazing. But sometimes she knows just how fabulous she is, and it shows."

Bixby placed a crown on her head.

Cantor wondered how much it weighed. The massive headdress combined filigreed gold, plush red velvet, emeralds, rubies, and diamonds. Only Bixby could wear the monstrosity and not look absurd.

By all rights, she should. He'd known ten-year-olds taller than she was. And since he'd carried her all the way down the running hill, he knew she didn't weigh as much as a feather pillow. And her hair? Well, maybe her bushy blonde explosion of hair actually helped offset the size of the crown.

His mind came back to the missing Totobee-Rodolow. "Well?"

Bixby scowled at him. "Wait a minute. I just put it on. And be quiet."

She closed her eyes and looked beautifully serene. He was about to quiz her when she frowned.

"What is it?" he asked at the same time Bridger demanded, "What's wrong?"

Her eyes flew open, and she glared with her lips pressed together in an angry line. "Would you take it easy? Let me concentrate."

She returned to her closed-eyed, meditative look. Cantor

had to remind Bridger twice not to speak. The dragon would open his mouth and Cantor would pinch his arm, along with shaking his head and putting a finger to his lips.

At last, Bixby opened her eyes. "Nothing."

Cantor pushed his plate away. "I think we should take this seriously. Let's go to the markets."

Bixby's eyes glowed. "All of them?"

Cantor laughed in spite of his concern. "Yes." As he stood, he slapped Bridger on the back. "You'll have to fly us, Bridge."

Bixby stood and looked around the room. The servants were now having their dinner at tables lined up against the wall right outside the kitchen door. Everywhere she went, Bixby had always had an easy camaraderie with the household servants. These men and women had snobbery down to an art. She didn't trust them to not snitch on her and her friends should they do anything unusual. "Don't we have to get permission?"

Bridger cast an eye at the servants as well. "I'm not sure we'd get it."

"Dukmee isn't in here." Cantor stilled. The tension from his two companions climbed his spine in a series of warning shivers. "Act natural. We don't want to draw attention to our departure. Let's just head for our rooms, and when we get to the dormitory wing of the vilta, we'll slip outside."

Before they left, Cantor got a jacket. Flying at night was cold business. Bridger tried to leave Jesha in their room, but the cat slipped out the door every time they attempted to shut her inside.

"I guess she's coming," said Cantor after the third try.

"You're a nuisance, cat." Bridger gestured. "Come on."

They got away without any interference from the staff.

Oddly, no one seemed to care whether they went to study or swim or run away completely. That by itself made Cantor suspicious.

Bridger enlarged himself so he could accommodate two riders comfortably. He also shape-shifted a double saddle with large handles to hold on to and slots in his sides to use as stirrups. When Bixby rode Totobee-Rodolow, she needed a girth strapped around the dragon.

"Bridger," she said, "*you* are a superior mor dragon."

"Tell that to the realm walker riding behind you."

"Oh, he knows."

Cantor ignored them. "Let's go to the market farthest away, then work our way back."

Bixby agreed. "That would be Plainsmen Plaza. Totobee-Rodolow and I have some favorite vendors there. If she's been there, it should be easy to find someone who's seen her."

The nighttime atmosphere of the market sparkled and chimed much more than the quiet daytime business. Housekeepers and serious customers had gone home to bed. Cantor remembered festivals back home where friends and neighbors danced through town. This crowd had a brittle edge to it, as if the revelers partied to relieve frustration, not to celebrate life.

In the evening air, the scent of fruits and flowers permeated the atmosphere. Each booth had strings of lanterns to light their wares. Bixby exclaimed over the dainty, more plentiful lights decorating some shops.

"I want to learn how to make these."

"Later," said Cantor, scowling at the people passing.

In the background, a band played with lots of flutes, bells, and handheld harps dominating the music. And under all the forced gaiety, the current of anger drained the atmosphere of joy.

Bridger had withdrawn in size and in manner. He stalked through the aisle, looking at everyone suspiciously. Bixby stopped to look at the merchandise.

Cantor took her elbow and steered her away from a table filled with patterned cloth. "Bixby, ask the shopkeepers and vendors if they've seen Totobee-Rodolow."

"I've remembered to ask. So far, no one has seen her." She bounced and pointed. "Look at those scarves."

"We aren't here to shop. Come on."

"All right. I know. It's just been a long time since we've been to market. If we were living at the Moor, I bet we'd get to walk around town more."

A hawker stopped his spiel to watch them. Cantor whispered, "Ask this man." And guided Bixby to his stall.

Bixby fingered the rows of braided material. Dozens of brilliant colors made up each cloth rope. She lifted her eyes to the surly man studying the group. "I think they're gorgeous. How much for this one?" After paying for her new bit of pretty, she smiled. Her relaxed manner gave no indication of her concern. "I'm looking for my dragon friend, Totobee-Rodolow. Do you know her?"

With his eyes narrowed, the man snarled, "No."

Cantor took a step forward, but Bixby seemed to take no notice of the man's tone. "She's absolutely stunning. You'd remember her if you saw her. She particularly likes to look at fabrics, jewelry, and gifts. She sends presents home to her family and friends."

"Listen, missy, if you're finished looking at my wares, go

away." His anger was out of proportion to the circumstances, and alarmed Cantor.

He and Bridger stepped up, taking protective stances beside Bixby.

Cantor's chin jutted out. "No need to be rude to the lady."

The vendor sneered. "You buying?"

"Not from you." Cantor guided Bixby away. "I'm sorry about that."

Bridger fell behind the two.

Bixby took hold of Cantor's arm and floated next to him. He could tell she no longer took steps, and her head was closer to his shoulder than when she stood on the ground.

"Don't worry." Her voice rang like the bells in the background music. "I really am a big girl, and I've traveled extensively. I can handle a gruff old man. I suppose he didn't sell much today."

"With that kind of salesmanship, it's a wonder he sells anything."

Bixby's eyes twinkled. "His ropes are gorgeous." She pointed up ahead. "There's a row of vendors down that side street. We bought a lot of things there."

They rounded the corner, and Cantor could tell why this was a favorite part of the market. Fabrics, laces, and ladies' apparel hung from every available spot.

Cantor and Bridger stayed back as Bixby approached the first booth. "Hello, Seller Dakkon. Have you seen Totobee-Rodolow today?"

The man, who had been wearing a smile, turned away and said, "Don't know who you're talking about."

"My friend, Seller Dakkon. She's a mor dragon. We shopped here often several months ago."

"Don't remember her. Don't remember you."

"But —"

Cantor took her arm. "Come on. Let's try another shop."

Bixby lowered her voice. "Why is he acting like that? What's wrong?"

Bridger poked his nose between them. "He's lying. And he's scared."

Bixby asked sharply, "Why?" Her companions shushed her.

She insisted on asking at the next stall. The woman said she hadn't seen Totobee-Rodolow and barely remembered what she looked like.

As they stepped back into the stream of nighttime shoppers, Bridger snorted. "She doesn't remember what my sister looks like? Another liar."

The next stop, the vendor loudly claimed he hadn't ever sold Bixby merchandise and hadn't seen any dragons all day. After looking around, he ducked his head toward Bixby and whispered. "Best go, miss. The crowd can get rambunctious. There's lots of drinking and they get stirred up. I wouldn't want you to be hurt."

"Thank you, Seller Wren. I don't think we're going to learn anything tonight."

The man's voice rose in volume. "That's right, miss. Too many citizens come through these aisles for anyone to keep track of who was here and who wasn't."

Again, Bridger expressed indignation. "Hasn't seen a dragon all day? That's a lie. There are always dragons in the market. We like the color and the frenzy of busy shoppers. It's stimulating. On Effram, most of the dragons in our valley went to markets for entertainment."

Bixby sighed. Her shoulders drooped, and her smile had

disappeared beneath anxious concern. "Should we go to the other markets?"

Cantor put his hands on her waist, picked her up, and deposited her on Bridger's back. "What do you think, Bridger? Should we look for Totobee-Rodolow in the other markets?"

"No. Wait until we get to the side street and I'll tell you what I think."

They walked in silence until they found a deserted street, wide and well lit by the moon.

"Tell us your theory, Bridger," said Cantor. "And I'll tell you mine."

"I think my sister was here today. I think something happened that no one wants to talk about for fear the same thing will happen to them."

Bixby gasped. She leaned forward to give Bridger a hug around his thick, scaly neck.

Cantor nodded. "That's much the same as I was thinking. I wonder if everyone saw, or one person saw and spread the word to take care."

Bixby sat up but stroked the back of Bridger's neck. "I want to go back to the vilta."

"I agree. Coming aboard, Bridger." He vaulted up as the dragon stood and enlarged his body.

Bridger flapped his wings as he often did to shake out the kinks before taking flight. "I suggest we find Dukmee when we return. Perhaps he can make inquiries."

Bixby shivered. "You don't think that maybe she just went home?"

Cantor put his arms around her for a reassuring hug. "No, people wouldn't be afraid if that were the case. Those people were scared. Totobee-Rodolow is in trouble."

38

MEETING IN THE NIGHT

Bridger winged over the city amidst trailing fogs behind thicker clouds. Like cumbersome mountains, the clouds piled up on the horizon and obscured the moon. The air chilled. The darkness deepened.

The yellow lantern lights of the city gave way to outlines of dark trees, ponderous rolling waves of tilled farmlands, and black ribbons of roads. Everything wallowed in murky hues of nighttime gray. Bixby's mood sank in the heavy atmosphere.

Ahead of her, Jesha sat between Bridger's ears like a sentinel. Behind her, Cantor provided a windbreak against the rush of the dragon's wings, and he'd also wrapped his arms around her. Comfortable and secure physically, she wished her imagination would let go of dire scenes in which Totobee-Rodolow suffered and needed rescue.

Bixby rested her head on Cantor's chest, closed her eyes, and tried to dream of a happy ending to this day.

The dragon's voice rumbled under her seat. "That looks interesting."

"It does, indeed." Cantor gave Bixby a little shake. "Wake up."

"I'm not asleep." She sat up, then leaned to look where he pointed. Far below she saw a farmhouse with all the windows lit and a dozen carriages standing along the road and in the yard. Small fires appeared as glowing gems dotting the open areas between the house and the coaches.

As she straightened, Cantor's excitement passed through her. His mind hummed with anticipation. "Bridger, let's go in for a closer look."

The dragon responded to Cantor's request, making a wide circle and a lower approach to the house from a different angle.

Cantor counted while Bixby looked for distinguishing marks on the vehicles.

"Eleven," said Cantor.

"No crests — I think they've been covered up. But every one of those carriages is expensive."

Cantor vibrated with excitement. "Let's land and see what they're up to."

Bixby caught his raging curiosity, but just for sanity's sake, she thought she should voice an objection. "You don't think we should check back with Dukmee first?"

"He'd say we should investigate."

"He might want to report to the guild and let them send full-fledged realm walkers."

"Bixby, I'm betting the men meeting in the middle of the night, in the middle of a rural area, are none other than realm walker councilmen up to no good."

"In that case, we better skip the formalities."

"Right!" cheered Bridger, and he dove for the nearest clear field.

A hill rose between the spot where they landed and the farmhouse. During their descent, Bixby had watched for any sign that they'd been seen. Some men, probably drivers and groomsmen, huddled together near the fires. Most seemed intent on the games they played, several slept, and two men watched the road. At the approach of the dragon, the horses skittered a bit, but not enough to alarm the men whose job it was to see to their welfare.

When she and Cantor stood beside Bridger, she relayed what she'd seen. "I don't think much of the councilmen's servants. None of them seem concerned about their masters' business being disrupted."

"That's good for us," said Bridger. "I propose that I sneak in and hear what they're doing."

Cantor cocked an eyebrow. "Sneak in as what?"

The dragon's arms held Jesha. "A cat, of course."

Bixby approved, and she almost gave a hurrah when Cantor agreed.

"Good idea," he said. "But first, let's get a clear picture of where everyone is from the crest of the hill."

They climbed the hill, then dropped to crawl the last few feet so they wouldn't be silhouetted against the sky. It was dark enough to make the possibility slim, but they chose to be careful.

Cantor pulled a spyglass from his store of realm walker gear. "What do you have in your tiara hamper to help us learn what these men are up to?"

"Listening, mind-probe, aura-reader, obscure, action control—"

"We don't need the aura-reader. We assume these men are all bent toward evil. If Bridger's going in, we don't need listener or obscure. Mind-probe?"

"Yes."

"I wouldn't recognize any of the councilmen. Would you?"

"No."

"Why don't you see if you can get a list of names? And also who tends to stick together. We can use it to our advantage if there is more than one faction."

Bixby fitted a crown on her head. "What are you going to do?"

"I'm going to be lookout. I don't want one of those men to spot us. I'll also use that ear focusing you taught me the first day we met. Remember?"

She grinned and nodded. "I thought you were pretty lame not to know how to tune in to a conversation."

She knew he wasn't offended when she saw a flash of his white teeth in the dark.

"I thought you were lame for wearing all those clothes."

"I've been lame once as a horse." Bridger's voice came from beside them. He sat with Jesha, two cats ready for an adventure.

Cantor reached out and stroked Bridger's head and shoulders. "You're a beautiful cat, but I'm not sure about your color. Even without the moon, I can tell you're greenish."

"Oh! I forgot." The cat's fur faded into a mottled, dark color.

Bixby picked him up and gave him a quick cuddle.

"Hey!" objected Cantor. "Leave the dragon some dignity."

Bridger purred and rubbed his head against Bixby's chin. "I don't mind."

Bixby stilled. Holding the cat close, she forced her question out. "Do you think these men had something to do with Totobee-Rodolow's disappearance?"

In her arms, the Bridger-cat bristled. Cantor's white smile vanished in the dark. "There's only one way to find out."

Cantor watched Jesha follow Bridger down the hill. They crossed the yard among the carriages, horses, and men without raising an alarm. Obviously, two cats on a farm were not noteworthy. As bold as a rooster in his own henhouse, the two pranced up the front steps, strolled along the veranda, leapt in an open window, and vanished from Cantor's sight.

Bixby wore two diadems now. She'd chosen bulkier crowns since she expected to see no one. These headpieces held greater power with their heavier frames. One would enable her to enter the men's minds, and the other was to help her remember the names she ferreted out of them. She placed the more sparkly crown inside the darker one.

Cantor took his leave and slinked from bush to bush to get closer to the carriages and men. When he settled between the wheels of one of their conveyances, he gently parted the tall sweetgrass to get a view of the closest group.

Four crouched in a circle with a pair of dice. Three other men stood, watching the play.

"I'm losing all my wages to you, Smitt." A man stood and offered his place to one standing. "You see if you can break his run of luck, Digger."

Digger hunkered down and tossed a coin in a hat, then threw the dice. A collective groan said the numbers weren't good. One of the other men scooped up the hat, dumped change in his hand, and pocketed his winnings.

Smitt laughed. "If the gents argue all night, I'll have everyone's pay, and me Sassy and I can go on holiday."

"Where'd you go?"

"I'd go to the sea and watch the waves and fish for those big 'uns they say run 'long the coast. Sassy'd want clothes, though, and prob'ly a trip to someplace cooler than the beach."

"I'd like to get away. My gent's been in a mood. Sometimes I think he's gonna grab me whip and use it on me. I seen him get after a footman with his cane. Temper's wild and close to the top."

"None of them that gets together has a soft word in 'em."

"But the pay's good."

A man laughed. "The pay's good 'cause *they* ain't."

A nervous laugh from the group answered the man's jest. "Best watch what we say even among ourselves. There be spies, most likely."

Cantor snickered softly. One spy was closer than they suspected. He waited until the game caught their attention again and moved to the next group of servants.

These men swapped stories, some funny and many stretched beyond what was believable. After a time, a man began telling of the spooky things he'd witnessed while working for his gent. These could be discounted as told for the drama, but the next man who spoke up told of cruelty and vicious attacks that rang true.

"So why do you work for him, Jost, if the blood and gore make you squeamish?"

"That's easy enough to answer. If I wasn't working for the gent, then the gent would be after me. I come from the folks he likes to hound and pummel. 'Work for the man who's stronger, and you're less likely to be battered.' That's what my old man said."

One man lowered his voice and jabbed a thumb over his shoulder at the farmhouse. "That's not going to be true for all of them."

"They'll kill each other?" A man squeaked his question. Cantor wondered if it was nerves that pinched his vocal cords or if the man always sounded like a rat.

"Sure, Nots," said the man who predicted a falling out. "Who's in there arguing is the ones you'd call the strongest. They's gonna hound and pummel their own. You know, the ones that ain't here, the ones that ain't the strongest and are getting in the way of what's they" — he jerked his thumb at the house again — "want to do."

"Anyone know anything about the explosion?"

A chorus of abrupt negatives met this question.

"Not me."

"Don't want to know."

"Healthier to be deaf and dumb to that one, buddy."

"Hauss knew something about it."

"Where is Hauss?"

"Exactly."

The voices dropped into the dark night. One man broke the silence with words as solemn as a dirge.

"Where is Hauss?"

39

KERNFEUDAL

Making a list of those present in the farmhouse proved to be difficult. Bixby discovered that when people think, they don't supply their own names. So she had notes like, "Subject *A* thinks Migal Trudge is an imbecile and not a leader and should not be a member of the Kernfeudal."

She concentrated on picking up the thoughts containing the word *Kernfeudal* and learned it meant the core of a feudal system. These men considered themselves the elite rulers of the Realm Walkers Guild.

As part of the instruction she and Cantor had received under Dukmee, she had learned the names of the councilmen and where they were from. That helped her identify some of the men whose thick accents she recognized. But the whole process was tedious and confusing. She almost despaired of ever figuring out who was who, until she caught on to the different patterns of thought and the individual tone imbued in each mind. Some thought in complete sentences, some in a kind of staccato, abbreviated string of words. Others mixed streams of thought, carrying on more than one idea at a time.

For the most part, these supposedly educated men used foul language in every sentence. Some of the names they called each other made her blush. She placed a hand on her cheek and felt the warmth. Even her ears tingled.

It didn't take long for her to grow impatient with them. To her, vulgarities and profanity demonstrated lazy thinking and posturing. She thought of street urchins who didn't have sufficient vocabulary to use a word that carried weight instead of some crude term. She saw the same youth using tough language to make themselves feel adequate and hoping others would not see through the shame.

She wanted to learn something important. These grown men wasted time with thinking derogatory thoughts about one another, boasting about how great they were, and using worthless language. Bixby wanted to take their dirty minds and scrub them in hot water and lye soap. Or maybe apply some harsh astringent. Or give them a lecture on orderly deductive reasoning.

One person did use his own name. His thoughts centered on himself.

"I am not Errd Tos if I fail to bend these fools to my will."

"The day we destroy the lesser members will be known as the day Errd Tos came to power."

"These morons only think they make plans. It is not they, but I, Errd Tos, who guides them into their decisions."

Bixby longed to see which one of these men was Errd Tos. He sounded absurd but she feared he was a lethal type of crazy. Would he look as pompous as he sounded? Did he look normal? She thought that was likely. If he looked like he thought, people would probably steer clear of him.

He sure loved the sound of his own name. Did he have Errd Tos spelled out on a fancy ring? She froze in her thoughts. The fancy ring blazed with fire and smoke, but still remained clear in her mind's eye. The ring was real. The wearer of the ring was using his mind to survey the area. She threw up a block and wondered if she'd been quick enough.

The men in the farmhouse talked on and on, but she stopped homing in on the speeches and instead took note of the reactions. Who sounded powerful and in control of their emotions? Who easily produced counterpoints to any argument? Who had the least amount of scruples? Who would be the most dangerous to confront? Errd Tos stood out, and she cringed at each encounter.

As the night dragged on, Bixby's head ached with the intensity of her concentration and the long hours. Just as she hoped the meeting would finally end, a new topic emerged. The spoken words hummed in the background as she directed her attention to thoughts. As the tenor of the meeting altered, the voiced comments dominated the thoughts of all the men. Fatigue, confusion, and the nagging sense that someone hovered at the wall of her mind wore at Bixby's concentration. She remembered the Aray Anona Yara instructor's word of choice. "Focus, focus, focus." She focused. The men had settled into a deep chasm of fear.

The Kernfeudal became less boisterous as a few men took over the discussion. So far, her surveillance had left her unimpressed, but now dread replaced her casual eavesdropping. Their thoughts had turned to very dark images. Even a few of these hardened men had qualms about the brutal force the leaders called for. The stronger led the weaker to embrace the evil plans needed to achieve the power they craved.

Generally, Errd Tos stayed on the sidelines, muttering to those who did not wish to be in the center. Most of the time, the men weren't even aware he had spoken, but his evil words buried themselves in the weaker minds.

And now a man spoke whose powerful influence drew every other man's thinking to pay exclusive attention to his words. Bixby drew in an alarmed breath. She hadn't noticed. When had he taken the new position? How did he avoid her surveillance? Errd Tos stood in the center. All listened, and few dared even think thoughts that countered his strong voice.

"We must address the event that will bring down the council as it is now."

"The less said aloud, the better," objected a man she'd named Snort. *"We've agreed to the day and time. Let the minions carry out the actual bombing."* He punctuated his statement with a snort, then sniffed and blew his nose.

"We all agree," said the man who constantly squirmed. His actions twisted his thoughts as well as his body. It set Bixby's teeth on edge just to listen to him. *"The brutes will have the blood on their hands, and we'll have only the scent of slaughter."*

An undercurrent of laughter sent shivers up Bixby's spine.

Deftal was one of the first she'd been able to put a name to. His thoughts dragged as if pulled over a gritty surface. *"The stench of death clings, Brother of the Kern."*

"But you can't use a smell as evidence in a court."

Impatience fermented in the mind of Errd Tos. Bixby recoiled from the writhing exasperation. She heard his unspoken complaint: *"These fools waste my time."*

Aloud his words sounded like blows of a hammer. "We

will eliminate those who are weak. The meeting will be called. The weak will assemble. The bombs will shatter the building. Destruction shall cull the unworthy."

A rumbling of voices reassured Errd Tos that these men would follow through.

"Let us go to our homes. Be not content. The shelter you take for granted shall soon be gilded with power and authority. We shall rise above the others. Each of us shall be as kings. Go."

Bixby sighed, relaxing as the men dispersed. Errd Tos spoke softly to a few men at his side. She found she could not resist his magnetic pull. And when he mentioned their mentor, the blood in her veins almost stood still.

"Dukmee was an advantageous choice. We can trust him to provide inadequate instruction so these four will be ineffectual in any plan to thwart our aims. The servants at the vilta report that he does not supervise their training closely, and he accepts substandard performance as the four are put through the rounds. We have nothing to worry us there."

Bixby cried out as an explosion of sharp pains ripped through her head. She dropped her pencil and paper and rolled onto her back, her hands pressed against her temples.

She heard him laugh, an evil, twisted sound. She heard him speak.

"You know the prophecy of Kern?"

"We're the Kern."

"Are we? They say the true Kern is of three. Three to cleanse."

"We're cleansing, getting rid of the weak."

A growl resonated deep in the soul of Errd Tos. His desire to kill the man he spoke to had to be leashed, tamped down, controlled. Bixby writhed as she encountered his wrath.

She lost the connection, struggled to erect her barrier. Had Errd Tos seen the breach? Had he *seen* her?

He knows me. Totobee-Rodolow, I need you. I'm not strong. He wants to know me, know my name. He digs at my mind. The wall. I need the wall. Primen, I am in your heart. You are strong. Protect me.

She groaned and tried to muffle the sound. Was she close enough for the men by the carriages to hear her? She rolled away from the top of the hill, trying to reach the pasture where they had first landed. Nausea stopped her motion. If she rolled again, she'd lose control. She'd retch. They'd hear. She stayed still, eyes clamped shut, trying desperately not to moan.

As the pain eased, the nausea loosened its grip on her stomach. Slowly, she raised her hands to remove the two circlets. Where was that pad of paper? If someone from the enemy camp found it, they would know they'd been spied upon. She must crawl back and retrieve her notes.

Bixby opened her eyes, then squeezed her lids shut as pain again blazed across her forehead. The agony spread behind her eyes and the bridge of her nose.

Where was Cantor? Where was Bridger? Had they learned anything? Was this a useless exercise? Surely nothing she had written down was important. She'd only learned these men were unspeakably depraved. They couldn't stop them. No one could stop them.

Hide. She should hide until someone came to help her. The wall. Primen's protection. But Dukmee had tutored in the use of the wall. Dukmee could not be trusted.

Caught. What if Cantor and Bridger were caught?

Would the councilmen catch her?

She needed something.

Something for the pain.

In a hamper.

She couldn't move.

Evil. She'd been touched by evil.

She must get rid of the touch. A hamper. Which hamper? What did she need?

Hide. She needed to hide.

Totobee-Rodolow was hidden. She needed to hide with Totobee-Rodolow. Totobee-Rodolow had run away. Too much evil. Wise to run. Hide.

Cantor had hidden under one of the coaches. Just after he'd gotten settled, two of the men came and sat down less than a yard from where he'd folded himself behind a long tuft of grass. He could hear their conversation well enough, and what they said was of great interest. But he feared if they stopped gabbing for a minute, they'd be able to hear him breathe.

Another man came by with small loaves of bread, bowls of stew, and a couple of bottles of foul-smelling spirits. The men guzzled the liquor and downed the meal with the manners of barnyard pigs. Luckily, their slurping and belching covered any noise Cantor might have made.

The bottle must have loosened their tongues as well as warmed them. Cantor listened and congratulated himself on picking the right carriage.

"Hey, Bolar. Do you believe that stuff about dungeons under the realm building?"

"Why wouldn't I believe it?"

"I sometimes think they tell us those things to make us toe the line. That most of it's not true."

"They don't need stories of torture and endless years in dark holes to keep us in line."

The first man remained silent.

"You've never thought about breaking their trust and running away, have you, Kreeg?"

Again the man was quiet.

"That kind of thinking will get you killed. You know that, don't you?"

The first man's answer was barely above a whisper. "I'm tired of being afraid all the time."

"You're afraid?"

"Yes, I am. And if you want to say you're not, go ahead. But I won't believe you."

Now the second man took a turn at being quiet. Finally he cleared his throat. "Yeah, I'm not stupid enough not to be scared. But there's nothing for it, Kreeg. We're stuck."

"Sometimes I think being in the dark hole would be better than being in the light, working with fear riding on your back."

"We get paid. We have uniforms and good grub."

"Listen, Bolar. When was the last time you went someplace just because you wanted to? Like to the market. Or to visit someone."

"You mean you want to visit Kinni. All this is about Kinni, isn't it?"

Kreeg didn't answer.

"We knew when we got chosen —"

"Taken."

"All right, taken. We knew when we got taken that

everything before was gone. You can't go seeing Kinni or anyone without making it dangerous for them."

"I know. They find out I've gone to see Kinni, then they think I told her something to tell someone else. Then she's dead and I'm dead."

"Right."

"But I don't even know anyone to tell something to. And I don't know what the something is that I'd be telling."

"That's good, Kreeg. It'll keep you alive."

"You think the dungeons are real?"

"I know they are."

"How?"

Bolar looked around, then shrugged his shoulders.

Kreeg poked him. "How do you know they're real?"

"I saw the door."

Kreeg lifted his head and surveyed the area around them. Cantor slowed his breathing, willing the tiny puffs of air silent. Kreeg bent his head back to his friend. "Tell me."

"This morning, the main guard brought in a dragon. She was knocked out. Drugged, I think. When they unloaded her, the cart shifted. One of the guards had his foot under the wheel, and it got smashed. They made me take his place."

"I don't believe you."

"It's true."

"They had a cart with a drugged dragon in it for all to see?" Kreeg shook his head. "Right, Bolar."

"No, no. I didn't say that."

"You did."

Bolar wiped his hand down his face. "She was covered up with a tarp."

"So how'd you know it was a drugged dragon? How'd you know it was a she?"

"Because I went with them. I helped carry her. We came to the door, and we put her down. The tarp slipped and I saw her tail, but I just pretended I didn't see anything. They told me to go back. I started to walk away, and I heard one of them say she'd never get out of the dungeon."

Kreeg didn't speak.

"I know a dragon tail when I see one, Kreeg. And the guard said it was a she."

"You better forget you saw or heard anything."

"I forgot it already."

Silence filled the night air. Kreeg stirred. "Where was that door?"

"Under the bridge, through a tunnel, and into a cellar where they keep stuff for the kitchen. Behind the sacks of flour."

"I thought you said you didn't remember."

"I don't."

"I think you do."

Kreeg made a swift movement. Bolar grunted. Kreeg stood. Bolar fell over. Kreeg wiped his knife in the grass and sheathed it. He picked up the bowls and walked back to the carriages closer to the house.

Cantor's leg had gone to sleep. He moved out anyway.

40

TROUBLE, DEEP

Cantor inched up the hill, keeping to the bushes and tall grass. His leg tingled as he approached the top, and he felt he could stand now if he had to. Two small furry creatures sped past him. The second one spoke in a high, raspy voice, but still managed to sound like Bridger. Ahma's Tom would have barked, but Cantor did not expect Bridger to meow. His dragon seemed to have better control while shifted into another shape.

"Hurry!" said Bridger-cat. "Bixby's in trouble."

Cantor stood and hobbled as quickly as he could over the remaining few yards. He flattened himself just before the crest, then rolled to the other side. He studied the decline and spotted movement. Cautiously approaching the nearest bush, he waited to see if these were his friends or an enemy. One form in the shadows looked like a pile of clothing. When he saw two smaller shadows circling and sniffing, he decided the cats had found Bixby. A plaintive moan prodded him to his feet.

As Cantor rushed to Bixby's side, Bridger transformed into his dragon shape. "It'll take me a few minutes to get myself big enough to fly with all of you on my back."

Cantor nodded and knelt beside Bixby. She'd curved herself into a ball and held her head with both hands. Jesha rubbed against her.

He turned Bixby into his arms and cradled her head against his chest. "What happened?" His breath stirred the wild curls on the top of her head. He couldn't see her face.

"My head. That man! He tried to get into my brain."

Cantor held her with one arm and struggled to retrieve his water bottle with the other hand. "Here. Drink this."

Tipping her face up, she took a few sips, but the grimace twisting her face didn't lessen. "Pour it on my head."

He dribbled some over her hair and on her neck. She sighed with relief. He gave her another sip.

"Keep pouring," she begged.

Bridger hovered close by, gradually increasing. "I'm trying to hurry. It takes a while to go from cat to flying dragon size."

Cantor was about to snap at him for chattering at his back when he realized something. He glanced up at the dragon. "I'm rushing you, aren't I?"

"You're radiating urgency like the sun puts out light. A constant, even if a temporary constant, can't help but feel these things."

Cantor closed his eyes and took a precious moment to order his thoughts. He needed to work *with* Bridger. Bixby's life might depend upon it. "Dukmee will have something to heal her."

Bridger leaned closer. "Do you have a spare cloth?"

Shifting Bixby again, Cantor handed the dragon a wash-cloth out of the hamper that had held the water bottle.

Bridger took it and trotted down the hill and across a field. When he returned, the rag was soaking wet.

"There's a stream down in the glade."

Cantor took the cloth, folded it, and draped it over Bixby's forehead.

Jesha jumped onto Bridger's shoulder. The dragon stroked her. "She's nervous."

Cantor poured more water into Bixby's hair, ignoring the cold trickles that ran down his arm where he held her. "Why?"

"Those men are evil. That house has a malevolent air."

"Did you learn a lot?" Cantor looked up at his friend.

Bridger nodded yes and then wagged his head no. Then shrugged. "Bits and pieces."

"Me too." He took off the cloth, turned it over and replaced it with the cooler side down. "Maybe when we get back to the vilta, we can put all the pieces together."

"I'm almost ready. Can she fly?"

"If I hold on to her. Dukmee will know what to do."

Bixby moaned. "No, no, no Dukmee."

Cantor propped her up a bit more. "What's the matter, Bix? You like Dukmee."

Her head flopped to one side, then back. "No."

Bridger frowned. "Has she ever had to drink a healer's potions?"

"I don't know."

"Well, that would explain her not wanting to go see Dukmee. His potions are sometimes abominable." Bridger flapped his wings. "I'm going to make a seat and straps. Then I'll be ready."

Cantor realized the dragon had been stretching diligently. He was now the size of an elephant. Jesha sat on his head.

He had to depend on Bridger to get Bixby to safety. "Are you all right? You didn't do that too fast, did you?"

"I'm fine, but I couldn't do this over and over without making myself sick. The shifting isn't hard, but changing sizes is tricky."

Cantor gently laid Bixby down, stood, and then scooped her up.

"I don't know how I'm going to climb up there and carry her."

"That's no problem. Or I guess it could have been a problem, but I thought of it and so it's not now. Put her down on my wing, climb up, and I'll lift her to you."

Bridger stretched out a wing so the tip rested in front of Cantor.

Cantor followed the instructions. When he was settled, Bridger rolled the tip of his wing over Bixby. As he raised his wing, Bixby slid toward Cantor.

"Be careful!" Cantor unhooked one leg and reached toward the slipping girl. "She's going catawampus."

Bridger deftly tilted the wing and corrected her wobbly descent. "Got her?"

"Yes. Wait until I get us situated again." He pulled his cloak from a hamper and draped it over Bixby's still form. He put a jacket on, and invited Jesha to come ride in Bixby's lap. Her furry warmth would help.

When Cantor gave the signal, Bridger jumped into the air and circled higher and higher above the hill.

Cantor watched the scene below grow smaller. He wrapped his cloak tighter around Bixby and Jesha in response to the chill in the higher air. Now that they flew just below the clouds, he expected Bridger to take off in the direction of the vilta. Instead, he continued to circle.

"Bridger, do you know which way to go to the vilta?"

"Of course I do."

"Then why are we going in circles?"

"I put a powerful amount of muscle in that wing to lift Bixby. Now I have to balance the pull so we can go straight."

"Oh, like rowing with only one oar." Cantor accepted that as a logical outcome. Earlier in their acquaintance, he would have chalked the mishap up to Bridger's ineptitude. "Did you know that was going to happen?"

"Well, no." Bridger's loop became wider. "But I'll know next time."

The dragon managed to straighten his path after several more orbits.

Bixby moaned.

Cantor held her closer. "It won't be long now."

All the lights were out at the vilta. Cantor used the electricity generated from his hands to jolt the lock of one of the side doors. Bridger carried Bixby into Dukmee's library and laid her on the couch. Jesha leapt onto the sofa and found a place next to Bixby's shoulder to curl up and keep watch.

Cantor went to wake the healer.

He knocked softly on the door to the man's bedroom.

"Coming," Dukmee called from inside. The door opened, and the healer appeared, looking disheveled. He pulled on his robe and tied the sash. "You're distressed. Tell me what's happened."

"It's Bixby. She's ill."

"Where've you been?"

Cantor explained as they walked through the corridors. "We discovered Totobee-Rodolow was missing, and after dinner, we went to find her. We thought first she would be at a market, but at the first one we checked the merchants behaved strangely whenever we mentioned her. We decided the situation was worse than we first thought, so we headed for the vilta to consult you."

"You might have consulted me before you left."

Cantor didn't answer. They both knew the three had made a poor choice.

"As we flew back, Bridger noticed a farmhouse with carriages gathered around it. Some sort of meeting was going on, and we decided to investigate. Bridger and Jesha went inside as cats. I hung around the grooms and drivers. Bixby used her crowns to find out who was in the building."

Dukmee quickened his step. "She strained her mind by using her skill at too great an intensity and for too long."

"She mumbled about a man attacking her, trying to get into her mind, find her identity. At least, that's what we think. She hasn't been very coherent, but it's obvious her head hurts."

Moments later, Dukmee walked into the library with Cantor directly behind him. "Help me find the hamper that holds her crowns."

Cantor knew where it would be. He remembered from the many times he'd seen her pull it from between folds of her skirts. Gently shifting her position on the couch, he drew out the hamper. Dukmee took it from him, sat on a chair, and rummaged through the bag. "Two are missing."

"She didn't have them on when we found her."

Dukmee chose a thin circlet with a few diamonds attached at even intervals around the rim. He placed it on her head.

"That will help, but we need to retrieve the other crowns."

Bridger had put himself out of the way. At the edge of the room, next to a wall filled with portraits, he came to attention. "We'll go."

Cantor started for the double glass doors that led to the veranda.

"Wait. First tell me what you learned at this meeting."

Cantor sighed. He wanted to go *do* something, not stand around and talk. "I learned there's an entrance to the dungeons near the kitchen storage room." He looked at Bridger. "Totobee-Rodolow's been taken there."

Bridger caught his breath. He sagged against the wall, knocking two portraits of distinguished realm walkers askew. Jesha leapt from her position on Bixby and darted to sit on the dragon's shoulder. She leaned against his neck.

Dukmee sighed and turned to Bridger. "The best way to help your sister is by ..." He paused. "Bridger, tell me what you learned. When we have facts, we can act."

Bridger shuddered, then took a deep breath and drew himself erect. Stroking Jesha, he carried the cat over and replaced her next to Bixby.

"A group of councilmen plot to kill the others. They can gain more control when they divide the power among thirty-six instead of ninety-nine."

Dukmee nodded and turned to scrutinize Bixby. "And do you know what Bixby learned?"

"No." Cantor looked at his dragon friend. "Didn't she have a notebook?"

"Yes. But I didn't see it anywhere around her."

"She'd rolled down the hill."

Dukmee went to a cabinet and opened the doors. "I'm going to give her an elixir. Hopefully, she'll be able to answer questions by the time you get back. Find those crowns and her notes. We don't want those men to know we were the ones spying."

He glanced toward the glass doors. "It's almost dawn. I suggest you hurry."

41

GATHERING
FORCES

Bixby sat up. Jesha stretched beside her. The room was cool and dark with the drapes pulled over the many long windows and glass doors — Dukmee's library. Where were Cantor and Bridger?

She tried to stand, lost her balance, and sat down hard on the couch. The jolt rattled her brain, and she remembered how very sick she'd been. She lifted her hand to her head and found a healing circle tangled into her hair. She must have tossed a lot while she was unconscious.

She remembered Errd Tos. Her arms folded across her midriff. It was her mind, not her stomach, she should be protecting. Strings of pain and terror still threaded through her thoughts. She collapsed back onto pillows and blankets.

Jesha leapt aside as Bixby thumped down almost on top of her. The cat stared at the girl reproachfully. With a haughty turn of her head, she licked a front paw and began her morning ritual of putting herself in order.

Bixby stroked the cat's head between her ears. "I need to do some grooming as well."

A glass and pitcher sat on an end table. She scooted along the cushions until she could reach them, drank the full glass of clear liquid, then refilled it from the pitcher. An elixir. She remembered Dukmee holding her in a sitting position so she could sip the tart fluid.

Where was he now? Something niggled at her brain. Something about Dukmee and those horrid men.

The doorknob rattled, then the door opened. Dukmee entered, followed by a servant with a tray.

The servants were spies. She remembered a statement made by Errd Tos that confirmed their suspicions. He had said something else, but the memory shivered and hid from being ferreted out.

"You're awake. Good. Head any better?" Dukmee gave her a searching look, and she was sure he'd analyzed her state of health.

He gestured for the man to place the tray on a small round table near the windows. Then he came to her side and took her wrist, resting his fingers on her pulse. After a moment, he gave a nod of approval. "Good, good. Can you sit at the table?"

He helped her stand and supported her to where the servant held out a chair. "Thank you, Seymour. That will be all."

Before he left, the servant put a dish of milk on the floor. Jesha sauntered over and sniffed his offering. She waited until the door closed behind him to lap the milk.

Bixby sat and placed her hands in her lap.

Dukmee folded his long frame into the other chair. "You haven't said a word."

The memory twitched. Bixby snatched it then tossed it away. Too late. She knew what she had learned at the farmhouse. A storm brewed in her chest as Bixby focused on the one horrid bit of knowledge. "You work for them."

"Them?"

"Those wicked councilmen."

He frowned, picked up her toast, and spread bright red jam across the golden top. "Bixby, you've always known I was in the employ of the guild."

"The servants spy on us, and you make sure we aren't equipped properly for the job."

He put the toast back on her plate, but continued to hold the knife as he gazed at the door to the hall. "Of course the servants spy on us." He paused, then set the knife on the tray. He scooped sugar into her tea. "Do you want cream as well?"

"Yes."

He poured the cream from a small china jug, then stirred the brew. "Ah, that smells like a flower garden."

She picked up the delicate cup and sipped the warm tea. The flavorful taste pleased her, and the warmth soothed her raw throat. She realized the outside muscles of her neck were tight and sore. But her head hurt only if she moved quickly, and the nausea had disappeared. She was better, and her regained health was probably due to Dukmee's healing gifts.

She dipped her spoon in the bowl of porridge. Dried fruit and crumbled nuts floated on the top of the thick, creamy crushed grain and oatmeal mixture.

Dukmee watched her. "You don't think I'm doing an adequate job as your mentor?"

"*They* are counting on you to *not* do your job."

"I see." He tapped a finger on the table, then abruptly stopped. "The servants spy. The spies report to the councilmen that I am not preparing you properly. The corrupt Guildsmen are pleased, and you are not."

She nodded and ate more of the porridge.

"Number one. You are wondering if I am fulfilling my obligation to get you ready for the arduous tasks of being a realm walker.

"Number two. You've heard I'm doing a poor job. If so, you're wondering if it's deliberate negligence on my part, because I desire to please the corrupt guild. Or, if I am doing a poor job without malice, is it because I am inadequate to train you and your cohorts?"

Bixby fixed her eyes on her teacup, and she swallowed a large amount. She put the cup down but avoided Dukmee's eyes. Picking up the jam-covered toast, she nibbled with deliberate concentration.

Dukmee poured himself tea and spent some time preparing it to his liking.

He stirred well past the time the tea was blended with the sugar and cream. "We can't answer number one until we've answered number two. I have three statements that can put your mind at ease, *if* you believe them to be true."

She looked up, wanting to read honesty in his eyes.

He smiled. "I'm not interested in pleasing the guild members. To my own pleasure, I've enjoyed feeding them false information through their spies. I'm perfectly capable of training you and the others in the ways of a realm walker. I'm convinced that your training will equip you to either handle a situation with expediency, or to evaluate a problem and determine an adequate response."

Bixby tried to keep her expression neutral, but it was no use. She frowned as she contemplated their time at the vilta. She'd witnessed Dukmee allowing the servants to overhear half-truths, not lies, but misleading statements. That much would be true. And as for his allowing them to be slack in their training, weariness, sore muscles, and hours of study proved that accusation wrong.

Unprepared? She knew cocky Cantor thought he was more than able to level forests and build cities. Any more certain of his ability to do the things he'd trained for would cause problems. They'd have to widen doors to get his head through.

She'd been confident when she started the training. If she'd been prepared then, now she should be able to knock down mountains.

In her hamper, Bixby had a crown that enabled her to discern whether or not a person told the truth. She smiled at Dukmee. She didn't need the crown.

Light burst into the room as the doors to the outside swung open, and Bridger and Cantor stepped in. Cantor stopped and held the door as he watched out across the veranda. Jesha darted out.

Bridger came to Bixby's side. He took her hand. "Are you all right? You look a lot better. You looked bad before. Not bad as in ugly, but bad as in sick. Well, looking sick did look ugly, but you're all right now. Right?"

She smiled. "I am much better. Thank you."

"You're welcome, but it wasn't just me. Cantor helped, and of course, Dukmee took care of you once we had you here."

He turned his head as if listening to a noise from outside.

"What is it?" asked Bixby.

"We have a visitor." He smiled, flashing rows of pointy teeth.

Could it be Totobee-Rodolow? Bixby held her breath.

Cantor stepped back and Feymare entered with Jesha in his arms. Of course, it wasn't Totobee-Rodolow, but Feymare could help find her, couldn't he?

He greeted Cantor, Bridger, and Dukmee, then came to sit with Bixby.

"Have you had breakfast?" asked Dukmee.

"No." He placed a hand on the side of Bixby's face, cupping her chin. "You're doing well. I was alarmed to hear of your experience."

"I forgot to be cautious."

"That's true, but the endeavor was exacerbated by the content of the minds you probed. They are truly depraved men, and their evil is a malady of hedonistic hearts."

"I'm hungry," said Bridger. "I'll go to the kitchen and have breakfast brought to the library."

Bixby wondered how the Primen warrior would take this mundane statement. After the delivery of his explanation of her severe reaction and the thorough corruption of these men, surely a comment about food was out of place.

She needn't have worried. Feymare bestowed a glowing smile on the dragon. "Thank you, friend. I'm hungry too. Food sounds utterly practical. And then we must talk."

While they waited for Bridger to return, Cantor sat across from the Primen warrior, determined to find out about Ahma and Odem. They all sat at the small round table. Dukmee had moved Bixby's tray out of the way.

Feymare answered Cantor's question even before he could ask it. "I'm sorry, Cantor. I've heard nothing. But the fact that we haven't had news is actually news in itself."

Cantor tried to form an optimistic expression but knew he was scowling. "How so?"

"There are only a few places they could be hidden from my ability to locate them."

The scowl slipped. "So you can guide us to these places, and perhaps we'll find them."

"The first one is right here in Gilead."

Dukmee leaned forward. "The dungeons."

The possibility of rescuing Ahma and Oden within the next few hours excited Cantor. "We've had information that Totobee-Rodolow has been taken there. And I heard directions on how to enter the dungeons."

Feymare's eyebrows rose. "Indeed, this is good news. I heard yesterday about Totobee-Rodolow's disappearance. I was able to find out who kidnapped her, but not why, and not where she'd been taken. I was coming here anyway to suggest we look for Ahma and Odem under the Guild Center. And I had a message from Toolooknaut. He has more information and will meet us here later in the morning."

Dread squeezed the joy out of Cantor's expectation of finding his friends. What would their state be after so long in such a wretched place? Were they even still alive? His fault if they were ill. His fault if they were beyond regaining health. A discreet knock on the door, followed by the arrival of breakfast, cut off the blame Cantor heaped on himself.

The servants brought a long table and trays of food. While

they worked, Feymare examined each one in turn. Cantor wondered what interested the warrior.

The men filled plates from the impromptu buffet, and Cantor brought Bixby a fresh cup of tea. She sat back from the table, cradling Jesha in one arm. The cat spilled onto Bixby's lap as a furry, limp, and happy feline.

After the servants left the room, Bixby repeated what she'd learned. "The servants are spies for the guild."

"You're correct, Bixby." Feymare gestured toward the closed door. "Only one of those who were just here is truly evil. The others have fallen away from righteousness, but they could be brought back if circumstances offered them a way out of serving the councilmen. And there's one who secretly yearns to shed himself of this company. I believe he might generate enough courage to change without aid."

Bixby was silent for a moment. "The shorter one who looks like he's ten years younger than he really is. He often has a pleasant expression."

"That's the one."

Dukmee looked around the table. "One of the talents you'll develop as you mature as realm walkers is the ability to discern the basic character of a person." He smiled at Bridger. "Or a dragon."

Feymare agreed. "It's part of being in tune with Primen. His wisdom, His insight will guide you. I knew of your troubles before any concrete evidence came to me."

Cantor turned to Bridger. "Last night, how did you know Bixby was in trouble?"

Bridger looked embarrassed. His eyes darted around the room, and he wouldn't meet any of the others' gazes. He twitched as if he suddenly wanted to go do something any-where but there.

"It's all right, friend." Feymare clapped him on the shoul-der. "You did well."

He looked at his cat, who showed no evidence of shar-ing his embarrassment. "Jesha and I had been in the room with the councilmen for a long, long time. Jesha went to sleep. The men talked and talked, and it seemed they said the same things over and over, just in different words. My mind drifted away from my assigned task, and after some time, I sort of dozed. Something stirred me out of being half-asleep. I felt a twinge of anxiety. Then Bixby's distress hit me like she stood beside me wailing. I woke Jesha on my way out of the room."

Cantor gave Bridger a look.

He heard the dragon's thought, loud and clear in his mind. *"What?"*

He couldn't resist teasing his friend and answered. *"Asleep on the job."*

"They were dreadfully boring."

"They talked about murdering people, and that was boring?"

"Boring after you heard the same thing over and over. It wouldn't have been boring if they'd actually been murdering people, but it was all talk. They'd think of a method to deliver the bombs, then think of reasons why that idea wouldn't work."

"Did they ever come up with a plan?"

Bridger looked uncomfortable again. *"Ummm? I was asleep."*

Feymare interrupted their silent conversation. "I'm sure the information you gathered, Bridger, will be very help-ful. Combined with the others' input, we'll have a firm understanding and can plan accordingly. But first, this break-fast calls me."

After they'd eaten, noises from the hallway announced servants had moved in to work, or perhaps to listen. The friends moved to the veranda where no one could overhear without obviously being close. Over the next several hours, the five discussed in detail all the things they had learned the night before. Feymare and Dukmee shared knowledge they had from previous experience.

"Tonight," said Feymare, "we'll enter the dungeons and free all we find."

Cantor clenched a fist. "Hopefully, that'll include Ahma and Odem."

Bixby stared off toward the road to Gilead. "Didn't you say that Toolooknaut would be coming?"

"Yes." Feymare turned so he could see the road. "But it looks like Ponack is coming instead."

"Why is he walking?" Bridger asked.

"I'd hardly call that walking. He's almost trotting." Bixby grimaced. "He's too old to be in that big of a hurry."

Cantor squinted to get a good look at the man. "He looks upset."

Bixby shook her head slightly. "When I met him before, he seemed like 'upset' was his normal way of dealing with things."

Dukmee sent a servant with a pony cart to meet Ponack and bring him the rest of the way to the vilta. As soon as the pony slowed, Toolooknaut's employee climbed off the seat and hurried to join them.

Ponack took Feymare's hands. "I'm so glad you're here. Toolooknaut was to come and tell you the plot." He panted as he spoke. "Some of the councilmen are going to cause an explosion. Gas and fire and such. At the guild building this evening, before the dinner hour. Today! Hours from now."

Bixby reached to take Cantor's hand. *"They talked about this. Those men. Errd Tos. I remember now. Glee. Evil, maniacal glee over the destruction of so many. And shattering the foundation of what the guild has been."*

Cantor squeezed her hand. *"We still have time to save them. Ahma, Odem, and Totobee-Rodolow. There's time."*

Bixby stared into Cantor's eyes. He saw terror and panic. *"What is it, Bixby?"*

"Errd Tos was in my mind. He blocked the memory of the bomb plot. Does he know who I am, Cantor? Will he destroy us all through my weakness?"

Ponack reclaimed their attention with his dramatic gestures and shrill voice. He let go of the Primen warrior and turned to the others, wringing his hands, whining his news. "Toolooknaut was arrested. He was coming here. They arrested him right on the street outside his quarters. And where did they take him? To the guild building!"

Now he paced and wrung his hands. "We must free him. An explosion. Enough power to knock down the whole building. No respect for life. No respect for our history. The Realm Walkers Guild stood for honor and generosity and forbearance. But that was years ago. Now it's nothing like it should be. Rotten. Rotten!"

He stopped and shook his head slowly, as if in disbelief. Then he resumed pacing — pacing, shaking his head, and wringing his hands, muttering. "Good men will die. Records, artifacts, history will burn as if they never were. And that's what they want. They don't want reminders of the past when the guild ruled justly. A sad day. Sad. We must rescue Toolooknaut."

Bixby came to her feet. Her dragon's name came like a soft stutter to her lips. "Totobee-Rodolow." She looked around the room, seeing the strength and purpose in her comrades. Her voice gained intensity. "She's there! We can save her."

Bixby grabbed Cantor's hand. The current he used to unlock doors and move objects tingled in his fingers. The energy grew as it passed back and forth between the two realm walkers. She looked intently into his eyes and he knew what she would say. "And Ahma. And Odem."

Feymare's gentle voice sealed their intent. "So be it."

42

IN SHADOW INN

Feymare, Dukmee, and Ponack rode to town together in a closed carriage. Bixby, Cantor, and Jesha traveled by horse, or rather, by dragon — Bridger. They took a longer route and had agreed to meet Feymare and Dukmee at the In Shadow Inn across from the guild building.

Bixby fidgeted in front of Cantor. Her nerves wouldn't let her settle. She held back a stream of chatter, knowing Cantor would not find her way of relieving tension to his liking. She stroked Jesha, then patted Bridger on his neck.

"Can't you hold still?" Cantor asked.

"I can be quiet or hold still, but I can't do both when I'm so nervous."

"Your jumpiness is driving me crazy. Try talking for a while. That might be better."

"All right. What do you want to talk about?"

He made an exasperated noise. "Not me. You. It doesn't

matter what I want to talk about. You're going to talk instead of twitch."

Bixby sighed and tried to think of something they hadn't talked about for hours already that day.

"I know!" She wiggled a bit to get comfortable before she switched from shifting to speaking. "I heard one of the farmhouse men say that Dukmee was on their side."

"Dukmee? You jest."

Bixby twisted in Cantor's arms so she could face him. "No, but I misunderstood what he meant."

"You're supposed to be still."

She faced front again. "He said that it was a good thing Dukmee was our mentor, because he wouldn't train us properly."

"How could he know that?"

"I thought he meant Dukmee would deliberately leave things out of our rounds so we'd make bad mistakes when we went on missions."

"I think we're learning more than we have to know."

"But," said Bixby, ignoring the interruption, "he meant that Dukmee was an inadequate mentor. He thought that he didn't have the qualifications to be a mentor and Dukmee was too caught up in his own interests to pay much attention to us."

Cantor's chest jostled Bixby's back as he laughed. "You have to admit he reads a lot."

"That's probably why they gave him that huge library. To keep him preoccupied."

"But why would they think he's not qualified?"

"They know him as a healer. And they successfully had him contained for years. If he couldn't get through an evil wizard's ward, how could he be an experienced realm walker?"

"He knew how to do it, he just needed more power — us — to make it work."

"I know that, but just hearing someone say Dukmee wasn't fit made me doubt. We don't know what a realm walker mentor is supposed to do. How would we know if he is inadequate? And it is feasible that every mentor has a different agenda."

She felt Cantor nod his head. "And the whole thing about being at the vilta instead of in the hall is strange." He sputtered and wiped her hair away from his face. "But, in spite of that, I think we're making progress."

Bixby did too, and she'd had a lot of experience under mentors. She was about to rattle off some examples, but Cantor had a question.

"You really thought he had given his allegiance to the corrupt councilmen?"

"For a little while."

"That's why you didn't want to go to Dukmee when you were sick."

"I didn't? I don't remember that."

"You were pretty out of it." He paused. "What made you change your mind?"

"He talked to me. He knew I was upset, and I could feel him looking through my mind for clues. I was too weak to stop him. So he kind of outlined what I was thinking, and then reassured me I was wrong."

"And you just believed him?"

Bixby shrugged. "He's Dukmee. How could he be anything but what he is? Do you remember how forthright he was when we needed his help to rescue the young men? He doesn't prevaricate. And I suppose I dabbled in a little logic as well."

This time Cantor's laugh sounded more like a snort. "Dabbled, eh?"

"Don't tease. I actually have a very fine intellect." She knew better than to wait for him to agree. "The things that Errd Tos said were a result of Dukmee's ineptitude weren't true. Dukmee worked us hard, demanded perfection, and spent time addressing our specific needs. He wasn't slaphazard in any way. Besides ... Feymare trusts him."

"Well, that makes sense." His sarcastic tone scraped her nerves. "If Feymare trusts him, then we should too."

"Of course we should! He's a Primen warrior. Do you think His warriors are easily fooled? They do take orders directly from Primen. Some people believe these warriors have actually stood in the presence of Primen."

"I haven't been all that impressed by Feymare."

"Why?"

Cantor didn't answer.

"Why, Cantor?"

He still remained silent.

"Come on. You can't just say something like that and not say why. Why is it that you're not all that impressed by Feymare?"

"He hasn't done much good in keeping the councilmen under control."

"Maybe Primen didn't tell him to keep the councilmen under control."

"Why wouldn't He?"

"Seems to me, Primen is interested in citizens working through problems and causing their lives to line up with His standards. He doesn't do it for us."

Bixby heard the low growl that oozed from Cantor's tense throat.

She poked his arm that wrapped around her waist. "What else? There's something else, isn't there?"

"Feymare didn't have a clue as to where Ahma and Odem are. He still doesn't know for sure. You'd think a Primen warrior would be more useful in finding lost realm walkers. Realm walkers take a vow to serve Primen. After a life of faithful service, Ahma and Odem don't seem to rank much attention."

"Oh, that's all twisted, but I'm not sure what to say to get it untwisted."

Bridger shuddered beneath them. "Ask Cantor about the man who was murdered a couple of feet away from him."

Bixby gasped. "When?"

Bridger answered. "Last night."

"Last night? Cantor, what is he talking about?"

"The man who talked about seeing Totobee-Rodolow taken into the dungeon was stabbed for knowing too much."

"You didn't say anything about that when you told us about his information."

"Why should I report it? His being killed didn't change what he'd said."

Bixby pondered his words. What was he not saying? And why was he not saying it?

"You saw a man get killed, and you didn't mention it?"

Cantor lowered his voice. "It's the first time I've seen a murder. I felt sick. I couldn't get away fast enough. Your being wiped out gave me something else to think about, something to do. The urgent need to find care for you helped me focus. And I didn't want to talk about it. I still don't want to talk about it."

Bixby wanted to hug him. Of course she couldn't. First of all, it would be embarrassing for Cantor. And second, she would have to turn all the way around and that would be awkward. Really her position was a good thing, because if she'd been facing him, she would have thrown her arms around him and held on until he admitted he'd been distraught. Being a man, he probably thought he shouldn't react to what he'd seen.

She felt herself blush. Realm walkers should remain stalwart and not go throwing their arms around others.

She cuddled Jesha closer to her and cooed in her ear. "Cats are very useful."

Jesha purred.

Congested traffic clogged the road closer to Gilead. Their progress slowed, and Cantor realized the crowd pressed in on them.

"Bixby, you had better quit talking now. Someone might overhear you."

"You know I'll twitch."

"That's all right. I'll handle it."

If he was forthright like Dukmee, he would have told her he was nervous too. Instead, he busied himself watching the crowd for anyone who looked suspicious.

He noticed several citizens taking unusual interest in Bixby. He'd forgotten how bizarre her appearance was. He'd grown used to the layers of clothing, the additional bits of lace, the trailing ribbons, and the embroidered flowers cascading off of sleeves or from her waist or down her back. Her flyaway, corkscrew curls just looked like Bixby. The only way she could somewhat tame it was by smashing it down with a crown or a hat.

Her face turned as she watched a family in the back of a wagon. Oh, and she had a flower painted on her cheek today. And of course, the paint glittered.

"Bixby, put on that crown that obscures your presence. I'd rather people were a bit hazy on whether they saw us together since a lot of things are going to happen. Confused witnesses might come in handy."

She quickly donned the proper headdress.

"That's better." Cantor observed the citizens on the road. "They seem to look right through you."

She giggled. "Handy for our purposes, but I wouldn't want to be ignored all the time."

"Little chance of that."

Bridger shifted back into his dragon form soon after they entered the city.

Bixby changed from fidgeter to chatterer. "Which is more comfortable, Bridger? Horse or dragon?"

"Definitely dragon. I always feel better in my own skin."

"Which does Jesha prefer you to be?"

"Probably a sheep. More comfy to sleep on."

Bixby laughed, but Cantor tossed them an impatient look. "Come on. They're probably already there."

When the hall came into view, all three friends stopped at once. Cantor drew in a sharp breath as the combined impact of his and Bridger's reactions clenched his stomach. The avenues around the Guild Hall were packed with people.

Very few had business at the guild building itself, but markets and shops, restaurants, libraries, and museums lined the surrounding streets. Gilead was the capitol city, and this district was the cultural center. Unless the catastrophe occurred late at night or they could stop the explosions , the carnage would be unspeakable. They could not fail.

Setting his mouth in a firm line, he led Bridger and Bixby straight to the In Shadow Inn.

From two o'clock on, the establishment squatted in the shadow of the guild building. The owners of the inn played upon their location by keeping the inn in darkness most of the day. The elite members of the guild strutted past this inn, seeking more elegant establishments beyond. Roobsters made up the clientele of the inn, men and women of the lower class: the drivers, lackeys, grooms, and lowly messengers who served those of the guild without expectation of a better life.

The innkeeper gave Jesha a rude greeting. "Anyone notices the cat, out it goes!"

"*She*," said Bridger. "Not it, but *she*. Out *she* goes."

"That's right," said the grumpy man. "Out she goes."

Cantor decided it was time to take the attention away from Bridger and his cat. "We're looking for friends."

"I don't know who your friends are. Go ahead and look for 'em." The innkeeper stomped away.

Cantor, Bixby, and Bridger stood near the door, surveying the room. No lamps were lit. Massive windows lined the street wall, but the grimy glass let through little sun. The common room of the inn was dim. As soon as Cantor's eyes adjusted, he pointed to the opposite wall. Dukmee held a large table for them, but Feymare was not with him.

"I've ordered a meal," said Dukmee as they gathered. "We're likely to be busy the rest of today, and we may not get another chance to eat."

They settled around the table. Jesha prudently sat in Dukmee's lap under the red-checked tablecloth.

"Where's Feymare?" Cantor asked.

"Out gathering information." Dukmee looked behind Cantor. "Where's Bixby?"

"Right here. Oh, I still have on the crown." She took it off and grinned at their mentor. "You knew I was here."

His eyes twinkled as he teased her. "I did."

Bridger laughed. "Dukmee's got a sense of humor. I didn't know."

Bixby gasped.

"I suppose you knew." Bridger twisted his lips in a frown. "You don't have to act so surprised just because it took me a while to figure it out."

She shook her head at him and pointed to the door. Cantor and Bridger turned to look.

Feymare stood with the sun shining behind him. He glowed.

Cantor blinked. He should be able to see only the Primen warrior's silhouette. But light poured from his entire body. The backdrop of sunshine highlighted his outline. Then it occurred to Cantor that there was no sun behind him. The inn was in a shadow.

He turned to look at his companions. Bixby and Bridger were awestruck, but Dukmee sat with an amused, content look on his face. Cantor surveyed the rest of the clientele of the inn. No one else seemed to notice the astonishing figure at the door.

Feymare stepped in, and the glow diminished somewhat, but now his apparel could more clearly be seen. He wore burnished armor. From his side hung a white shield with a bright blue, rearing horse emblazoned on the front. He wore a gleaming sword, and his long hair was braided for battle. Even the cloth of his garments and the shoes on his feet gleamed as if polished with moonlight.

Cantor swallowed the lump that came to his throat. The aura around the warrior proved his status. Only those following Primen would see the glory given the man by their creator. Even though Cantor had thought Feymare less than capable, this showed how little Cantor understood. Dazzled and humbled, Cantor almost rose to his feet and bowed. He remembered in time that the honor should not be given to the gifted but to the giver.

The closer Feymare came to their table, the less distinctive he looked.

Dukmee leaned forward. "No one else can see him as you do. Primen has revealed his status to us to give us confidence. It's heartening to have a Primen warrior on our side."

Feymare took the last seat available at their table.

"Did you learn anything?" asked Dukmee.

"Yes." He closed his eyes and took a deep breath.

When he opened them again, his demeanor had subtly changed. Tranquility had been added to authority, confidence, and purpose. The peace on his face was at odds with the nature of their task. Cantor wanted to fold his hand over that quality and use it for his own approach to the rescue attempt.

Feymare spoke quietly. "A meeting has been called for the councilmen this afternoon. It's most likely that once the men are gathered in the forum, the Kernfeudal will make their move."

Bixby whispered. "Not tonight?"

"This afternoon."

Cantor glanced around the room, his mind on the crowds outside. An explosion large enough to bring down the huge structure across the street would surely damage all the buildings around it. "What about all the people?"

"We will rescue the prisoners, then try to stop the explosion."

Bixby's voice quivered. "Can't we warn those in the forum?"

"Yes, but first we will see the prisoners safe. If anyone knows of the escape plan, they will do their best to stop us. If they stop us there, then we will have no opportunity to thwart the destruction of the Guild Hall."

Dukmee stood, holding Jesha in one arm. He searched the crowd, and found what he wanted. He raised a hand and, although he did not raise his voice, Cantor heard him call as if his were the only words spoken in the room. "Yo, innkeep!"

The man turned. However, none of the other patrons of his tavern seemed to notice. Dukmee tossed a bag across the room. Oddly, Cantor heard the coins clink within. Traps, enough to pay for the meal being prepared, but they would not stay to eat. He wondered if they were gold or silver. Ahma had always preferred to deal in gold.

He breathed a prayer. Let Ahma be there.

Dukmee indicated the door. "It looks like our business takes us away from our supper. Let's hope later tonight we can sit down to a celebratory feast."

The others rose as one and filed solemnly out of the inn.

43

UNDERGROUND, OUT OF SIGHT

I t has to be this bridge." Cantor stood at the apex of the river crossing. At one time, the river had been used as a moat around the building. Now the water flowed only on one side. "There should be a tunnel that leads to a cellar under there."

Feymare turned to Bridger. "Why don't you stay here and create a diversion while we sneak inside?"

"What kind of diversion?"

"Can Jesha help you?"

The ridges above Bridger's eyes lifted. "I have just the thing. We'll play keep-away. She likes that."

Bixby and Dukmee strolled to the end of the bridge closest to the Realm Walkers Hall.

As they had planned in order to remain inconspicuous, Cantor and Feymare waited a few minutes, then started to leave.

Bridger grabbed the Primen warrior's arm. "Wait!"

Cantor turned back. What was wrong? Had Bridger seen a threat of some kind? Why wouldn't the dragon let them go?

"I want to help rescue my sister."

"You *are* helping." Cantor blew out his breath in frustration. If they had to go into a long, persuasive argument to get away, they would lose valuable time.

Feymare looked Bridger in the eye. "I need you here because you'll be best at causing the distraction. Give us thirty minutes, then walk away from here, double back, and follow us into the tunnel."

For a moment, Cantor thought the dragon would be stubborn, but after a brief hesitation, he agreed.

"All right."

Feymare clapped him on the upper arm. "You and Jesha can start your commotion now."

Cantor watched over his shoulder as he and Feymare joined Bixby and Dukmee. Bridger whispered something to the cat and put her down. Jesha leapt onto a passing cart.

"Stop!" yelled Bridger. "You have my cat."

He ran to the man leading a donkey. Bridger grabbed the man and forced him to stop.

He pointed to the cart. "My cat!"

"Well, get your cat."

Bridger scurried to the side of the cart, but just as he reached for Jesha, she jumped to a man passing the other way. The man screeched and tried to knock the cat off his shoulder. Bridger had raced to intercept Jesha, but she bounced back to the cart and then onto one of the struts that held up a side of the bridge.

Another traveler bent and tried to catch the cat for Bridger. She scratched him, jumped to the side railing of the bridge, sprang from there onto the man's back, and then launched herself onto another, larger conveyance. Several people joined in the attempt to corner the cat. Bridger couldn't reach the vehicle's roof where Jesha perched. She looked calm, but the end of her tail crooked and straightened in subdued excitement.

A small boy clambered up the side of the carriage and tried to creep up behind her. Waiting until right before the boy pounced, Jesha cleared the space between vehicles and boarded a wagon headed the other direction.

Jesha had landed on a small cart overloaded with round fruit. Apples, oranges, and melons tumbled down and hit the bridge with force. The avalanche picked up speed and fruit bounced in all directions. Jesha continued bounding hither and yon, Bridger continued following, and more citizens joined in the chase.

Cantor chortled at his last sight of the keep-away game. The four rescuers would have no problem leaving the bridge unnoticed.

Below the bridge, Feymare found the opening to the tunnel behind a collapsed section of brick. The bridge had been supported by another column replacing the damaged buttress. The tracks behind the pile of bricks made it obvious that the tunnel was used. Cantor and Bixby followed the older men into the dark recesses. Feymare and Dukmee produced lighted orbs, giving two to the initiate realm walkers and keeping two for themselves.

Bixby wrinkled her nose. "It doesn't smell very nice down here."

Cantor followed close behind her. "Makes me think we must be in the right place."

"The storage rooms beneath my parents' palace have

a fresh, organic fragrance. A little clean dirt and lots of vegetables."

"Clean dirt?"

"Oh, you know what I mean. You've grown crops with Ahma. The soil has nothing rotten or moldy in it. Anything like that has broken down into mulch and loam."

Dukmee spoke softly over his shoulder. "We're coming to the storeroom. Hold on a minute while I scout ahead. And be quiet."

Feymare moved to stand behind them. Cantor saw Bixby open her mouth. He suspected she would ask him why Feymare had taken the rear position. They'd studied strategic positioning in the tactical planning round. She always had questions. He glared and put a finger to his lips. She grimaced and nodded.

Dukmee came back. "I don't see anyone down here, but it is evident that it is frequently used. There's a series of smaller closets all around the periphery of the main storage room. We can go from closet to closet all the way to the other side where the flour is stacked and a door leads to the cellar. Keep your ears tuned to pick up the slightest noise."

"Aren't the closets full of stuff?" asked Bixby.

"Some hold a few supplies, but most are empty."

"Let's go," said Cantor. "We can figure out why the hall is so low on supplies later."

Feymare crowded them from behind, urging them forward. "Agreed. We want to find the prisoners and get them out before the building above comes down on us."

The globes they'd brought gave off enough light for them to see in their immediate vicinity, but not across a room.

However, when they stepped into the closets one at a time, the small space lit up with a glow that was almost too bright.

Cantor tried to discern what was originally kept in each area. First he decided they weren't closets so much as connected cupboards. One room had shelves and a few glass jars containing interesting vegetables, most he couldn't name. It was a relief to see green beans on one of the shelves. He left the door behind him open so that Bixby could enter, while he went on through the open door to the next storage unit.

Ahead of him, Dukmee stepped through the next door, and Cantor knew immediately that something was different. Instead of the bright glow in a confined space, the light from his globe showed dimly.

Cantor followed and found they had entered the large storage room around which the smaller closets circled. Stacks of flour bags reached almost to the ceiling. He and Dukmee hid there, waiting for Bixby and Feymare.

As soon as they grouped together, Feymare held his finger to his lips and tilted his head, listening. Dukmee leaned around the towering bags. He crept forward into the main room.

In a moment, he was back. "Cats. They must keep them here to thwart a community of mice springing up."

Whistling from beyond the flour raised Cantor's eyebrows. "Talented cat," he whispered.

Bixby clamped her lips together and glared at him. He grinned at her, enjoying her outrage at his disregard for their successful hiding. He didn't think they were in danger from one whistler, one who was still some distance away.

At Feymare's signal, they dimmed their light orbs. The whistling came closer, joined by a metallic squeak. A pale light illuminated the rest of the room. The whistling ceased. The harsh squeak ceased.

"Hello, cats." A young voice, probably a boy's. Cantor wanted to see him. He crouched low and crept around the edge of the flour stack.

The boy wore all white clothing, although the white wasn't pristine. Smudges decorated his chest and elbows. The rest of his outfit was cleaner, but still a far cry from fresh. A small baker's hat sat on his head, and a too-big apron that hung around his neck reached below his knees.

The cats came to wrap around his ankles, weaving around and around in a typical feline demand for attention.

The boy dug in his pockets and sprinkled handfuls of unidentifiable crumbs on the floor. Whatever it was pleased the cats. The young baker put his hands on his hips and with a big grin watched his offering disappear.

"There's a big do in the Hall this afternoon, cats. A special meeting's been called, and we're making a tea. It'll be fancy. Little cakes, sandwiches, crackers, jam, cheese, and cookies. I'm helping with the little cakes. I'll be pouring the glaze on them, so I've been sent to get the soft sugar. I'll come back when it's over and tell you all about it."

He heaved several bags into the wagon he'd brought, turned it around, and moved down a dingy corridor. He whistled. The wagon screeched under its heavy load.

As soon as he was out of sight, Cantor backed up and ran into Bixby.

"He'll be killed, Cantor." She pointed toward the gap in the other wall where the boy had gone. "There are lots of people in this building that only work here. They aren't bad. We must warn them and get them out."

The rustle of movement sounded loud as the four, who had remained so still, shifted to continue their mission. Bixby stood and faced Cantor.

She pushed her hair out of her face. "Nobody should be blown up. Not even the bad people."

She sounded a little hysterical. Cantor put his arm around her shoulders and turned her to the closed door leading to the dungeons. "I agree. Let's get the prisoners, then spread the word."

Dukmee bent to put his hands on the door. A small flash passed between his fingers, followed by a click as the hidden bolt moved out of the doorjamb.

Feymare pushed the door open. Hot, putrid air flowed out and enveloped the four. Bixby clapped her hand over her mouth and nose. Cantor pinched his nostrils. Feymare and Dukmee waved their hands in the air, and the thick cloud dissipated.

Cantor lowered his hand and blessed his companions. The smell was gone.

Silently, they entered the hallway and began their search. Many of the cell doors stood open with no one occupying the tiny, squalid rooms.

"I hear her," exclaimed Bixby. "Totobee-Rodolow is down this way."

Feymare put up one hand to stop her. "Wait one minute." She paused.

"There are five spokes going out from the central location. One we just used." His thumb over his shoulder indicated one. "There are four of us and four more to explore."

He handed each of them a small glob of pliable material. "Roll this between your hands into a long, narrow cord. Wrap it around a lock, tap it with your fist, and the lock will snap.

It's much faster than generating your own force to pop open a door. Free everyone you come to. Send them back to this hub. I've communicated to Bridger to guide the prisoners to freedom. He's left the bridge and is now doubling back to help us."

Dukmee nodded. "Choose your tunnel and run."

Bixby sprang into the one she believed would lead her to Totobee-Rodolow. Cantor didn't wait to see where Feymare and Dukmee went, but plunged into the nearest opening.

As he ran past open doors, he reached with his mind, trying to contact Ahma or Odem. He got no response. This part of the dungeon rang hollow as if no one with life dwelt here. He ran into the wall that ended this spoke and turned, panting, to lean against the stones.

Nothing. He prayed the others hadn't also come up empty-handed. He pushed off from the wall and ran back the way he'd come.

44

EXPLOSION

Bixby struggled to keep Totobee-Rodolow on her feet. The dragon's body was heavy, and her friend was too ill to shift herself into something easier for Bixby to handle. She'd tucked the light orb into her lace vest so she could use both hands to help Totobee-Rodolow. The globe slipped, and she used her forearm to nudge it back into place.

"We're almost there." Bixby spoke to encourage herself as much as Totobee-Rodolow.

The dragon hummed an answer. It sounded like, "Yes, darling."

She paused, thinking she'd heard a sound in the long corridor ahead of her. She peered out from under her burden and spied a globe shining on the chest of a man, then revealed his face as he came closer. Cantor.

"Did you find Ahma? Odem?"

He shook his head and put his shoulder under

Totobee-Rodolow's other arm. With a quick adjustment, he carried the dragon's weight. Bixby stood aside and flexed her shoulders.

"Thank you," she whispered.

He thrust his light globe toward Bixby. "Can you carry my orb as well?" He turned his face toward the dragon's. "Totobee-Rodolow, are you in pain?"

Her lips moved but only a hum came out.

"What did she say?"

"I'm pretty sure she said, 'No, just weary, dear one.' Her thoughts aren't much clearer than her tongue, though."

Cantor nodded. "Lead on."

She held up both light orbs and hurried toward the center of the dungeons. "How much time do you think we have?"

"No idea."

Bixby turned and trotted backward a few steps. "What kind of explosives do you think they'll use?"

"Dynamite, maybe."

She faced forward again, and her clothes fluttered around her. "Who would light the fuse? Do you think there will be one explosion or several?"

"They couldn't bring the building down with one."

"So, several. That would mean several people to light the fuses. How could they synchronize the blasts?"

"I don't know, Bixby."

"I don't think it's dynamite. They'd need it to be a chain reaction-type setup. You know, one person sets off the first explosion and then boom, boom, boom, the rest go off in order. Quickly! It must happen quickly so the victims won't hear the first explosion and have time to get out."

Cantor grunted.

"If we could find the first blast, we could stop the whole thing before it even began. Even if we found one in the middle, we could limit the damage. One of us could follow the trail back and dismantle whatever they're using, and another could go forward to disrupt the explosions that way. We can do this. We just have to find whatever they're using."

She pondered the possibilities as they traveled the last few yards to the center of the spokes. Light orbs illuminated the center room. She saw the glow and hurried forward, forgetting that Cantor carried no globe.

"Bixby."

She turned and saw the problem, hurried back, and apologized.

"You're going to be all right now, Totobee-Rodolow. Dukmee is there, and he'll give you something to strengthen you. We'll get you out of here."

This time Totobee-Rodolow's hum definitely had the rhythm of, "Yes, darling." Bixby threw her arms around the dragon and gave her a quick squeeze.

Cantor grunted. "That doesn't help."

Bixby stepped back. "You're panting."

Cantor stopped. "Bixby, I ran all the way down one corridor and back, and then halfway down this corridor, and now I'm supporting a very limp and heavy dragon."

Totobee-Rodolow made some comment that Bixby didn't understand. She swallowed a giggle and choked when she realized the hum was an objection to being labeled heavy.

"Are you okay?" asked Cantor.

"Of course. A hiccup caught in my throat."

Bixby smiled at the dragon, but Totobee-Rodolow's eyes

were closed. She patted one scaly arm. "We're almost there. I can see the light ahead. That's the core of the dungeon."

She squinted as a bulky shape obscured some of the light. Bridger rushed out of the central room to meet them. Without a word, he embraced his sister, then picked her up and carried her the rest of the way. Following several paces behind, Bixby smiled as Totobee-Rodolow nestled against Bridger's chest and rested her head on his shoulder.

Without thought, Bixby reached over and took Cantor's hand. She had plenty of family, but no one close. Cantor had a family of sorts, but they were displaced. He squeezed her hand, and she knew. Sometimes friends are the only family one really has.

When they reached the hub, Bridger sat on the floor and held his sister, a low, soothing sound emanating from somewhere in his throat. Dukmee immediately knelt beside them to assess Totobee-Rodolow's condition.

"She can't be a party to the rest of the rescue. We need to get her away. No more stress. She's had no food or water, and I believe they used a gas to keep her sedated."

Cantor passed a drinking flask to Bridger, who tilted the water into Totobee-Rodolow's mouth. The she dragon smiled sweetly at her brother and reached to touch Bixby's arm.

"I knew you would come. It hasn't been days, has it, darling?"

Bixby shook her head. The lump in her throat kept her from speaking.

Totobee-Rodolow closed her eyes. "It felt like *weeks*."

Feymare arrived from the spoke he'd examined, followed closely by Toolooknaut, who looked disheveled and tired, but not ill.

Bixby saw a quick exchange between Cantor and Feymare. Cantor raised his eyebrows as if asking a question. Feymare's eyes held a shade of sorrow, and his chin jerked once from side to side. No. He hadn't found Ahma and Odem.

Bixby moved back to Cantor's side, but she didn't grasp his hand. That's not what he needed now. Focus. Ahead, not to the side where spokes had already been queried and the answer was no. Ahead, not behind.

Dukmee checked Toolooknaut over and pronounced him well enough if he downed some water. "They didn't have to use much force to subdue him, and they didn't gas him to keep him in line. They used excessive force on Totobee-Rodolow since she was a serious threat."

"I can be a serious threat." Toolooknaut blustered a bit, then dropped the performance and looked sheepish. "I suppose I'm more of a threat when I've a pen in my hand. I did run quite a bit ahead of them. I'm fast when motivated. And I made them a wretched chase. But once they had me surrounded, I had no defense."

He surveyed the others and evidently found no condemnation. He didn't offer any more explanation. His eyebrows pulled together. "Feymare, what's that you have?"

The Primen warrior held up two hard-skinned, bulbous objects. Large, smoothly shaped, and colorful, they looked like the seed pod of some exotic plant. "I picked them up in the corridor. These are kantablash gourds."

Cantor caught his breath. "Those are illegal."

Dukmee went over and took one. He sniffed it, turned it over carefully, and sniffed the other end. "It's primed."

Bixby watched the interaction between the men. Their concern for a vegetable seemed out of line. What was so unusual about finding a gourd in a tunnel next to a food storage? And why illegal? "Primed? What does that mean?"

Cantor answered. "They don't need dynamite, Bixby. Kantablash gourds when permeated with the acid from bun-tornut berries form a highly explosive liquid. Very unstable. This would easily start that chain explosion you spoke of. And who is going to be suspicious of a plant pod?"

She gingerly touched the smooth hard skin of the gourd in Dukmee's hand. "So how do they ignite the first one?"

Dukmee sighed. "They shake it vigorously and put it down."

"Then run like a bull is chasing them," Bridger added.

Bixby looked from one man to the next. "What are we going to do?"

Feymare smiled without any joy in his eyes. "Same plan. We evacuate as many people as we can and disarm the weapons."

He turned to Bridger. "You and Toolooknaut will take your sister and find Ponack. You'll be in charge of moving the people in the immediate vicinity away from the Hall."

He gestured toward the building above. "The rest of us will move the servants and staff."

"What about the other prisoners?" asked Bixby.

Feymare herded his people toward the hall leading to the storage area. "There weren't any other prisoners."

Bixby resisted the gentle push on her back. "What about the councilmen in the forum?"

"We'll get to them."

"Will it be in time?"

Feymare stopped and turned Bixby so he could look in her eyes. She found his gaze patient and sad.

"Your heart is in the right place. We mustn't allow anyone to remain in danger by not warning them. You can go back through the entrance we used. Go to the front of the hall. Find someone who will tell the gathered councilmen of the danger. I don't think they would believe you."

"Penny Lunder?"

He shook his head. "Find a councilman. The councilmen gathered above us are the ones to be eliminated. One of these condemned men might be willing to risk his life to save the others."

Bixby followed the others who had already entered the hall leading to the storage room. Cantor, Dukmee, and Feymare headed off in the direction the boy baker had taken. She and Toolooknaut went with the dragons to the tunnel under the bridge. From that point, she left her friends and tore along the river, up an embankment, and down the street to the front of the Hall.

The congested traffic slowed her down. She wanted to yell warnings, but knew she should follow the directions given her. If she caused a commotion and was arrested by the city guard, she wouldn't be able to relay her message to the councilmen. Toolooknaut and Ponack were assigned to these people.

She ran up the steps of the hall where she overtook a man dressed in the robes of a councilman. She grabbed his sleeve and forced him to stop.

His face reddened as he glared at her. "What is the meaning of this?"

"Sir, are you going inside?"

"Yes."

"To the forum?"

He shook his arm, trying to dislodge her hold. "What is it to you?"

"You have to warn the councilmen. Tell them to get out of the building. There are explosive kantablash hidden inside. It's a plot to kill you all."

"That's ridiculous."

"No, no, it's not."

He studied her face for a moment. "You're one of the new realm walkers. An initiate. Princess Bixby D'Mazeline."

"Yes." Bixby bounced on her toes.

"Explosive kantablash?"

"Yes. Do you believe me? You *have* to believe me, or all those men will die."

"It is rather a bizarre story to make up." He frowned and pinched his upper lip, where a bushy mustache hung below a pointed nose.

She saw when he made his decision. His hand came down and clamped on her shoulder. His fingers pressed into her bones.

"I'll tell them. If we get out and there is no explosion, at least we'll be alive. Looking foolish, but alive."

He released her shoulder and sped into the building.

She charged the door, opened it, and yelled after him. "And the staff. Not just the councilmen, remember all the people working in the offices."

He waved his hand, indicating he'd heard, and dashed on.

Bixby turned and leaned against the closed door. The glass felt cool against her back. This side of the building was shaded. Soon the traffic would abate as all the citizens went to their homes for the evening. She could join Toolooknaut and Ponack now in their efforts to clear citizens from the area.

Rushing down the steps and across the avenue, she entered the In Shadow Inn. Pushing past the customers standing near the entry, she launched herself up on a chair and then a tabletop.

"Everyone out. There are explosives in the Realm Walkers Guild building. Everyone must flee. Get away." She looked around at the skeptical faces below. They didn't believe her. "Go!"

A man in a city guard uniform plowed through the crowd and swept her off her platform. She felt a prick in her thigh and a hot flow traveled across her skin, leaving her numb. He had her by the legs, and she fell over his shoulder, draped down his back.

"Let me down!" She tried to beat on his back, but her arms whipped at him like two strings on a wet mop. "Let me down. I have to warn them."

He didn't stop, but carried her out into the street.

He'd disabled her, probably with essence of pardox leaf. She wouldn't give up. If he wasn't going to let her down, she was still going to warn as many people as possible.

"Get away from here. The Guild Hall will explode. Run!"

She didn't quit. She wouldn't. Even as the burly guard carried her away from the cultural area and toward the city jail, she cried out. Still no one listened, only scoffed and turned away. She hoped Toolooknaut and Ponack were having more impact.

Only one man seemed to heed her calls. A councilman followed them.

With hair in her eyes and tears streaming down her face, she couldn't see him well, but the robes were unmistakable. If he could catch up to them, he could help. He must have been warned in the forum and dashed out.

The guard rounded a corner, and Bixby lost sight of the man behind them. She searched the throng of people until the councilman came around the corner.

Grabbing the guard's belt, she shook it. "Stop! Stop! A councilman's coming, and he'll tell you I'm telling the truth."

The guard slowed, but she soon realized that it wasn't because of what she'd said, but because they'd reached a paddy wagon. He fumbled with the door. He would throw her in and she'd never be able to get these people to safety. She thought of her friends. Would they waste time looking for her? Her heart froze to think of them lingering in danger because of her. She sobbed. Choked on the emotion, then with all her will banished the weakness. Part of it must be the pardox leaf she couldn't control. But part of it was her, and all her training enforced the concept of self-control. Now was not the time to doubt.

"Please, just talk to the councilman. He's coming. We have to move these citizens."

The guard grunted. The iron door screeched as it opened. He tossed her in and slammed it shut. The chains rattled, and the key turned in the lock. The man tested the door to make sure his prisoner was secure.

"What's the matter, guard?"

The councilman! Bixby pressed her ear to the door. Tiny slits close to the floor allowed air to waft through the enclosure, but the paddy wagon was built without a window to see through. Bixby stretched out on the grubby floor and put her eye to the vent. She could see both men from their shoes to their knees. She abandoned her position as uncomfortable and useless.

"The girl made a fuss at the In Shadow Inn. Brackett doesn't put up with any disturbance. He tips us to take care of things quick."

Bixby opened her mouth to beg for aid.

The councilman spoke. "That's good. That's good. Everything should be done in an orderly manner."

His voice! He was the councilman who had said he would warn the others. She closed her eyes and leaned her forehead against the metal wall. She'd enlisted the wrong man. He hadn't warned anyone.

Sobs shook her to the floor. Collapsed against the narrow vents, she called out. "You didn't help."

"Oh, I helped, child." He laughed. "I'm the fastest, you see."

He shook the gourd.

No sooner had the thought registered than an explosion knocked the paddy wagon on its side. The pardox leaf was wearing off, but Bixby still had no coordination to speak of. As the prison cart tumbled, she bounced against the walls. She heard the horse's panicked squeal over her own shout of alarm. Screams from all around. A second explosion followed the first. And then a third. And a fourth.

Each blast rocked the iron cart. Bixby curled up in a ball. Seven … eight … fifteen explosions in all. She heard wails and moans outside her prison. If people were injured badly so many blocks away, was anyone alive in the building or near it? They couldn't be.

Cantor? Dukmee? Feymare? Had they escaped?

Totobee-Rodolow? Bridger? Toolooknaut? Ponack? Had they been far enough away?

She heard the building next to her cry out as brick and mortar were torn asunder. Falling objects cracked in deafening blows against the wagon. The last one flipped the vehicle again. Bixby bounced against the hard walls, crying out as her cheekbone struck and the rough metal scraped her face and the back of one hand.

A seam burst at the corner of the paddy wagon. Cradling her face in one hand, Bixby squinted at the dust motes whirling in a narrow light ray. She could see outside. But powdered debris filled the air. Paper thin shards of plaster, paper, and cloth floated on the heavy air.

The prison cart had saved her life. She put her hand on the open ridge and pulled it back with a slice of red across her palm. She was alive enough to bleed, but was she alone?

45

WHERE ARE
THE FRIENDS?

Bixby huddled on what was now the floor of the cart and cupped her stinging hand in her lap, pressing it against her legs to stop the shaking. The shallow cut bled just a little, but the jagged metal edge had made a tattered wound. The pain was significant, proof that the pardox had completely worn off.

So many people ...

Opening her hamper containing medical supplies, Bixby found disinfectant, ointment, and bandages.

How many dead? Maimed?

Clumsily, with one hand, she cleaned and bandaged her palm.

Why wouldn't they listen?

Taking a deep breath, she put her supplies away and crept to the narrow opening to survey her surroundings. Few people walked the street among the litter of rubble and huddled forms. She wondered how far the devastation reached from the guild building in the center of Gilead. Time to leave her prison shelter.

Primen, give me strength.

Bixby braced her back against one side of the box and pushed against the torn edge with her booted feet. The gap widened. Muttering voices came from the street.

She pounded on the side of the prison cart. "Help! Help. I'm trapped."

No one came to peer in the slice of an opening she could see through. The people who were within feet of her metal box moved on by. Frustrated, she flung herself back and kicked the damaged metal. A bolt popped out, and the side bent farther away from the frame.

With renewed hope, Bixby applied more pressure. Her thick leather boots protected her feet so she wouldn't end up with another cut. Although she heard people passing from time to time, no one stopped to help. When the escape hole gaped open, she slid through, avoiding the sharp edges.

The first thing she saw was the uniformed body of the guard who'd arrested her. Beside him lay a still form draped in the black robe of a councilman. The treacherous man must have miscalculated how far away he had to be from the building to be safe. She shuddered and turned away.

Twilight shadows cast the deserted street in somber shades of gray. A haze of dust blanketed the scene. Bixby paused to cover her mouth and nose with a large handkerchief, then chose the route back to the guild building. If she were to find any of her friends, it would be there. She walked a few steps, picking her footing carefully in the debris.

A low moan stopped her. She tilted her head and located

the source. Off to the side, she found an unconscious woman holding a child. The child was dead. Bixby removed the little girl from the woman's arms and looked for injuries.

Aside from a nasty, bleeding cut on her scalp, the woman had a broken arm and a mangled leg. Bixby could stop the bleeding, but couldn't do any of her healing arts on the street. She wished she'd already had a mentorship with Dukmee. She knew basic aid for minor wounds.

The woman didn't regain consciousness, and when Bixby had done all she could do, she continued her way to the center of town. The five minute walk took over two hours. Citizens from the outskirts of Gilead came in to see what had happened, look for friends and family, and help.

Bixby stopped for every injured person. She gave what comfort she could, and found some survivors who were able to help the more seriously wounded. Purposely thinking like her mother, she quickly took charge, delegating responsibility to those who reacted in a sensible manner.

As she entered the avenue that ran to the front of the building, she found no more survivors. The destruction broke her heart. No sign of life. None of the fine cultural sites standing. One building was indistinguishable from the next.

She guessed where the Hall had stood. The area looked like a giant had dug under the building, lifted it up, and then thrown it down. The river that flowed around the back side was damned with debris and overflowed its banks, creating more mess.

Where were her friends? Did any of them get out?

A tabletop lay across a mound of plaster, broken wood, and crushed stone. Bixby tested it for stability, then climbed up to perch where she could see in all directions.

She sat with her legs crossed and her arms folded around her middle. Staring at the scene around her, she begged for someone to walk out of the wreckage. She swiveled her head, looking one way along the shambles of the avenue, and then the other.

If someone had gotten out, wouldn't they come back here to look for her?

A brilliant red and orange glow filled the western sky as the sun set. Bixby coughed. The same dust that irritated her lungs refracted the light and produced unbelievable colors above. Bixby shivered and waited. Her hand throbbed. The scrapes on her face tingled unpleasantly.

Her thoughts went over all she knew about the pardox leaf. The essence would affect her for days after the initial numbness wore off. Her body, which should be safe with her thermea on, felt cold. She fought back waves of emotion, which were probably evidence of shock, but heightened by the pardox. Sleep would ease the effects of the drug, but right now, Bixby wanted to be alert.

With a muddled mind, she thought about cleaning her wounds and covering the deeper ones with a bandage. She'd only tended the hand before. Infection would be a bother later on.

A groan escaped her lips as she forced herself to shift. She pulled out a hamper, but it wasn't her supplies. She looked for it again and found other hampers. But not the one with salve and cloth wraps. She'd probably left it with the last man she'd treated.

Out of the clothes bag, she pulled a knitted cap that fit like a tight helmet. She tugged it onto her head, flattening her hair, and buttoned the strap under her chin. She wrapped a woolen cloth around her waist and a thick shawl over her shoulders. Two striped tubes in faded shades of pink and rose provided more warmth for her legs. After she'd tidied everything, repacked what she wasn't going to wear, and hidden the flat hampers away in her skirts, she pulled on long gloves ruffled from wrist to elbow.

There. At least she looked like she wanted to look. She didn't feel like she wanted to feel. Her heart ached. Parts of her body complained about being tossed about in a big tin box. Her stomach rumbled. Hungry, but her stomach was not the only thing that was empty. All the unpleasant sensations couldn't be tossed aside, because she was hollow. Nothing distracted her from the uncertainty of her situation.

A thump on the tabletop jerked Bixby around to see what had landed behind her. Jesha swished her tail and promptly climbed into Bixby's lap. She voiced several rowly complaints, turned about, rubbing her tail under Bixby's nose, then settled down. Her purr indicated she was content to have found at least one warm body she could count on to provide comfort.

Bixby stroked her. She had trouble speaking through her tears. "I'm just as happy to see you."

They sat together long after the sun had dropped beyond the rim of their plane.

A swoosh of noise turned Bixby's head. A short distance away, a portal opened, showing a bright and fancy room populated by people in wondrous garments. A man and woman came to the portal and stepped through.

Bixby leapt to her feet and jumped off her platform. She darted through the littered avenue.

"Mother! Father! You came."

Without any regard to royal etiquette, or her mother's

preference for clean gowns and capes and everything else, Bixby threw her arms around her mother and then her father and then her mother again.

Her mother stroked her head, her fingers running over the bumpy cap again and again. "You're safe. Thank Primen."

"Let us get out of the way," her father said quietly. Then his voice took on a kingly tenor and he boomed, "We have brought aid to Gilead." He pulled his wife and daughter to the side. A squadron of men marched two by two through the portal and advanced into the city. They carried bundles of supplies. Tears rolled down Bixby's cheeks as she saw her countrymen disperse to give vital aid.

When the soldiers had cleared the portal, her father led her and his wife back through to the splendor of their throne room.

"Don't cry, Bixby. I have news I think will lighten your heart."

She turned her face up to look in his kind eyes. "My friends?"

He nodded. "Yes, your friends. Bridger brought Totobee-Rodolow through a portal to the court and told us of the happenings in Gilead. He asked about his cat. Have you seen a cat?"

Before she could answer, her mother, having regained her royal reserve, continued. "Some minutes later, Dukmee and Feymare lead a motley group of servants and unnamed strays into the battalion quad."

"Cantor?"

The king looked at the queen with an arched eyebrow.

She nodded decisively. "Yes, there's a young realm walker named Cantor D'Ahma." Her expression changed to one of contemplation. "But I don't remember who he came with or when."

Bixby looked intently at her mother and father. "But he's here?"

"Oh, yes, my dear," said her mother. "He's here. I think he's with the mor dragons and Dukmee." She gently touched her daughter's cheek. "I'm sure you can find them. Bridger tells me his sister is your constant." She frowned. "You really should learn to write letters, Bixby. A mother likes to get letters from her daughter."

"Yes, Mother. I will." She pulled away and headed for the door to the main palace.

"Is that the cat?" Her mother pointed at Jesha, who sat just inside the portal on the gleaming, polished floor. She posed with her tail wrapped around her and an exaggerated calm expression on her face.

Bixby scooped Jesha into her arms. "Yes, this is Bridger's cat."

Her father's voice carried across the room even when he muttered. "A dragon with a cat?"

Her mother called after her. "You could do that fancy writing like the scribes do on scrolls. That would be pretty, and I know you're capable."

"Yes, Mother."

"Oh, Bixby."

She stopped and turned at the tone in her mother's voice.

"Say good-bye to your father. He's going to Gilead to do kingly things."

She ran and enveloped her father in another hug. "Take care. There are some truly awful people on Dairine."

"I will. And Feymare has already returned. I'll be in good

company." He hugged her close and put his lips close to her ear. "And you shall give me your report at a more convenient time."

"Yes, Father."

Her father passed through the portal with a royal guard of six men.

Bixby returned to her quest to find her friends. She located them in the west tower, in three connected rooms, resting and eating.

Dukmee and Bridger played a game of cards. Cantor lay on a bed.

Bixby put Jesha down, and the cat ran to her dragon.

"There you are." Bridger picked her up, gave her a hug, then put her down beside a plate. "I saved you my cheese."

Bixby smiled at the normalcy of her friends' activity. Satin drapes, cushioned seats, polished wood, curlicues of burnished metal on lamps and candlestands. Her normal world. Nothing broken, nothing crushed. No one holding on to his last bit of strength. A moment of guilt almost knocked her down, but she knew what Primen said in His Book. She would recover in order to enter the trials of tomorrow. That was not only allowed but also commanded.

And her friends. Bridger's color was off, each scale seamed with gray. Dukmee's powerful hand shook as he put down a card. She heard Totobee-Rodolow's gentle whoosh of breathing as she slept. Jesha leaned against her dragon, not settling down, but maintaining contact.

Then Bixby took a good look at Cantor.

"You're hurt."

She rushed to his side and sat gingerly on the bed beside him. His eyes were closed. A cloth wrapped around his head, and a bit of dried blood trailed down his cheek. She could see bruises under the skin, rapidly darkening.

"You're hurt." Bixby's voice broke his intention to stay asleep.

He pinched his face muscles. "You already said that." Opening his eyes, he examined her. "You're hurt as well."

"I'm not."

"You are."

"Not much."

"Have you looked in a mirror?"

Bixby backed off the bed and stood by his side. "I'm glad to see you too. I'm glad you're alive."

The frazzled tone in her voice alarmed Cantor. He peeked around her to where the dragon and healer played cards.

"Dukmee, you'd better come see to Bixby's injuries. She's not quite herself."

Dukmee abandoned the game and came to examine Bixby. "Just scratches and bruises."

Bixby cried. Tears flowed from her eyes, and her shoulders shook.

Panic rose to Cantor's throat and caused his one word to squeak. "See?"

"I cry," she said to Dukmee. "It was pardox leaf. I just keep crying." And in defiance of her wet cheeks, puffy eyes, red nose, and voice laden with grief, she stated emphatically, "I never cry."

She glared at Cantor. "There were people dead everywhere. And people hurt. Badly hurt. I couldn't help them all. And I couldn't find you. I couldn't find any of you. Then Jesha found me."

She sobbed.

Totobee-Rodolow came from the next room and gathered Bixby into her arms.

"You're better," wailed Bixby. "I'm glad. I'm so glad. You aren't dead."

Cantor raised his eyebrows when he looked at Bridger. In his mind, he clearly heard Bridger's response. "I don't know. I guess it's one of those woman bones."

He shifted his gaze and saw that Bixby had intercepted their exchange of looks. This was not a good thing. Her face proclaimed it was a very, very bad thing.

"Don't you understand?"

He and Bridger shook their heads in unison.

"Some people are dead. Some people are alive. Some people who were just there are dead. Some people who were wicked and horrible are alive. I know one of the bad, bad councilmen is dead. He was supposed to be alive. And maybe the three good councilmen are dead. And maybe they are alive. And those farmhouse councilmen are probably alive. And what did we do to help? And was it enough? And it's not over, because some people who want people dead are still alive."

She collapsed on the side of Cantor's bed. Cantor scooted away, giving her more room.

Totobee-Rodolow sat beside her, keeping an arm around her shoulders. He relished the relief he felt. The dragon had stepped in with comfort. He graciously allowed her to do all she could. He'd observe and stay close for support.

Bixby now faced Dukmee. Dukmee could take care of it.

The healer asked Bridger to bring over his healing

supplies. Totobee-Rodolow and her brother helped as Dukmee unwrapped Bixby's hand, cleaned it, oozed ointment on the jagged tear, and re-wrapped it. He calmly washed the scrapes on her face and put a soothing lotion on them.

She sniffed and shuddered, sighed and squeaked once, and slowly calmed down.

Dukmee packed his unused supplies and gathered up the material that needed discarding.

He straightened and turned away.

Where were the words of wisdom that the healer should say? Wasn't he going to point out a couple of things designed to make Bixby feel better? Oh, where was Ahma when he needed her?

Disappointment slammed into Cantor's heart. They hadn't stopped the explosions. They hadn't found Ahma and Odem. With the guild in shambles, his likelihood of achieving full realm walker status was nil. For once in his life, instead of looking forward to the next stage of his training, all he could do was look back. He saw in his mind's eye, his mentor and caretaker. She'd raised him. Her smiles were rare, but her eyes always glowed with love. He remembered her soft voice as he went to sleep. Talking. Not really *to* him. But the sound of her voice eased him to sleep.

Cantor reached out and cradled Bixby's hurt hand.

"This is what Ahma said:

'Forget the past, both the fame and the shame.
The fame and shame of yesteryear are not suitable
*   foundation for today.*
Carry with you the lessons you learn each day,
for each lesson is a brick,

solid and true.
Press on to finish the task set before you,
building today for the needs of tomorrow.
Don't eye tomorrow with impatience in your heart.
For an eye on tomorrow's journey
will cause you to stumble
over a rock at your foot.'"

He caught and squeezed her other hand. "It's the last one I never get quite right."

Bixby's big eyes were still sad. "Do we know what happened to Toolooknaut and Ponack?"

Cantor shook his head slowly. Ahma's words had comforted him, but not Bixby.

Bridger spoke up. "We don't know, but Primen does. If I had a choice of who was to know where I am, I'd pick Primen over you two."

"We'll find them, Bix. We'll find Ahma and Odem too. As Odem would say, 'If you're walking with Primen, you will reach the desires of your heart.'"

Talk It Up!

Want free books?
First looks at the best new fiction?
Awesome exclusive merchandise?

We want to hear from you!

Give us your opinions on titles, covers, and stories.
Join the Z Street Team.

Visit zstreetteam.zondervan.com/joinnow
to sign up today!

Also—Friend us on Facebook!

www.facebook.com/goodteenreads

- Video Trailers

- Connect with your favorite authors

- Sneak peeks at new releases

- Giveaways

- Fun discussions

- And much more!